*Praise for Art Ross: The Hockey Legend Who Built the Bruins*

"No one would believe this wild tale if it were a movie (and maybe should be). A child of the Canadian wilderness, who may well have been the country's greatest athlete, becomes a player, coach, manager, and inventor who likely affected the game of hockey more than anyone else. Those who say they should change the Art Ross Trophy to a more recognizable name would cringe in embarrassment after reading Eric Zweig's magnificent biography."

— Roy MacGregor, bestselling author and *Globe and Mail* columnist

"A fascinating read. In fact, when I started reading it I could hardly put it down until I completed it. What a pioneer Art Ross was … a great story."

— Scotty Bowman, Hockey Hall of Fame builder and the winningest coach in NHL history

"With his wonderful, many-layered, anecdote-rich study of Art Ross, author Eric Zweig does a masterful job of profiling an important figure who was a player, coach, executive, inventor, and innovator during the professional game's crucial, formative years. In Montreal, more than 50 years after Ross's passing, this hockey pioneer has been forgiven — almost — for having been an architect in the building of the Boston Bruins."

— Dave Stubbs, *Montreal Gazette*

"It is hard to talk about the history of hockey without mentioning the name Art Ross … from being a player, coach, manager, and on-ice official, to the history of the goalie net, to having a trophy named after him … just to name a few things Art Ross did over his years. Zweig has uncovered some great stories. A must for all hockey fans."

— Phil Pritchard, Vice President and Keeper of the Stanley Cup, Hockey Hall of Fame


"A diligently researched portrait of a canny, controversial, colourful hockey icon. Recognition for a hockey genius long overdue. As Cherry would say, 'Two thumbs up, Eric!'"

— Brian McFarlane, bestselling author and former sportscaster


"I enjoyed it very much. I had no idea Art Ross had been such an athlete in his day before he came to Boston. I think this book really has a place in Canadian history, in hockey history, and in NHL history. It was fascinating."

— Harry Sinden, senior advisor to the owner, and former coach, general manager and president, of the Boston Bruins


"No, Art Ross didn't invent hockey. You can forget that, sometimes, reminded of the extent to which he shaped the game we know today. On the ice, he was as skilled and as wily a goal-scoring defender as there's ever been. Off it, a tireless innovator of rules and equipment, he also coached, managed, and gave the Boston Bruins the feisty spirit that defines them still. It's high time his formidable tale was told; Eric Zweig does it with a vim and an eye for detail that delights the fan in me as much as the historian."

— Stephen Smith, author of *Puckstruck: Distracted, Delighted and Distressed by Canada's Hockey Obsession*

# ART ROSS

## The Hockey Legend Who Built the Bruins

## Eric Zweig

With a Foreword by
Ron MacLean

**DUNDURN**
TORONTO

Editor: Michael Melgaard
Design: Laura Boyle
Cover design: Laura Boyle
Cover image: Courtesy of Art Ross III
Printer: Webcom

**Library and Archives Canada Cataloguing in Publication**

Zweig, Eric, 1963-, author
        Art Ross : the hockey legend who built the Bruins / Eric Zweig ; with  a foreword by Ron MacLean.

Includes bibliographical references and index.
Issued in print and electronic formats.
ISBN 978-1-4597-3040-3 (paperback).--ISBN 978-1-4597-3041-0 (pdf).-- ISBN 978-1-4597-3042-7 (epub)

1. Ross, Art, 1886-1964.  2. Hockey players--Canada--Biography.  3. Hockey coaches--Canada--Biography.
4. Sports executives--Canada-- Biography.  5. Boston Bruins (Hockey team)--History. I. MacLean, Ron, 1960-, writer of foreword  II. Title.

GV848.5.R68Z84 2015          796.962092          C2015-904686-6
                                                 C2015-904687-4


1   2   3   4   5     19   18   17   16   15

  Canada

We acknowledge the support of the **Canada Council for the Arts** and the **Ontario Arts Council** for our publishing program. We also acknowledge the financial support of the **Government of Canada** through the **Canada Book Fund** and **Livres Canada Books,** and the **Government of Ontario** through the **Ontario Book Publishing Tax Credit** and the **Ontario Media Development Corporation.**

Care has been taken to trace the ownership of copyright material used in this book. The author and the publisher welcome any information enabling them to rectify any references or credits in subsequent editions.
                                                        — J. Kirk Howard, President

The publisher is not responsible for websites or their content unless they are owned by the publisher.

Printed and bound in Canada.

**VISIT US AT**

Dundurn.com | @dundurnpress | Facebook.com/dundurnpress | Pinterest.com/dundurnpress

Dundurn
3 Church Street, Suite 500
Toronto, Ontario, Canada
M5E 1M2

For Art and Kathy, Victoria and Valerie, and MacKenzie

# CONTENTS

# FOREWORD
## by Ron MacLean

Eric Zweig, who has endlessly provided me with wonderful historical hockey anecdotes in return for nothing save the joy of a shared story, has produced a touching and extraordinary book examining the life of hockey's most important figure, Art Ross. Ross was a human workshop in which the game's best implements — the nets, the pucks and the painted lines — were designed, and then, under Art's direction, implemented by players such as Eddie Shore, Milt Schmidt, and the Patricks.

Art Ross is a classicist and a romantic. The kind of man who could not only buy a violin and play it, he could build the violin. I have a metaphor in my mind. In our hockey cathedrals we honour the greats by raising their numbers to the rafters. Those simple rooftop banners distill talents and traits symbolizing what that player must have been. Michelangelo, in a far different cathedral, took a complex story of sin and the human struggle for salvation and managed to express it in a painting on the ceiling of the Sistine Chapel. His genius lay not in the incredible renderings, but in the brilliant grasp of the story he was portraying. That is what strikes me about Ross. He figured out what the point of it all was, and he displayed it. The sport, the business, the life. He knew how hockey should look. And he knew what a player should look like. He could spot the prodigy and the beginnings of decline. A remarkable life imbued with struggle and success.

A few years ago at the NHL Awards, we had Russell Crowe lined up to present the Hart Trophy, awarded annually to the NHL's most valuable player. As always, the Hart Trophy is presented last, but Crowe had to return to a movie set that night and couldn't stay until the show's end. As we debated backstage which award to switch him to — timing worked best for the Lady Byng Trophy — Crowe was clearly enamoured by another. I recall him emoting the name Art Ross. I swear it lasted ten seconds. Each word, a delicious two or three syllables, "Aaah-rrr-Te' Rrrgh-aaa-Sss!" All of us on the production team buzzed at that moment. The name never sounded so big, so important — until now.

Ron MacLean
July 2015

# PROLOGUE

He was into his seventies now and no longer the athlete he'd once been. But he could still move when he needed to. It was nearing game time, so he made his way quickly to the living room of the Wadsworth suite, his apartment in the annex building behind the Hotel Kenmore.

The broadcast would begin at 1:00. His beloved Bruins wouldn't be in action until evening, but watching the Rangers face the Black Hawks was better than watching nothing at all. Especially today. For the first time, a hockey game was being broadcast from coast-to-coast in the United States. CBS was to air games on Saturday afternoons for the next 10 weeks, but even network executives were surprised by the reaction from their affiliate stations across the country. "The response is better than we had for Big Ten basketball," announcer Bud Palmer told reporters.

The elderly gentleman settled himself down in front of the television set in a living room that could have been mistaken for a hockey museum. There was a small keepsake trophy he'd been given to commemorate his first Stanley Cup victory a half-century before, and tokens from the three championship teams he'd run for the Bruins. Other mementos marked his induction into the Hockey Hall of Fame. Everywhere, it seemed, there was a trophy or a photograph from his lifetime in sports. He hadn't been able to keep them all. Some resided with a daughter-in-law. Others had simply disappeared as the years went by. He still had the photographs of his sons, dressed in their uniforms as pilots with Royal Canadian Air Force during the Second World War, but he lived alone in his apartment now — he'd been a widower for nearly four years.

It was January 5, 1957, and though he was indoors, in Boston, in the dead of winter, the gentleman wore dark glasses. "My eyes get tired quickly these days," he would later explain to Arthur Siegel of the *Boston Globe*. "I wear dark glasses when I'm not reading. I wear regular reading glasses otherwise." He switched to his reading glasses to watch the game. And as he watched, he noticed something. It wasn't just that his eyesight was failing — he'd been watching hockey for close to 60 years and could follow it even if his eyes were closed. Yet on a small black-and-white television, especially when the camera showed a player in a close-up shot, it was impossible to tell if the line that player was crossing was red or blue.

The man had been a tinkerer most of his life. Over the years, he'd devised all sorts of strategies and gadgets to make hockey better — or to give his team an advantage. Immediately, his mind seized upon the solution. First thing on Monday he picked up the telephone and dialed the National Hockey League office in Montreal. When Mr. Campbell, president of the NHL, came on the line, the gentleman suggested to him that the league ought to dash, or checker, the line at centre ice. Within a few years, the checkered red line was a standard feature in hockey rinks all around the world.

Throughout his career, Art Ross had always been conscious of the bottom line, whether fighting for the top dollar as a player, or forcing down costs as a coach and a manager. When he thought back on his conversation with Mr. Campbell afterwards, Ross told his son John he realized what he should have done. "I should have called him up and said, 'Hey, Clarence, I've got a great idea — it'll cost you $500 to use it!'"

# INTRODUCTION: BIG GAME PLAYER

The big game was set for 8:30 on Saturday night, February 29, 1908. The Montreal Wanderers and the Ottawa Senators were tied for first place, each with six wins and two losses so far in the 10-game season. Both teams would still have another game to play afterward, but no one expected either team to lose it, so whoever won was all but assured of the title in the Eastern Canada Amateur Hockey Association, and with it the Stanley Cup.

"Who's going to win?" asked Wanderers captain Cecil Blachford when questioned by reporters before the game. "Why, we are, of course. We're a better team than Ottawa."

Not surprisingly, Senators captain Alf Smith felt the same way about his squad. "I tell you we can beat them," Smith said, "and we're going to do it, too."

More impartial observers were also at odds. Referee Bob Meldrum wasn't working the big game, but he still refused to take sides. "It's going to be a good fight," he said, summing up nicely what everyone believed. "I think the game ... will be the best of the season."

All week long, the management of the Arena in Montreal worked to ensure that tickets got into the hands of the proper subscribers, and not speculators (who would be known as scalpers today). Even so, tickets that normally sold for 50¢ or $1 were being resold for anywhere from $5 to $15. Some reports put the price as high as $20. The *Globe* in Toronto stated that a box holding six seats was sold for $125. This at a time when the average Canadian worker would count himself lucky to bring home $1,000 in pay for the entire year.

Were the prices justified? Well, for sheer intensity over a brief time, the rivalry between the Wanderers and Ottawa was as good as any in hockey history. It was similar to the animosity between the Detroit Red Wings and the Colorado Avalanche from 1995–96 through 2001–02, seven years marked by bad blood, brawls, and five Stanley Cup championships between them. One particularly violent game between the Wanderers and Ottawa, on February 11, 1905, was described by a Montreal newspaper as "a saturnalia of butchery." Another meeting on January 12, 1907, was even worse, with the *Montreal Star* describing at least three major stick assaults by Ottawa players. "They should get six months in jail," read part of a *Star* headline. Even the *Ottawa Citizen* described much of the game as "disgraceful."

It was familiarity that bred contempt between the Wanderers and Ottawa. This was an era when rosters were small because the seven men who started the game (the seventh player was the now-defunct rover position) were expected to play a full 60 minutes. Leagues were small because train travel meant teams had to be close together. Freezing temperatures were the only way to maintain ice in an arena, so schedules were short. The Wanderers and Ottawa were regional rivals that had faced each other at least twice every season for a number of years. And there was more than just violence to their rivalry. These were two of the best teams in hockey. One or the other finished in first place in the league standings, with their rival second, in every season from 1904–05 through 1909–10. Between them, they held the Stanley Cup for all but a few months from 1903 through 1911.

Heading into the 1907–08 season, the Senators realized that changes were needed to their veteran lineup if they were going to keep up with the Wanderers. In modern terms, Ottawa decided to reload instead of rebuild. They brought in two young stars to energize their aging core. Tommy Phillips — a man considered by many to be the best player in the game — was lured away from his hometown Kenora Thistles for a record salary, usually reported at $1,800 for the 10-game season. Fred Taylor, who would eventually earn the nickname Cyclone for his amazing speed, was not yet a star and signed for just $500.

The Wanderers entered the 1907–08 season as defending Stanley Cup champions for the second year in a row, but they'd also brought in new players as well. The best of their newcomers was Art Ross. When the Wanderers won their season opener against the Montreal AAA on January 8, the *Gazette* reported that Ross, "… was sure in getting the man or the disc in Montreal attacks and time and again he dashed down the ice on end to end runs."

Ross had spent the previous two years in Brandon, Manitoba, but returned to Montreal to play for his hometown team. Ross played point — in this era the two defencemen lined up one in front of the other with the man closer to the goalie known as "point" and the one further up the ice called "cover point." Cyclone Taylor was a cover point. Both were inclined to rush the puck whenever they could, which was not yet the norm for defencemen.

Before the Wanderers' first game against Ottawa on January 11, the *Gazette* boasted that Ross on defence was already the finest player at his position in the East, but was curious to see how he'd stack up against the Senators' new star. "Taylor, according to Ottawa men who saw [the Wanderers' previous] game, is faster than Art Ross, but not the same finished stick handler." One area where Ross definitely had the advantage was in size, standing 5'11" to Taylor's 5'8" and outweighing him 190 pounds to 165.

Taylor and Ottawa certainly got the better of Ross and the Wanderers during that first game, with the Senators scoring a stunning 12–2 victory in front of an overflow crowd on the opening night of their brand new 7,000-seat Arena. Despite the blowout, "Ross was one of the stars of the game," the *Gazette* reported, but his reviews were nothing like the glowing reports Taylor got in the Ottawa papers.

For the rest of the season, both Ross and Taylor had played brilliant defence while managing to score almost a goal per game. Both became stars, but only one man's team could win the championship, and the lopsided result of the season's first meeting between the Wanderers and Ottawa added extra fuel to the fire when the rivalry was renewed in the big game in Montreal on February 29.

The game was rough, although not particularly dirty. In fact, most of the violence took place outside the Arena where fans were desperate to get in. A huge crowd had gathered outside long before the doors opened at 6:05 for the 8:30 start. It took about an hour for the patrons rushing for a spot in the Arena's ample standing-room section to make their way inside. The trouble began around 8:00, when the reserved seat ticket-holders seemed to arrive at the corner of Wood Avenue and St. Catherine Street all at once. The pushing and shoving was intense as those without tickets tried to sneak inside with those who had them. There were 30 members of the Montreal police on patrol, as well as 10 Westmount officers, in addition to the 80 ushers working inside, but it was impossible to get everyone into the rink safely.

"Holders of choice seats were held up in the crush at the front," said the *Gazette*, "and in some cases it took half an hour for a party to work its way to the front and gain admittance to the vestibule of the rink. Hats were broken, clothes torn and [galoshes] lost in the scrimmage." Despite reinforcements of 15 more policemen, the angry crowd began smashing windows and breaking door panels. "The St. Catherine Street doors of the Arena look as if they had been attacked with a gatling gun." Though the damage report of $300 sounds insignificant by today's standards, it was enough to warrant its own headline in the *Gazette*. The start of the game was delayed until 8:55, and yet there were hundreds of ticket-holders among the 7,000 paid fans still waiting to get in when the Wanderers' Bruce Stuart and Ottawa's Marty Walsh lined up for the opening faceoff. Several thousand more without tickets had to be turned away.

Once the game started, each team made several rushes up the ice before Alf Smith finally launched the first shot, which Wanderers goalie Riley Hern handled easily. Play continued quickly from end to end, but the Ottawa defence of Cyclone Taylor and Harvey Pulford, and the Wanderers tandem of Art Ross and Walter Smaill, made it difficult for the forwards to break through. Ross also made several rushes that brought the crowd to its feet, but Ottawa had the best of the play for the most of the half. The Senators' Tommy Phillips scored near the midway mark, and his team went to the dressing room with a 1–0 lead. In the battle between Ross and Taylor, the Wanderers' star sent his Ottawa counterpart crashing to the ice twice with heavy checks. Taylor got in one good hit of his own that, according to his biographer Eric Whitehead, brought blood streaming from Ross's nose and left a trail of red on the ice as Ross went after Taylor.

Following a 10-minute break, the Wanderers came out fast to open the second half. They seemed determined to wear down their opponents, but a string of penalties slowed their momentum. The game got rough and the penalties continued to pile up as the second half went on. Still, the Wanderers maintained a brisk pace, and were finally rewarded with the tying goal after 13 minutes of play. Four minutes later, both teams were two men short when Ross rushed the puck from end to end. His shot was blocked, and there was a lively scramble in front of the Ottawa net before he batted in a rebound. Pandemonium erupted, but the fans — except for the 600 or so who had travelled from Ottawa — fell silent just two minutes later when Alf Smith scored for the Senators.

The big crowd was tense with the game tied again. Another wild celebration ensued when Montreal's Walter Smaill went end to end and whipped in a shot just under the crossbar.

It was 3–2 Wanderers with seven minutes remaining, but referees Percy Quinn and Claude Spafford refused to put away their whistles. Tommy Phillips was banished for five minutes after a hit on Ernie "Moose" Johnson, but the sides were evened up a short time later when Stuart was issued five for pulling down Taylor with a hook around his throat. No sooner had those two returned to the ice then Pulford was sent off for tripping. The Wanderers clearly had the better of the play now, but couldn't get the goal that would clinch it. And then Phillips was banished for another penalty. The final blow came shortly thereafter when Ross once again rushed the length of the ice and fired the puck past Ottawa goalie Percy LeSueur. Thirty seconds later, the final gong rang and the Wanderers had a 4–2 victory.

In their dressing room afterwards, the Senators put the blame on the referees, but at a team party for players and family later that evening, the Wanderers expressed their belief that they had won it on merit. Reporters believed that the key to victory had been that, even with all the penalties, neither Walter Smaill nor Art Ross had been whistled for any infractions. They were the only skaters on the ice for the entire 60 minutes, and their stellar play made all the difference.

"The most popular hockey player in Montreal, or for that matter anywhere else," reported the *Toronto World* after the season ended,

> is likely Arthur Ross. One of the Ottawa players thus describes his effect on a crowd in the Arena: When Arthur Ross skates down the ice the crowd in the Montreal Arena stands up and yells. As he returns to his position, he is showered with hand claps. Should he indulge in that excusable habit of passing the sleeve of his sweater across his nostrils, everybody says: "Good boy, Arthur." When he retires at halftime he gets a hand. On his reappearance, a bevy of hands. Should he be ruled off the crowd cheers, then hisses the referee. When his time expires, another hand. He receives enough attention to spoil a whole family, but strange to say the big fellow takes it all in good part, and only wears a [size] six and seven-eights [hat].

After just one year in the game's top league, Art Ross had established himself among the best players in hockey. It was a position he retained for nearly 10 more years in a playing career that earned him his place in the Hockey Hall of Fame. Yet those who know his name today are most likely to know him for the 30 years he spent in management with the Boston Bruins from 1924 to 1954. Even more will know him only because of the award he donated, which has been handed out each season since 1948 to the NHL's leading scorer.

But Art Ross was so much more than a name on a trophy.

# PART 1:

Becoming a Legend

# 1

## GROWING UP IN THE
## HUDSON'S BAY COMPANY

All hockey records that list birth dates say Art Ross was born on January 13, 1886. However, there's a compelling argument that Art Ross was actually born in 1885. This comes from fellow hockey legend and childhood friend Frank Patrick, who was born on December 21, 1885. In the first of an eight-part autobiographical series that ran in the *Boston Sunday Globe* beginning on January 27, 1934, shortly after Ross hired him to coach the Boston Bruins, Patrick had this to say about his boyhood chum:

> When I first met Art Ross he was 12 years old and I was 11. Between then and now, Art seems to have lost time. He now claims he is a year and 23 days younger than I. My belief is that he is that year, less 23 days, older. But Art has lost his birth certificate (accidentally?) somewhere en route, so he has the edge on me there.

Of course, even Frank Patrick seems a bit confused, because if Ross was claiming to be a full year and 23 days younger than Patrick, that would mean that he was born on January 13, 1887. Clearly, though, Patrick recalled that Ross had been older than he when they were boys, and he believed him to have been born earlier in the same year that he was, and that year was 1885. In addition, records from Ross's one year at Bishop's College School and from the Merchants Bank of Canada, where he was first employed, show his birth date as January 13, 1885. When the grandchildren of Art Ross commissioned a new headstone in 2014 to mark his final resting place in the Mount Royal Cemetery in Montreal, Art Ross III had the birth year 1885 etched into the bronze.

Regardless of the date, the place of birth for Art Ross has always been listed as Naughton, Ontario. In fact, it's likely that Naughton — which since 1973 has been a part of the town of Walden, itself a community within the city of Sudbury — was merely the closest white settlement to the Hudson's Bay Company (HBC) post a few kilometres away, near the First Nations reserve on the western shore of Whitefish Lake where Ross was actually born. Ross's father had worked at that HBC post as a clerk since the late 1870s, and though the post was eventually relocated to Naughton, that was not until 1887.

Art's father, Thomas Barnston Ross, was born in February or March of 1844 in Chicoutimi, Quebec. His father, Simon, was a Scottish-born HBC employee who had worked in Canada since 1839. Thomas followed his father's footsteps, taking a job at the HBC post at Lake St. John, on the south shore of what is now known by its French name, Lac-Saint-Jean, some 70 kilometres west of the current city of Saguenay, in June of 1864. According to the HBC records, he was there for 12 years. On February 3, 1868, Thomas B. married Marguerite (Margaret) McLeod at Ste. Anne church in Chicoutimi. Margaret was said to have been the most beautiful woman in the Saguenay region, elegant, friendly, and very popular. To marry her, Thomas B. had to promise under oath and sign a document with the Catholic Church stating that their children would follow and practise the Catholic faith. However, only their first child was baptized a Catholic. This may have been due to Simon Ross's hatred of Catholics. He did not allow his own Irish Catholic wife to attend church and even refused her deathbed request for a priest to absolve her of her sins. He likely put pressure on Thomas B. to have his wife leave the church.

Whatever the reason, it's clear that Margaret McLeod-Ross had a falling out with her priest, Father Durocher, at some point, and chose to raise her children as Protestants. Her next four children, all born in the Saguenay, were baptized in the French Presbyterian Church and there is no baptismal record at all for her subsequent children. Many years later, John Ross (Art Ross's second of two sons) heard a story about his grand-mother's conversion. He thought it was one of the funniest stories he'd ever heard, and enjoyed telling it:

> She was attending a Roman Catholic Church in a small town in Quebec, with the priest threatening to call down the ashes of hell on the congregation if they didn't contribute to something or other. They didn't and the next week, the priest *did* call down the ashes of hell on everybody. A fog of ashes started to descend upon the congregation … until they heard a small voice from a helper, asking in French, from the attic, "Is that enough ashes, Monsieur?"

Margaret apparently got up from her pew and walked out of the church forever.

The first child of Thomas B. and Margaret Ross came barely 10 months after their wedding, when Simon Peter Ross was born on December 27, 1868. Hockey sources have long claimed that Art Ross was the 12th of 13 children; however, it appears that Thomas B. and Margaret had "only" nine sons and a daughter. George Munro Ross was the couple's second child, born May 19, 1870, the day of the Great Fire, which destroyed everything in a 150-kilometre stretch of the Saguenay, including Simon Ross's farm, Gladfield. Thomas Robert Ross, who was born on December 6, 1871, came next. Charles William (August 18, 1874) and daughter Sybil (March 21, 1876) followed. These five children were all born in Quebec, which is in keeping with the information on Thomas B.'s HBC biograph-ical sheet saying that he transferred to the Huron district in 1876.

Thomas R. Ross was interviewed about his early life at his home in Calgary, Alberta, in March of 1957 when he was 85 years old. In an arti-cle about him one month later in the HBC periodical the *Bay News*, an unaccredited author writes that when "Ross was a boy of eight the family was moved from the Saguenay to Huron district, where his father took charge of Whitefish Lake post, north of La Cloche, the district headquarters." (That would indicate Thomas R. remembered his family moving in 1879 or 1880 — although 1876 seems correct.) Today, La Cloche is unsupervised bush, located on the north shore of Georgian Bay directly above Manitoulin Island and not far from the towns of Espanola and Massey. Fairly remote even now, "it was," notes the *Bay News*, "an isolated region before the coming of the railway."

"The country over which my father presided," wrote Thomas R. Ross in 1906 while attending Queen's University in Kingston, Ontario, "is now the well known Sudbury District, famous for its nickel deposits. We lived in that country ten long years before the Canadian Pacific [Railway] passed through it. Our only means of travel and communication with the civilized world was by birch-bark canoe in the summer time, and by dog-team in winter."

All items of trade for the post, and all of the goods for the Ross family, were brought in every six months, in the fall and in the spring. The voyage to get supplies began with a canoe trip of 70 kilometres to the town of Little Current on Manitoulin Island. It was usually made by Thomas B. in the company of a team of Ojibwe from Whitefish Lake, but was sometimes made by Margaret in his place. From Little Current, Thomas B. or Margaret would travel 300 kilometres south by steamer on Lake Huron to Goderich, where a six-month cache of supplies was purchased. After the return trip to Little Current, Mr. or Mrs. Ross and the First Nations team would transport the goods by canoe to the post. It was a difficult journey that took many days and included many portages where everything had to be carried while on foot.

As for life at the post, "We had no schools," writes Thomas R., "no churches, no white companions. The only evidence of civilization were the few books, magazines, and home comforts we had brought with us."

Life at the post on Whitefish Lake was decidedly different from what the Rosses had been used to in the Saguenay district. In Chicoutimi, the Ross's had enjoyed a much more affluent and middle-class life. There were other family members around, and Margaret Ross oversaw a fine house with servants. She had a good social circle and a school for the children. After the move, as Thomas R. writes, "We stepped out of our one-storey log house into what seemed an unbounded wilderness."

Margaret gave birth to five more Ross sons in this wilderness: Roderick Reddie (1878), Alexander Sinclair (August 17, 1880), Colin Eric (October 3, 1882), Arthur Howey (not Howie, as it is often misspelled), and Donald Walter, who was born on September 8, likely in 1886, which is further circumstantial evidence of Art being born in 1885.

"There was a large family of us," writes Thomas R., though in this essay he is referring to a time when there were still only seven boys and one girl. "We played with the Indian children and learned to speak their language fluently. I can speak that language today as well as my own, possibly better."

Art Ross could also speak First Nations languages fluently. In the first installment of a seven-part series telling the story of his life, published in 1949, Ross told writer John Gillooly, "I could talk Indian at the age of 10." Arthur Siegel of the *Boston Globe* would later write that Ross could speak English, French "and Indian." Siegel noted that Ross and his brothers would still talk "Indian" over the telephone when they wanted to keep the conversations confidential.

"I can actually talk both Ojibway [sic] and Montagnais," Ross told Siegel. The two tongues, he explained, "were very similar." Ross also claimed that Ojibwe Indians had made his first pair of skates with items obtained at his father's trading post.

Margaret Ross was most responsible for what her children learned. "I owe my early education to my mother who taught us daily, reading and writing, in both French and English," Thomas R. writes. And although the Ross children had a tutor for a few months around the time Thomas was 14, his mother's lessons must have been remarkable, as sons Simon, George, Thomas, and Colin all grew up to attend university and become doctors.

The Rosses had not quite been living at Whitefish Lake the "ten long years" Thomas R. wrote about before the Canadian Pacific Railway came through. By 1883 railway surveyors had blazed their way some 90 kilometres west from Sturgeon Falls, now a community within the municipality of West Nipissing, 38 kilometres west of North Bay. A tote road was cut by February of 1883 and equipment and materials were being moved into a hastily built new company town for the summer construction season. In mid February, the new village was named Sudbury.

"Rough and rugged in the extreme," was the way Provincial Land Surveyor Francis Bolger described the area. "[T]he terrain," writes C.M. Barrie in the book *Sudbury: Rail Town to Regional Capital*, "dominated by gigantic rock outcrops interspersed with extensive swamps and endless lakes, was the most difficult imaginable for railway workers." The land was too rocky to be of much use to farmers, and though the area around Whitefish Lake remained almost untouched, bush fires destroyed most of the timber in the region during the summer of 1883. The burned-out land was a boon to the railway workers, as it required less work to clear.

During the summer of 1883, some 3,350 workmen arrived in the Sudbury area. However, by the time trains rolled through in December of 1884, the population of the village had shrunk to only 200 or 300 people. Meanwhile, there were still only the Ross family and the Ojibwe living in the neighbouring area on the western shore of Whitefish Lake. On October 27, 1883, Ontario Provincial Land Surveyor W.O. Johnson wrote that "the Hudson's Bay Company have a very neat little post, under the very efficient care of Mr. Thomas B. Ross." Besides the Rosses, "there are no other settlers in [Graham] township."

Among the large group that descended on Sudbury in the summer of 1883, and part of the smaller contingent that remained, was Dr. William Howey, who came to Sudbury with his wife on July 1, 1883. Dr. Howey had been tending to the ailments of workers as a physician for the Canadian Pacific Railway since December of 1882. In 1933, Florence Howey (godmother to Art Ross and the source of his unusual middle name) began writing *Pioneering on the C.P.R.*, which was published in 1938, two years after her death at the age of 80. Among the slim volume's 141 pages are some very vivid accounts of what life was like for the Ross family at Whitefish Lake.

During their first summer in Sudbury, Dr. Howey was told of a lake beyond the hills, and the sights to be seen there. "It sounded like a story book," writes Florence, "real Indians and a real Hudson Bay Post. We decided to visit it at the earliest opportunity."

The Howeys set out in a borrowed canoe with directions for how to find the portage to Whitefish Lake. "We found it without much trouble," she writes, "a narrow footpath over a steep hill to the Indian Reservation. On reaching the top we looked down to the other side equally steep, upon a beautiful little lake.... Opposite were the buildings of the post, some children were playing on the beach."

A "hello" attracted the attention of the two young boys, who ran inside to announce the presence of visitors, they came out again, pushed a canoe into the water, and paddled out to greet their callers.

"Arriving at our side, they took off their hats greeting us most respectfully. They said they were Simon and George Ross, sons of the trader in charge of the post and asked if they could do anything for us."

Upon learning the names of their guests, the Ross boys told them that their mother had heard of Dr. Howey and would be pleased to welcome them for dinner.

"We were surprised," Florence admits, "at so much courtesy, from such little fellows reared in such an isolated place."

Writing about her visit some 50 years later, Florence Howey appears to get some facts confused, stating that the Rosses had been at the post for 12 years. She also names all 10 Ross children, plus a baby, while describing a New Year's Eve party in 1883. Even so, her account of the day she met the Rosses is remarkably vivid. Florence was amazed that Margaret Ross had borne eight children in the wilderness, which would be the correct number for 1883 (although only three had been born at the post by then) "with no doctor and no one but Indian women to care for her." She recalls being given "a good dinner" and that she and the doctor were shown around the post afterwards.

"There was a garden, and there were hens and a cow. There was also the store, where all kinds of dry goods required by the Indians were kept, and sold to them in return for furs."

Life was definitely rustic in the Huron district, even with Sudbury beginning to grow, but Thomas B. was good at his job. An inspecting officer based at the Hudson's Bay Company's Commissioner's Office in Winnipeg wrote the following report about him in 1888:

> Thos. B. Ross, Clerk, 45 years of age, 24 years in service, contract expires 1888, one hundred and twenty pounds per annum, married, 7 children resident, a very good trader, intelligent and deeply interested in Company and well worthy on account of the past as well as his capabilities of some promotion.

The contract was obviously renewed, and a promotion to junior chief trader came through in 1890. Yet his biographical sheet from the HBC states that Thomas B. Ross resigned from the company just a few years later, on June 30, 1896. The resignation was accepted on August 14, but he "stayed on the books" — meaning that he was still paid — until 1903. Other HBC sources claim he "retired on pension on May 31, 1904." All of this is may well be true. Still, by the end of 1895, Thomas B. Ross's marriage had fallen apart and he disappeared from his family's life.

Art Ross's son John had some idea of what happened. Though admitting that his father did not welcome questions about it, John believed that, Thomas B. Ross "left [the family] early and penniless," after suffering "devastating financial losses." John believed — erroneously it turned out — that Thomas B. had taken his own life.

Art Ross III offers a theory as to how one might succumb to "devastating losses" in the wilderness, despite a thriving market for one's goods, and no significant conflicts, droughts, or other natural disasters. It involves mining, and the difficulties encountered by those working in other professions who chose to moonlight as prospectors.

Tales of copper being found in the area that would become Sudbury date back to the 1630s. By 1856, there was an official notation of iron, copper, and nickel in the district in the Geological Survey of Canada. Nothing of note was found in observations of the area in the early part of 1883, but by that fall, talk of valuable rocks was in the air. Legend has it that a blacksmith named Thomas Flanagan swung his pick while working on the railway and struck a mineral vein. Florence Howey writes that her husband had found bright specks in bits of rock he had picked up while blasting was going on. Though it was wrongly declared to be of no value, prospectors came to see for themselves and in October of 1884 the first mining patents were issued.

It would take years — and huge companies with enormous capital — to mine the riches of the Sudbury region, but amateur prospectors couldn't know that at the time, and they began staking claims. According to Hudson's Bay Company records, on July 15, 1889, "an Indian named Michel Winde-Kenisaw" discovered a deposit. Fifteen months later, on October 21, 1890, a patent was issued "to Thomas Barnetson [sic] Ross and Donald Campbell MacTavish." Ross and MacTavish, who was the chief factor of the Huron district, named their site after Lord Strathcona, the long-time governor of the HBC.

Michel Winde-Kenisaw (this time identified as Winge-kissinaw, but almost assuredly the same person) made another discovery in 1890, which he also disposed of to Thomas B. Ross. A grant from the Crown was received on May 23, 1891, and this site became known as the Ross Mine. Some exploration went on in 1891 and 1892, but the Ross Mine wouldn't see production until 1943. Similarly the Strathcona Mine seems to have been a bust until Falconbridge Limited finally developed the site, but not until 1968.

Did Thomas B. Ross invest the family fortune in land rights, mining equipment, and whatever else a prospector might need in the hunt for nickel and copper in the 1890s? Did he squander his money and leave his family destitute before moving on? Mining fever quite possibly hurt the family's finances, but regardless of the possible loss of the family's money through speculation, it appears that the family's problems were compounded by Margaret falling in love with another man — though perhaps Thomas B. pushed her to him.

Peter McKenzie was an HBC man for most of his life. He spent nearly 40 years at posts in northern Quebec, near Ungava Bay, moving up the ranks from clerk to chief factor. However, for a brief period beginning in 1890, McKenzie returned to the Huron district, where he had been born, to work as chief factor there. This would have made him Thomas B.'s boss.

McKenzie was only in Sudbury about a year. It's impossible to know how much contact Peter McKenzie had with Thomas B. Ross and Margaret, but it's likely to have been a lot. Was there an actual affair between McKenzie and Margaret, or merely a mutual attraction? In any case, it seems that Thomas B. Ross was no longer comfortable in the Sudbury area even after McKenzie was gone. Within a year, he asked for a transfer back to the Saguenay district, apparently in the hope that the more comfortable life his family had known there would help heal the relationship between him and his wife.

On June 9, 1892, the *Sudbury Journal* reported that, "Mr. and Mrs. T.B. Ross, with the younger members of their family leave by the Soo train Saturday night [June 11] for their future home at Lake St. Johns, Que." A week later, the same paper reported that speeches were made at a going-away party given in their honour, after which Thomas B. thanked everyone for the magnificent set of silverware given to the family as a present and Margaret extended, "a cordial invitation to those present to visit them at their new home."

The report hardly makes it sound like the couple was in crisis or facing the public scandal of indiscretion. And yet, the next few years in the Saguenay district would play out like a soap opera. One thing that's certain during this time is that on April 25, 1894, Roderick Ross, the couple's sixth child, died of a burst appendix. This could only have added stress to a marriage that was coming apart.

Once stationed at the Pointe Bleue post on Lake St. John in the Saguenay district, Thomas B. Ross took to drinking. He also began to suffer from mental problems and became prone to violence. According to a friend's account, when Thomas B. got drunk he could sometimes be found in the company of another woman, identified only as Obéline. Apparently, after one particular incident with Obéline, Margaret forced Thomas B. to move out. It's unclear exactly how many Ross children were still in the family home at the time, but before Christmas of 1895, Margaret took those children and moved back to Naughton, near Whitefish Lake and Sudbury.

From 1867 to 1968, it took an Act of Divorce in Parliament to nullify a marriage. As a result, divorces were difficult to obtain, and no record has surfaced confirming whether Margaret and Thomas B. officially got one.

Despite this, on December 26, 1895, in the bottom right-hand corner of page one of the *Sudbury Journal*, the following wedding notice appears:

> McKenzie — Ross — At Naughton on December 23, by Rev. S. Roundeau, of Sudbury. Mr. Peter McKenzie Chief Factor Hudson's Bay Co'y, Montreal to Margaret McLeod Ross of Naughton, Algoma

The wedding is confirmed in the marriage records on file with the Archives of Ontario. Margaret is listed with an "S" for spinster (meaning she was single), not with a "W" for widow. There is no designation listed for divorce. However, reading between the lines in a letter written by Margaret a few years later, it would seem there had been an official dissolution of the marriage, though it wouldn't likely be recognized in Catholic-dominated Quebec, which probably explains why she married Peter McKenzie in Naughton.

Regardless of how it ended, Thomas B. Ross didn't take the breakup of his marriage well. It seems he had truly loved his wife and never got over her leaving him. Soon after her marriage to Peter McKenzie, Thomas B. suffered a long and severe nervous breakdown. He was committed to a mental asylum for a time. When he got out, there are more stories of drinking and violence. He was arrested for disorderly conduct several times, and it was said to be common to see him crying while looking at the faded picture of Margaret he always carried with him. In a letter written in 1947, a man by the name of Ernest Bilodeau relayed a story about Thomas B. told to him by his father, who had served as the justice of the peace in one of his cases. The two men apparently entered a room to talk, and Thomas B. removed the picture of Margaret from his pocket. "Bilodeau," he said gravely, "when I lost this, I lost everything."

Eventually, Thomas B. Ross was legally required to leave the Saguenay district. By 1903 he was living in Seven Islands (Sept-Îles), Quebec, and had married a woman named Mabel Eunice Mason in Quebec City that October. They already had a child together — or perhaps Mabel had one previous to their relationship — but the marriage appears not to have lasted. Margaret wrote that Thomas B.'s drinking took its toll on his health and that his new family moved to Los Angeles before the end of 1903 for the benefit of its warmer climate. However, by 1904, Thomas B. was apparently living alone in the Old Men's home in Victoria, British Columbia. He'd live out the rest of his days in that city, all but forgotten, before finally dying on May 19, 1930.

Thomas R. Ross's granddaughter Helen Webster recalled that her grandfather "never mentioned his father, at least in my hearing, nor directly to me." She does state that Thomas R. had contempt for HBC men who left their families to take Indian wives. "NOT because of the Indian wives," writes Helen, "but because they abandoned first their own families, and then in some cases, abandoned their Indian wives and children when white women 'became available to them.' (His words, not mine.)"

Is the implication, perhaps, that Thomas B. drove Margaret into the arms of Peter McKenzie, and that, perhaps the mysterious Obéline was a First Nations woman?

"Pure speculation," Helen admits, "though my mother also spoke of hearing a rumor to this effect."

Another family member had similar memories, though she makes somewhat different deductions. Audrey Gardiner-Tierney's mother, Eleanor, was the youngest of five children born to Simon Peter Ross (the eldest son of Thomas B. and Margaret) and his wife Ella. In September of 1901, just 11 months after Eleanor was born, her mother died of pneumonia and Eleanor was sent to live with Margaret and Peter McKenzie. Audrey says there was one supreme family law that nobody ever broke: you didn't talk or ask questions about what had happened to Thomas B.! However, Audrey's mother told her that when she lived with Margaret, there were certain times when she made pointed observations about her past life and Eleanor was able to draw some conclusions. As she understood it, the problems began almost as soon as Thomas B. accepted the transfer from the Saguenay to the Huron District. Margaret didn't want to go and was never happy with the loneliness and hardship of life there, or with her seemingly endless periods of pregnancy. Eventually, she couldn't stand it anymore, and even the return to the Saguenay district couldn't fix the damage.

"I feel that slowly she had begun to despise [her husband]," writes family historian Serge Harvey. "The cost [to their marriage] was enormous."

# 2

# THE MOVE
# TO MONTREAL

Peter McKenzie must have been a remarkable man. Far from being a home-wrecker who appears as a villain in the Ross family saga, he seems to have been truly in love with Margaret, and good to his new family.

Though he had a grown son he remained close to from a relationship with a First Nations woman in northern Quebec, McKenzie had never married before. Now, he found himself with a wife (whom he called Maggie) and at least five of her 10 children. He brought them all to Montreal in 1896, just as Art Ross was turning 11, and bought a big house for them at 4492 St. Catherine Street West in Westmount. He seems to have been a happy man. In a letter dated January 28, 1900, the former Jennie Ryan, who had married Thomas Robert Ross four days earlier and was honeymooning in Montreal with her new husband, writes that, "all the brothers and everyone else here have been the soul of all that is good and kind." Jennie also describes her delight in the gifts presented to the newlyweds by the family, including "from Arthur a linen five o'clock tea cloth."

In his own writings, McKenzie mentions his wife and her children in a letter to his brother George (another long-time HBC employee) dated June 29, 1900. It is a small, but insightful look, into the life of his new family:

> Sybil leaves on the 2nd for some damn place on the Main
> [sp] Coast called Kennebunk Beach, the Schultze girls per-
> suaded her to go down there. Arthur & Donald are going to
> their brother Robert [Thomas R. Ross], & Colin to Seven
> Islands. Maggie and I will wander along the coast as far as
> Seven Islands, Mingan, and St. Augustine…

In his will, dated May 29, 1903, McKenzie made provisions for all nine of the Ross children then living, as well as Maggie, his own son Charles, his brother George, an aunt living in Scotland, and a few others. Though the shares were small, being split 16 ways, McKenzie expected to leave a sizable sum when he departed. He believed his estate would be worth upwards of $20,000 by the time he died, which could be valued as high as $9 million today.

It's apparent the Ross children loved their stepfather. Perhaps the best indication of the feelings they had is the fact that, in 1919, Art Ross named his second son John Kay McKenzie Ross. And, of course, if Peter McKenzie hadn't married Margaret and brought the Ross children to Montreal, Art Ross's life — and the history of hockey — would have been very different. For even though Ross had learned to skate on boots and blades bought from his father and built by the Ojibwe, it was not until he moved to Westmount with his stepfather that he discovered his abundant talent for sports.

There is no record of any culture shock when Margaret Ross and her children came to Montreal, though there must have been some period of adjustment after moving to the country's biggest, richest, and most import-ant city. Art Ross grew up in the most affluent of Montreal suburbs, and it was in Westmount that he first met other future hockey stars such as Frank and Lester Patrick, Sprague and Odie Cleghorn, and Walter Smaill. "Hockey wasn't the only sport on our minds," Frank Patrick would write of the group of friends who grew up together in Westmount. "Almost every young boy competed in football, baseball, basketball and [track] as well as hockey." In a 1900 letter, Jennie Ross writes: "Arthur has asked us to go to the gymnasium tomorrow night to see himself and some other boys play basketball." But it was baseball that first brought Art Ross and the Patricks together.

"I soon learned that those of us that did not have baseball or bat had better tie up with a certain youngster who had a monopoly on the game," said Lester Patrick in a short summary of his life he wrote around 1947. "He was Mr. BIG. He would not like me to refer to him as a rich man's son but we certainly thought he was just that. He had ball, bats, gloves, catcher's mitt, mask — he had everything. And that's where I first met up with a gentleman that was to cross my path for the rest of my days — MR. ARTHUR HOWIE [sic] ROSS."

"When he showed up," writes Lester, "the game could start. He also had a lot of talent. He was a fine athlete, even then."

As Frank Patrick indicated, Ross played everything. It was said he could kick a ball 40 or 50 yards without much effort and he could kick equally well with either foot. He was also ambidextrous in baseball.

"We were playing a game one day," Ross related to John Gillooly for the second part of a series on his life, which appeared in the *Boston Daily Record* on December 5, 1949. "[T]he score was close and Les Patrick was on third. He didn't know I could throw with each hand. I was pitching, and he was taunting me from third. So I made the customary throw from the mound to first to keep the runner close to the base there. Les took a big lead off third. I took the return throw from first with my left hand, my glove under my arm, and whipped the ball to third and picked Patrick off by a couple of yards. The things he called me you couldn't print in that newspaper of yours."

Other stories claim Ross would sometimes start games pitching right-handed but finish the last few innings as a lefty if his team had a safe lead. Andy Lytle, writing in the *Toronto Star* on October 20, 1949, quoted Lester Patrick with a story to tell about that! As Lester related, Ross was pitching right-handed and beating his team pretty badly when Lester started needling him about his boast that he could pitch equally well as a lefty. "Well, Ross switched to left-handed and began to get hit all over the lot. Having switched, he wouldn't reverse, and we trimmed his club to a fare-thee-well." When he wasn't pitching, Ross was a heavy-hitting first baseman and, according to Gillooly, once had a tryout with a top minor league team in Minneapolis.

In addition to team sports, Ross excelled at boxing and wrestling. Later, he would become a pretty good bowler, a champion trap shooter, and an excellent golfer. He once enjoyed driving balls into a lake with Babe Didrickson Zaharias, perhaps the greatest all-around female athlete of the 1930s and a championship golfer of the 1940s and 1950s. Lytle also quoted legendary Montreal sportswriter Elmer Ferguson (for whom the Hockey Hall of Fame's writing award is named) saying that he considered Ross to be the greatest and most versatile of Canadian athletes. "[Lionel] Conacher was great," said Ferguson of the man who was named Canada's Athlete of the Half-Century in 1950, "but Ross even more so."

Not surprisingly, with Montreal teams winning the Stanley Cup virtually every year from 1893 to 1903, hockey was the game that excited the boys in Westmount most. "I developed 'hockeyitis' with the other kids in my gang," Lester Patrick writes, "and played at every opportunity." Roads paved with Macadam allowed the boys to play hockey games year-round if they chose to. "We played street shinny in Westmount each year until the rinks froze," Lester remembered.

By the time a state-of-the-art Arena opened in Montreal at Wood Avenue and St. Catherine Street on December 31, 1898, Lester was playing hockey for Montreal High School and got to play at the Arena on occasion. He also began to operate a successful ticket scalping business with his pal, Art Ross.

"I applied my savings to buying the 35¢ reserved tickets," Lester remembered, "and sold them at $1 per. Terrific prices in those days."

At a game in 1899, Lester recalled clearing $15 in profits. "It was so much money that I was in a dilemma as to how I could spend it without having to explain to my father."

Not all hockey-related enterprises were as lighthearted.

On March 1, 1900, news that the British army fighting in South Africa had finally ended the 118-day siege by the Boers on the town of Ladysmith was telegraphed around the world. French Canadians had not been pleased in October of 1899 when Prime Minister Wilfrid Laurier had committed 1,000 Canadian troops to the British war effort. Many Quebeckers sympathized with the Boers, a Dutch minority population who only wished to live free of British rule. When news of the Relief of Ladysmith reached Montreal, English students from McGill University rushed into the snowy streets to celebrate. A parade of revelers waving Union Jacks — many of them flying from hockey sticks — caught the attention of Art Ross and Lester Patrick, and they fell in with the rowdy crowd. When the McGill students reached the French and Catholic campus of Laval University, things got ugly.

Writing in his biography of the Patrick family, author Eric Whitehead said: "The ensuing battle lasted for more than an hour, and it took a squad of 50 policemen to restore peace. Dozens of combatants were hauled off in paddy wagons, and in one of those, nursing a bruised eye and a bloody nose respectively, were Curtis Lester Patrick and Arthur Howie [sic] Ross of Westmount. They were later claimed by their parents and taken home in disgrace."

Recalling the incident, Lester Patrick said, "My father didn't speak to me for three days while I sweated over what punishment I would receive. I guess he figured this was punishment enough, and on the fourth day everything was fine again." There is no record of how Peter McKenzie or Maggie dealt with the incident, or what punishment, if any, Ross received.

In addition to the pickup games he played with friends in the streets and fields of their neighbourhood, Art Ross honed his sports skills with the Westmount Amateur Athletic Association (AAA) and by playing for various teams while attending high school at the Westmount Academy. Ross played hockey for both Westmount institutions, as well as a few others. He later recalled a Saturday on which he played for a church league team from 8:00 to 9:00 a.m., for his academy team from 11:00 to noon, and for the Montreal Wanderers intermediate team, who were short a man, from 3:00 to 4:00 p.m. He then played basketball that night.

Ross would, of course, gain his lasting fame in hockey, but rugby was the sport in which he truly excelled in his younger days. "Football, or rugby," he explained to the *Boston Traveler* with a faraway look in his eye on the night of his induction to the Hockey Hall of Fame nearly half a century later, "was probably my best sport." Ross played a position known as centre-half (the middle of three halfback positions) and "while there were thirteen other members of his team on the field," a newspaper reporter once said, "he was reckoned fifty per cent of their strength."

In the early years of the twentieth century, the terms rugby, football, and rugby-football were used almost interchangeably. A fan today looking back at the game would certainly recognize it more as rugby than football, but the sport in Canada had already begun to change in subtle ways that were leading it from traditional English rugby to modern Canadian football. Ross excelled as a halfback in this rugged game, and in the fall of 1902, when he was only 17 years old, he captained the Westmount AAA junior team to the city championship with a perfect 4–0 record in the double round-robin series with the Montreal AAA and Britannia clubs. This title qualified Westmount to face the junior team from Quebec City for the Quebec Rugby Football Union (QRFU) junior championship in a home-and-home, total-points series. The series began in Quebec City on Saturday, November 8 and concluded in Montreal one week later.

Westmount won the opener 8–6 behind Ross's first-half drop kick for a field goal — worth five points then — and three single points in the second half after Quebec had scored the game's only touchdown (worth just four points, but with the chance for a conversion kick worth two more). Back home, Westmount scored a 19–4 victory to take the series 27–10. Ross's strong rushing, fine lateral passing, and powerful kicking leg were the keys to the victory, and after the game the *Quebec Chronicle* reported that he was "bounced by his team and carried in triumph to Victoria Hall."

A year later, Ross moved up to Westmount's intermediate rugby team, and captained them not only to city and provincial victories, but to the Canadian national title as well — although, at the time, only teams from Quebec and Ontario contested what was known as the Dominion championship. The big game was played at the University of Toronto's Varsity Field on November 28, 1903. Westmount defeated the Toronto Victorias 13–6. The *Toronto Star* reported that Captain Ross "was the pick of the back division simply because he did the bulk of the work." But according to Toronto's *Mail and Empire*, the Westmount captain was carried off the field at the end of the game not in triumph as he'd been the year before, but "suffering from an accidental kick to the head."

Art Ross appears to have begun his organized hockey career with the Westmount Amateur Athletic Association team in the intermediate division of the Canadian Amateur Hockey League (CAHL) during the winter of 1900–01 — though there was a player named Ross who appeared in some games with the Montreal Victorias' intermediate club in 1899–1900. Lester Patrick also played at least one game with Westmount in 1900–01, though he would spend the winter of 1901–02 winning a championship with the Montreal AAA junior team, which he considered to be his "first organized league hockey experience." Ross and Frank Patrick both played for the Westmount intermediates that year, and Ross and the two Patrick brothers all joined forces with the team in 1902–03. Despite the presence of three future hall of famers, Westmount couldn't top the Montreal AAA intermediate team for league honours that year.

Art Ross missed the entire 1903–04 hockey season, not because of any lingering concussion symptoms from the football kick, but because he and his sister Sybil had typhoid fever. Frank Patrick nearly led Westmount to the intermediate title during Ross's lost season, but Lester Patrick spent that winter playing senior hockey — the highest level of the game — in Brandon, Manitoba.

Lester was back in Montreal by the winter of 1904–05, and that year, he and a fully recovered Art Ross led the Westmount AAA team in its first season as a senior hockey club in the CAHL. (Frank would make a brief appearance as well.) Playing at the senior level qualified a team to challenge for the Stanley Cup, but it's doubtful Westmount had its sights set that high.

Ross had spent the fall of 1904 as captain of the Westmount AAA rugby team in its first appearance in the senior circuit of the QRFU. Westmount couldn't quite compete with the league's best teams that year, and the senior hockey team would fare no better. Westmount's cause wasn't aided during the 1904–05 hockey season by the fact that Lester Patrick spent the winter helping his father run the mill for the family lumber business in Daveluyville, Quebec, some 150 kilometres north and east of Montreal. "I played all league games for the Westmount Senior Club," Patrick writes, "but did not practice on a single occasion." Note, however, that the *Montreal Gazette*, in writing about a Westmount practice on December 16, 1904, states that, "Lester Patrick was out last night and did good work."

With or without Lester, practice certainly didn't seem to make perfect, as the *Gazette* of December 30 noted: "Westmount has the record for breaking globes at the Arena," which would indicate that their wild shots were breaking light bulbs above the playing surface. Still, as the team geared up for its season opener against the Montreal Shamrocks at the Arena on Saturday night, January 7, 1905, their fans were excited. "The Westmount slogan is: 'Shoot, Ross, shoot,'" the *Gazette* reported on the day of the game. But shooting wasn't the problem.

"A Record Game Won by Shamrock" read the *Gazette* headline atop the sports page on Monday, January 9, over the story about Westmount's 14–10 defeat in its senior debut. "While critics may argue that such a large score was due to weaknesses of defence on both teams, it may truly be said that the public has not been treated to such an exhibition of speedy hockey for many moons.... Both teams sent out fast lines, and both defences were strong.... The game was played almost with six forwards, because the defence men of both teams jumped into the fray so often that they were practically on the front line all the time...."

Playing defence for Westmount that night were Art Ross at cover point and Lester Patrick at point. The *Gazette* noted that they "could bring out the puck in fine style, but the pair did not prove to be so adept in useful checking...."

This would be a pattern throughout the season. Ross, who captained the Westmount team and lined up at point, cover point, and rover throughout the season, finished among the top scorers in the CAHL — although well back of the leader — with 10 goals during the eight games he played. That was quite a feat for a 20-year-old in his first year of senior hockey, but poor goaltending behind Westmount's offense-first approach doomed the team to a league-worst 75 goals against and a record of just 3–7, including one win by default. Westmount would never again place a hockey team in the senior division, but it would be onward and upward for Art Ross.

# 3

## GO WEST
## YOUNG MAN

Art Ross graduated from Westmount Academy in the spring of 1903. Guided by his mother and stepfather, he embarked on a career in banking. Ross began work as a clerk at the Merchants Bank in Montreal (likely at the head office on St. James Street) on October 4, 1903. During the winter of 1904–05, he played hockey for a Merchants Bank team in a local bankers' league in addition to the games he played for Westmount. An off-ice job was an important fact of life for all Canadian athletes in this era.

The first openly professional hockey league, the International Hockey League (IHL), started up in the winter of 1904–05 with a team in Pittsburgh, three on Michigan's Upper Peninsula, and another in Sault Ste. Marie, Ontario. It was the first opportunity many players had to earn an honest paycheque playing the game. While some players in Canada likely received small, under-the-table payments and others were over-paid for cushy off-ice jobs, hockey in Canada remained officially ama-teur, as did most sports in a country where many people of influence still clung to the British aristocratic idea of sports for sport's sake. Even when Canadian lacrosse teams began openly paying for talent around 1904, nobody earned enough money as an athlete that they didn't require employment elsewhere. So it was that Art Ross's job with the Merchants Bank soon played a key role in his hockey future.

In the meantime, as captain of Westmount's senior rugby squad, Ross began preparing his team in early September of 1905 for its season opener at the end of the month against the Rough Riders in Ottawa. Following three straight losses to open the season, there was dissention in the ranks. On October 20, 1905, the *Montreal Gazette* noted that, "Arthur Ross, centre-half and captain, has sent in his resignation to the club, and will [not] be seen in a Westmount uniform on Saturday.... As to the reasons that induced Capt. Ross to resign it is understood that there was some difficulty between the committee on the one hand, and the captains on the other, in regard to the running of the team. This difficulty finally resulted in the resignation of the captain."

Ross would referee football games in Montreal until the end of the local season in early November, but there were rumours that he'd leave the city for Ottawa and join the Rough Riders in their attempt to win the Canadian senior rugby championship at the end of the month. Then it was thought he would join the three-time defending Stanley Cup–champion Ottawa "Silver Seven" for the hockey season. Instead, Art Ross went west, to Brandon, Manitoba, as his friend Lester Patrick had done two years earlier. In fact, it was likely Lester who sent him there.

According to a story Montreal Canadiens general manager Frank Selke heard from Lester Patrick, "They were looking for a hockey player out in Brandon and a bank job was the bait." Brandon hoped Lester could be lured back, but he had a steady position in his father's lumber business. Patrick was also being wooed by the Montreal Victorias, whom he'd ultimately turn down in favour of an offer from the Montreal Wanderers. Lester turned down Brandon as well, "but he recommended Art, who was working in a bank at the time."

Mr. J.R. Little, manager of the Brandon branch of the Merchants Bank of Canada, made the arrangements for Ross's transfer out of Montreal, and at 9:30 a.m. on Sunday morning, November 12, 1905, Ross boarded a Canadian Pacific Railway train for the west. "His departure," noted the *Montreal Herald*, "will be regretted by hosts of friends, as he is very popular in Montreal." His arrival in Brandon on the afternoon of November 14 rated a small headline on the front page of the *Brandon Daily Sun*.

Brandon was a long way from Montreal, both figuratively and literally, but the second-largest city in Manitoba — though then, and always, much smaller than Winnipeg — was in the midst of an economic boom. As Ross stepped off the train in Brandon, he was greeted by officers of the senior team of the Brandon Hockey Club (commonly referred to as the "Wheat City" team) and by local bank officials. While in Brandon, he'd work as a clerk at the Merchants Bank and live above it with three or four of his fellow clerks. It's reasonable to assume that the room was a bonus in addition to the $600 annual salary he received from the bank — although a pay rate of $50 per month was then a fine wage for a young man of 20.

When he left Montreal, Art Ross was known as a great rugby player and a strong all-around athlete. By the time he moved to Brandon, he'd certainly reached his full height, which is usually listed in hockey records as 5'11" but was often noted as 6' in newspapers of the day. (His thick, wavy hair, which he tended to wear piled high to the right, could have added the extra inch!) He probably hadn't reached his full adult weight of 190 pounds, but he'd still have been quite large for a hockey player in this era. However, he was not yet a star on the ice. In fact, the Wanderers probably went after Lester Patrick because they felt Ross wasn't good enough. That all changed in Brandon.

Hockey in Brandon dates back at least to 1898 when the city had a team playing in the intermediate division of the Manitoba and Northwest Hockey Association. After winning the league title in 1901–02, the team moved up to the senior division the following winter and the city built the Caledonia rink, with a capacity of about 2,000 spectators. With Montrealers Lester Patrick, Harry Bright, and George "Doc" Smith added to the team in 1903–04, Brandon won the Manitoba senior title and challenged Ottawa for the Stanley Cup. When Lester returned home after the season, Brandon fell behind the Rat Portage Thistles in the 1904–05 standings. Brandon, Portage la Prairie, the Winnipeg Hockey Club (known as the Winnipegs), and the Winnipeg Victorias would all chase Kenora (as Rat Portage changed its name to in 1905) for the Manitoba Hockey League title during the Ross's first season there.

Practice for the new season began in Brandon on Monday night, December 4, 1905. Art Ross and his new teammates were on the ice from 7:00 to 8:00 that evening. A good crowd of fans was also on hand. The team would continue to practice on Monday, Wednesday, and Friday evenings. After the Wednesday workout on December 6, the *Manitoba Free Press* reported that "it looks as though the [Brandon] team will certainly be stronger than ever before." However, newspapers of the era rarely shied away from hyperbole and homerism, so it's impossible to know what the reporter really thought.

A schedule for the new season was drawn up at a league meeting in Winnipeg on December 9. Each of the five teams would play once at home and once away against their four league rivals for a total of eight games apiece. The season began on December 27, with Brandon on the road at Portage la Prairie. "Considerable interest is taken in the game," noted the *Daily Sun* that day.

The Brandon players were dressed in the club's traditional colours — yellow sweaters featuring black collars, shoulders, and cuffs, with "Wheat City" emblazoned on the chest in black. While Art Ross played cover point, lining up at rover for Portage la Prairie that evening was a smallish player making his debut in senior hockey. The young man from tiny Listowel, Ontario, had come to Manitoba after being banned from playing in his home province by the Ontario Hockey Association for alleged violations of residency rules after attempting to play in the town of Thessalon during the winter of 1904–05. This would be the first of many match-ups between Art Ross and Fred Taylor. Although he was not yet known by the nickname "Cyclone," Taylor's blazing speed was already in evidence, but it wouldn't help him much on the night of his debut. In its recap of the game, the *Portage la Prairie Semi-Weekly News* criticized Taylor for relying "too much on individual play."

Brandon took an early lead when Art Ross scored the opening goal at 2:30 of the first period. Play was rough throughout the first half, with seven players, including Ross, all penalized during the first 30 minutes as Brandon took a 3–0 lead. Both teams played better hockey in the second half, according to the Portage la Prairie paper, though the

*Brandon Daily Sun's* writer thought the home team only began to improve once the visitors eased up after taking a 4–0 lead. Ross's second goal of the night rounded out a 5–2 victory. "The Brandon team had the best of the game all the way through," reported the *Sun*, but the hometown reporter disagreed. "The game was hardly up to last year's senior standard," he complained. "Although the visitors won by a good margin, they did not have the best of the play by any means...." Still, "Brandon has a strong defence," the Portage paper admitted in its "Notes of the Game" segment, adding of Art Ross that, "Brandon's new man at cover point is quite a find and plays good hockey."

Brandon's next scheduled league game, at home against Kenora on January 8, would be a much bigger challenge. But first, there was a trip to Regina for an exhibition contest with the Capitals of that city. Again Brandon took an early lead, and was ahead 5–1 by the first few minutes of the second half before scrambling to hang on for a 6–4 victory. Ross, who scored twice, was referred to by the *Regina Leader* as "a wonder" who was "always making trouble for the boys in red and white, for he's there with the goods at every stage of the game." A story appearing in the *Manitoba Free Press* expressed similar sentiments: "Ross was undoubtedly the star of the visiting team," the Winnipeg paper reported, "treating the spectators to some most brilliant play."

After two road victories, Brandon fans were excited about the team's home debut against Kenora, who'd lost their opening game of the season. The *Daily Sun* promised a "hair-splitting contest," adding that, "the Brandon team are all in good shape and are prepared to put up the game of their lives and are confident of winning." They didn't.

Despite playing before a large crowd that filled every available space in the Caledonia rink, the hometown team fell to the Thistles 6–1. Ross scored the only Brandon goal and Winnipeg's *Morning Telegram* said he played "a splendid game," adding that, "it was seldom that any of the opposing forwards could pass him." When Brandon met the Thistles in Kenora a week later, the *Manitoba Free Press* noted that, "Ross was one of the fastest and pluckiest men on the ice, his rushes always being dangerous." Still the result was another 6–1 victory for the Thistles.

Kenora would not lose another game all season. The Thistles finished with a 7–1 record to win their second straight Manitoba championship, though it took a tie-breaking playoff against the Winnipegs, who also finished 7–1, to claim the title. Brandon finished the season with a record of 3–4–1, but when their tie with the Winnipegs was replayed (the game had been called when the lights went out with 12 minutes remaining and the score 2–2), the result was a 6–2 loss that dropped Brandon's final record to 3–5.

Despite the team's lack of success, it was a breakthrough season for Art Ross. The Thistles and Winnipegs dominated when critics made their selections for Manitoba Hockey League all-star honours, but Ross earned a spot as well. He had "done great stunts for Brandon at cover point this season and was pretty nearly the whole works on the Wheat City team," noted Winnipeg's *Morning Telegram* on March 12, 1906. "Most of the forwards in the league are agreed that he is about the hardest cover point to pass in the league, while his speed and skill in stickhandling make him a dangerous rusher."

All this had been noted with interest back in Montreal.

"Arthur Ross, the famous football player, is making a peach of a reputation out west as a hockeyist," the *Montreal Herald* told its readers on January 24, 1906. "He has been playing brilliantly for Brandon, and the sporting experts have lauded him skywards without hesitation or stinginess. Arthur would have been a tower of strength to any of the local teams, and certainly one or two of them think with regret of his departure."

In the words of Frank Selke — relaying Lester Patrick's 1951 story — Ross had been considered "a fellow who could stickhandle on a dime," when he left Montreal, "but couldn't skate, which kept him from being a first-class player." In discussing his improvement out west, Ross admitted to Lester that, "I can't really explain it. All I know is that there was nothing much to do after banking hours in Brandon except skate and I never skated so much in my life before. That must be it."

Between a full season of games and practices, his occasional appearances on the local bankers' hockey team, and plenty of work as a referee in intermediate and exhibition games across Manitoba, he certainly got plenty of ice time. Art Ross was still a great all-around athlete, but from this point on, he'd be thought of as a hockey player first and foremost.

# GOING
# PRO

Art Ross, hockey star, was in demand back east. The most serious offer he received during the summer of 1906 — when he also did some pitching for Brandon's bankers' baseball team — came not from any of the many teams back home in Montreal, but from the club that had been rumoured to be after him in the fall of 1905: the Ottawa Silver Seven.

After nearly four full seasons as Stanley Cup champions, Ottawa had relinquished the title at the end of the 1905–06 schedule. Lester Patrick and the Montreal Wanderers defeated Ottawa in a thrilling playoff after a season-long battle for supremacy in the Eastern Canada Amateur Hockey Association (ECAHA). The Stanley Cup now belonged to the Wanderers, but Ottawa wanted it back. Landing a youngster like Art Ross for the 1906–07 season would be a big boon to their aging lineup. The *Manitoba Free Press* confirmed at the end of August that Ross had "received a tempting offer from the Ottawa ex-champions" and that he had "partly decided to accept." The *Ottawa Journal* also reported on an offer to join both the Rough Riders and the Ottawa hockey club.

Without the ability to make an open financial offer, the Ottawa teams appear to have dangled the same type of off-ice job as compensation that would convince Fred Taylor to join the hockey team one year later. Ross's Merchants Bank of Canada employment file states that he resigned as a clerk in August of 1906, "to take place in Civil Service in Ottawa." Yet instead of leaving for the Canadian capital, Ross remained in Brandon and entered the employ of the Wheat City Flour Mills Company. The *Manitoba Free Press* noted that he was also purchasing an interest in the company, but it doesn't seem beyond the realm of possibility that someone with the Brandon Hockey Club might have arranged a deal with the milling company to provide both the shares and the job as a means of keeping their star cover point in town. It had certainly been an accepted practice in Manitoba hockey since at least the winter of 1903–04 — as it must have been elsewhere in the country — to overpay players with salaries they were not actually capable of earning at their jobs using the excuse that their names drew trade to a business.

However it happened, Art Ross was still in Brandon for a meeting at the Empire Hotel on the night of Monday August 27, 1906, when the decision was made to form a rugby football team and to apply for membership in the Manitoba Rugby Football Union. One night later, Ross took the minutes as secretary when the annual meeting of the Brandon Hockey Club was held in the office of team president Dr. John S. Matheson.

Hockey season was still a long way off, but rugby practices began on August 30 and continued throughout September. To no one's surprise, Ross, who was one of only a handful of Brandon players with previous experience, was named team captain in a unanimous selection on October 2. His skill would be praised in newspapers in Brandon and Winnipeg after he led his team to victories against the Winnipegs and St. John's College in games on October 13 and 18. Unfortunately, the short season came to an end on October 27 with a 20–1 loss to the Winnipeg Rowing Club, whose victory that day in Brandon clinched its third consecutive Manitoba championship.

There was plenty of excitement about the upcoming hockey season by the time the rugby season ended. Lester Patrick had passed through Brandon in mid-October on his way to British Columbia to purchase lumber interests with his father. This led to reports that Lester would return to Brandon to play hockey in the coming winter, or perhaps play in Winnipeg. Lester admitted that he'd been asked, and stated that Brandon was the only team in the west with whom he'd play, but said that if the business deal in B.C. played out as expected, he'd return to spend a final winter in Montreal before moving to the West Coast. Still, the executive of the Brandon Hockey Club was promising big changes to the team for the winter of 1906–07. Lester confirmed as much when he arrived back in Montreal a month or so later. "Brandon is going to have a cracker-jack of a team this winter," he told reporters. "The players already signed make that much plain, and more are in sight."

But before the season got started in Brandon, there would be even bigger changes to hockey all across the country.

*   *   *

The issue of professional hockey in Canada officially came to the forefront in the fall of 1906. For years it had been known, but not openly discussed, that some teams, players, or sports organizations were turning a blind eye to those who received money to play hockey or other sports. Once a player accepted money in any sport, it was expected that he could no longer compete as an amateur in any other. The Ontario Hockey Association was vigorous in banning any player who accepted money anywhere, but many other organizations were not. Some of those organizations were now calling for change.

On October 27, 1906, the question of professionalism was discussed in Montreal at the annual meeting of the Canadian Amateur Athletic Union (CAAU), which oversaw all of sports in Canada. The Montreal Amateur Athletic Association — the country's largest and most prestigious sporting organization — had proposed an amendment to permit amateur teams and players to play with and against professionals. An overwhelming majority voted down the amendment at the CAAU meeting, but the issue wouldn't go away.

Two weeks later, the Manitoba Amateur Hockey League held its annual meeting at the Leland Hotel in Winnipeg. In addition to taking care of various items of its own league business, delegates from the league's five teams discussed "the amateur problem" at length.

Dr. Matheson of Brandon felt it was time for the West to set its own rules. "The CAAU is an absolute farce," he argued. "This is a young man's country and why should we let some old fogies in the east sit up and tell us what we should do? There should rather be the same advancement in sport as there is in anything else."

R.H. Smith of the Winnipegs reminded the meeting that, regardless of what they decided, the CAAU was still the governing body in Canada. "We should not antagonize the CAAU at this stage," added Dr. Fred Cadham of the Victorias. A.C. Smith of the Winnipegs pointed out that some players on his team were nationally ranked oarsmen who wished to compete at the Henley regatta in St. Catharines, whose authorities recognized the regulations of the CAAU. John McGillivray of Kenora acknowledged that three Thistles were in the same boat, so to speak.

But the key issue was another one facing Kenora — with both the Manitoba title and the championship of the ECAHA having required playoffs, it had been too late in March to challenge for the Stanley Cup at the end of the 1905–06 season, but the Thistles had already had their challenge accepted for mid-January of 1907. The team had chased the Stanley Cup against Ottawa unsuccessfully in 1903 and 1905, and was anxious for another chance against the Wanderers. Knowing that the same issue was being discussed that very day at the ECAHA's annual meeting at the Windsor Hotel in Montreal, the question became what would the Thistles and the Manitoba League do if the Wanderers declared themselves to be professionals? It was decided to wait and see what actions were taken in the East, and what the trustees in charge of the Stanley Cup had to say about it, before deciding what to do out west.

A motion to withdraw from the CAAU and allow professionals to play alongside amateurs was moved at the ECAHA meeting by Ottawa delegate D'Arcy McGee, the brother of star player Frank McGee. "The public wants good hockey," he said, "and does not care whether a player is amateur or professional, as long as he can deliver the goods. To get good hockey we must pay the players. We have had much trouble over the athletic situation and I think my motion will clear up the tangle so far as hockey is concerned and will eliminate hypocrisy."

The delegates from the Montreal AAA, Montreal Shamrocks, Montreal Victorias, Montreal Wanderers, and Quebec Bulldogs voted unanimously in favour of Ottawa's motion, though the Victorias, AAA, and Quebec would ice rosters they claimed were composed solely of amateur players. The Senators, as the Ottawa team was increasingly being called, remained fairly quiet about whom, if any, of their players would be paid. It was the Wanderers who were known to have their eye on a couple of pros — goalie Riley Hern and defenceman Hod Stuart, who had both been playing for pay in the United States for several seasons.

ECAHA delegates continued to squabble about the issue well into December, but it was time for the hockey authorities in Manitoba to make their decision. A.B. Donley had written to Stanley Cup trustee P.D. Ross (no relation to Art Ross) who, as publisher of the *Ottawa Journal*, had written an editorial in December of 1905 claiming it was hypocritical to ask players to give more and more of their time to hockey at the expense of their off-ice careers without paying them. His reply to Donley was received on November 21:

> The trustees consider the Wanderers of Montreal, the present holders of the Stanley Cup, still eligible to defend same, despite the recent action of the Eastern Canada Hockey League in withdrawing from the CAAU.

And so, at another league meeting on December 1, 1906, the Manitoba Hockey League also broke ranks with the CAAU, but the acrimonious vote resulted in a split in Manitoba senior hockey. The Victorias and Winnipegs refused to go pro. They created their own league called the Western Canada Amateur Hockey Association along with the Winnipeg Shamrocks. Brandon, Portage la Prairie, and Kenora would form a new, professional version of the Manitoba Hockey League along with a new senior club from Winnipeg called the Strathconas.

The Stanley Cup, from this point on, would be the top prize in professional hockey, and the Kenora Thistles would soon be playing for it.

Art Ross would quickly embrace professionalism, but he couldn't possibly know how much this news would change his life.

\* \* \*

With the Brandon Hockey Club already promising a better team, going pro provided an immediate benefit. Out-of-towners Walter Bellamy (from nearby Virden, Manitoba), Jack Fraser, Roy Armstrong, and goalie Bob Mercer (all from Ontario) had already been brought onboard. Transplanted Quebeckers Art Leader and Doe Smith were both still in town from past years, as was Art Ross from the previous season. But now, a true local star was also available.

Though he was born in Milwich, England, and raised in Winnipeg, Joe Hall first made his name in hockey playing for Brandon in the late 1890s. He was a member of the Brandon team that won the intermediate championship in 1901–02 and earned a promotion into the senior ranks the following season. A cushy off-ice position lured Hall back to the provincial capital to play with the Winnipeg Rowing Club in 1903–04. He returned to Brandon for the 1904–05 season, but then elected to become a professional, and signed with the Portage Lake team of Houghton, Michigan, for the 1905–06 season of the International Hockey League (IHL).

While in the IHL, Joe Hall's reputation for toughness, if not outright mayhem, came to the fore, though Canadian newspapers always delighted in depicting the violence they believed ran rampant in professional hockey. Hall's talent was obvious too and he remained in demand over a lengthy career that concluded only with his death during the outbreak of Spanish Influenza that cancelled the Stanley Cup Final of 1919.

The city directory for Brandon shows that Hall had a job with local cigar-maker James Dillon, but newspaper reports beginning in late October had him preparing to return to Houghton for the hockey season. However, when the Brandon team began practice during the last week in November, Hall was on the ice with them. It was still expected he'd leave town until the *Brandon Daily Sun* noted: "If at the meeting tonight it is decided to pull away from the Canadian Amateur Athletic Association [sic], and thereby allow professionals to play with amateurs, Joe Hall will not go to Houghton, but will be seen on the Brandon team this year."

It's not clear whether Brandon paid Hall to play hockey or not. Even if they didn't, he would still be considered a professional for having played in the IHL the previous winter. Hall, Ross, Leader, and Smith all had jobs in Brandon, which may have constituted their only salary during the winter of 1906–07. After all, when Dr. John Matheson argued in defence of professionalism at the December 1 meeting in Winnipeg he said: "With so much demand on a player's time it is hard to secure suitable positions [meaning employment] for all the men. Why not have one, two or three paid men on a team?" This would seem to indicate that only those without jobs in town were paid to play hockey. Then again, as John McGillivray of Kenora opined, "a man who got a $75 job when he was only worth $40 was just as much a professional as the man who was paid directly for playing hockey," even if such behaviour had been winked at for many years.

Unfortunately, there's no record of what salaries the Brandon Hockey Club paid during the winter of 1906–07, nor of who received them. But there's no doubt that money changed hands. "The hockey boys are being paid off today by the treasurer of the club," reported the *Brandon Daily Sun* on March 30, 1907, after the season was over. "It is believed that the finances of the club will be sufficient to pay off all indebtedness, or at the worst the deficit will not exceed $75," the paper added. "This is a splendid showing for the club's first year in professional ranks," particularly in light of the fact that the team in Portage la Prairie was said to have "wound up the season $1,200 to the bad." Kenora was thought to be "pretty deep in the hole" as well. The Winnipeg Strathconas also "lost money for their manager."

After the pro/amateur motion was passed and the resignation and replacement of the Winnipeg teams was complete, the next issue to face the Manitoba hockey delegates was the creation of a schedule. With four teams in the league, a double-round robin format seemed in order. That would mean that each team would face the other three teams four times apiece; twice at home and twice on the road, for a total of 12 games for each team. Brandon, Portage la Prairie, and the Strathconas favoured this arrangement, but the Thistles were against it due to their aspirations for the Stanley Cup.

With three days of travel to Montreal and three more to get back, plus the possibility of a week's worth of games if the best-of-three series with the Wanderers went the distance, and the additional exhibition games Kenora expected to play on the road before and after the series to help fund the Stanley Cup journey, the team would be gone for nearly a month. The Thistles wanted a schedule with only a single set of home and road games for all four teams.

Kenora was the league's top draw, so the other teams weren't anxious to give up any games against them. After much discussion, a proposition by the Thistles finally prevailed. The Strathconas, Portage, and Brandon would all play a double round-robin schedule against each other, but each would face the Thistles only once at home and once on the road. This meant Kenora would play just six league games during the 1906–07 season while the others played 10. In order to balance the standings, total goals would be combined in the games between the other three teams so that each set of two home games and each set of two road games produced just one final score. For example, when Portage's home games with the Strathconas resulted in a 4–3 win and a 6–2 loss, the Strathconas were credited with a single 9–6 victory. Various postponements throughout the winter played additional havoc with the schedule, but the idea was sound and the final standings would be represented with six results for each of the four teams.

For the second year in a row, Brandon opened the season in Portage la Prairie on December 27. The team practised throughout December to get ready. The *Brandon Daily Sun* often commented on the workouts at the Caledonia rink and reported on an interesting new feature in its December 21 edition. Local jeweller D.A. Reesor had installed a large electric clock at the south end of the rink. The face was nine feet in diameter and divided into 60-minute increments. It was wired to the timekeeper's bench and could be stopped and started with the push of a button so that it kept the game time as accurately as possible. "The clock will no doubt be appreciated by both spectators and players," the paper said, "especially the latter, to whom it is often a help in winning a close game when they know exactly just how much longer they have to play."

Newspaper stories in Brandon leading up to the start of the season were generally positive, but the players received negative comments for their lack of teamwork. "Team play with a good combination is the only game that can possibly land the championship," said the *Daily Sun* a week before the opening game, "and it is to be hoped that this style of play will prevail among the Brandon players more than at the present time."

It certainly didn't on opening night.

Winnipeg's *Morning Telegram* said of the game in Portage la Prairie that, "The Brandon team tended to individual work," although added that, "their players were all speedy skaters and their rushes were always dangerous." Still, the result was an upset 8–5 victory for Portage la Prairie, which led to a shuffle of the Brandon roster.

Brandon's next game was their home opener against the Strathconas. It was originally scheduled for New Year's Day, but was pushed back to January 4, 1907 at the Winnipeg team's request. Art Leader at point and Joe Hall at right wing remained at the same positions, along with goalie Bob Mercer, who was said to have played well in the loss to Portage despite the eight goals against him. Art Ross had been working out at rover since the start of practice in November, but was back at cover point versus the Strathconas. The shake-up paid instant dividends. The revamped forwards displayed fine passing and excellent shooting, while the defence of Ross and Leader regularly broke up the Strathconas' rushes. The result was a 10–2 romp.

Brandon then played against Kenora at their home opener on January 7. The visitors jumped out to a 2–0 lead and were up 3–1 early in the second half, but it was all Thistles after that as eight straight goals led to a 9–3 victory. Despite the lopsided win, all was not well in the Kenora camp as their Stanley Cup challenged approached. The Thistles needed to find some new talent.

# SMALL TOWN
# GLORY

It was generally agreed in the many newspapers that covered the meeting when the Manitoba Hockey League went pro on December 1, 1906, that Kenora officials were not as concerned with salaries as they were with going after the Stanley Cup. If their players were going to be seen as professionals after facing the Wanderers anyway, the Thistles wanted to ensure they had a league in Manitoba to come back to. As to the question of paying for players, John McGillivray put it very plainly: "I do not say that the Thistles are going to be professionals," he was quoted as saying in the *Winnipeg Tribune* on December 3, "but if we want a man we wish to be able to go out and get him openly."

Kenora had begun the season with a win over the Strathconas, but had not played well. The Thistles also looked out of shape in a couple of exhibition games in December, particularly during a 10–5 loss to the Ottawa Senators in a game at Winnipeg. With their roster already hampered by the loss of two veteran players and their Stanley Cup dream in jeopardy, the Thistles looked to Brandon for help.

"Joe Hall Joins Kenora Thistles" read a headline in Winnipeg's *Morning Telegram* on January 9. Confusingly, a sub-headline and the body of the story, datelined from Brandon on January 8, made Hall's acquisition appear to be something less than a *fait accompli.* It also made it clear that Kenora was after Art Ross as well. "The Thistles want to take Arthur Ross and Joe Hall to Montreal with them to play for the Stanley Cup. Hall may go, but it is not probable that Ross will do so." Other stories that day reported that Ross and Hall would both go, which turned out to be true. "With the announcement that Kenora had strengthened up with Ross and Hall, there has been a noticeable return of the shaken western confidence in the ability of the Thistles to defeat the Wanderers," noted the *Winnipeg Tribune* a few days later.

There appear to be no contemporary reports stating what compensation Joe Hall and Art Ross received to join the Thistles for their Stanley Cup adventure. In fact, in detailed coverage of the Thistles' departure for Montreal, Winnipeg's *Morning Telegram* provided a very different reason for Ross to make the trip. "It is understood that his father is seriously ill necessitating his return home anyway." This seems likely to have been the case, although it was undoubtedly Ross's stepfather who was ailing and not his father.

Peter McKenzie would be admitted to the Protestant Hospital for the Insane in Montreal (today, the Douglas Mental Health University Institute, affiliated with McGill University) on March 5, 1907. He suffered from what was then called senile melancholia, which could have been Alzheimer's disease or another form of dementia. He would die of the disease on either April 30 or May 1, 1910. Family members in Montreal must have informed Ross of McKenzie's failing condition, so the offer from the Thistles certainly proved timely. A subsequent story in the *Ottawa Citizen* on January 23 also mentions a "sickness in Arthur Ross's family," though he himself never seems to have mentioned it in his many recollections of the Kenora Thistles over the years. Instead, Ross would choose to recall the trip as the first time he ever accepted money to play hockey. He told Art Siegel of the *Boston Globe* in 1960 that he received $1,000 per game for the two-game set, but it's more likely he received a flat rate of $1,000 for what was actually scheduled as a best-of-three series.

Despite agreeing to join the Thistles, both Ross and Hall played for Brandon in two exhibition games against Kenora before their departure.

The Thistles still won them, 7–5 and 7–3. "The team is back in its old-time form," Tommy Phillips assured the sports editor of the *Morning Telegram* in a long-distance call from Brandon to Winnipeg on the evening of the final exhibition game.

The Kenora Thistles' journey to Montreal began on Saturday morning, January 12, 1907. Arriving in Winnipeg around noon, they spent a few hours in the Manitoba capital before their scheduled departure on the Soo Line, which travelled to Montreal through St. Paul, Chicago, and Detroit. There were 19 in the Thistles' party, including nine players, manager Fred Hudson, coach/trainer James Link, and eight friends of the club. They travelled in their own railcar that displayed a huge banner bearing the words "Kenora Thistles."

By arrangement with railway officials, the Thistles' railcar was to bring up the rear of the train from St. Paul to Chicago, but their original train out of Winnipeg was late reaching the Minnesota city. The Thistles missed their intended connection and were forced to wait for the next train to Chicago. What seemed like an unfortunate delay turned out to be an important moment in hockey history. "When they reached Chicago," the *Winnipeg Tribune* reported on January 16, "they were informed that the rear coach on the train which they had missed had been completely wrecked in a rear-end collision on the outskirts of Chicago, so that the Thistles are figuring it out that if they had gone through St. Paul on schedule time their journey might have had a sudden and disastrous termination, a long way from their destination."

The Thistles arrived safely in Montreal on the evening of Tuesday, January 15 — two days before the opening game of the series — and took up residence at the Windsor Hotel. On Wednesday afternoon at 1:30, the nine players hit the ice for an hour-long practice at the Arena. Both the Wanderers and Thistles were known for their clean play in a violent era, and both were known for their team speed. The general impression in Montreal was that the Thistles were faster than the home team, but with their tendency towards individual rushes, Montrealers hoped the Wanderers' better team play would give their forwards an advantage. As for defence, "the Wanderers, with [Hod] Stuart and [Rod] Kennedy, would have a little on the opposing players, [Si] Griffis and Ross," believed the *Gazette*. "For one thing, Ross is playing his first game with Kenora, and for another, Griffis is playing for the first time at the point position."

There seems to be some confusion as to where Ross and Griffis actually played, with the majority of summaries from the games showing Ross at point and Griffis at cover point. Still, there are several stories and direct quotations — such as Tommy Phillips to the *Morning Telegram* — indicating that Ross played cover point. Perhaps the confusion was due to the style of defence the Thistles favoured. Most other teams might allow one of their defencemen to rush the puck on occasion, but the tradition was still to rely on long, high loft shots to clear their end of danger (rules against icing were still a long way off). As there was no forward passing allowed in hockey at the time, any forwards in front of the puck when it was lofted down the ice were offside and unable to play it until the other team did. Given that hockey's rules against forward passing were actually modeled on rugby, most teams believed the tactic of giving up the puck was better than risking a turnover, much like punting a football. The Thistles thought differently. "Kenora's tactics are well known," the *Gazette* reminded its readers. "There is no lifting the puck with the Western bunch; each time it is brought to the Kenora end orders call for the defence man taking it up himself, and, before getting rid of it, placing his own men onside." It was a high-risk proposition, but with the Thistles' talent and speed, it was often high reward.

\* \* \*

A crowd of about 6,500 began filling the Arena for game one at 6:30 p.m. on January 17, 1907. Although this was somewhat short of the big rink's capacity, it was seen as a testament to the Thistles' drawing power that such a big crowd turned out on so cold an evening, especially considering that the team from New Glasgow, Nova Scotia, had drawn tiny crowds to their Stanley Cup games in December. "All over Canada the struggle for the coveted cup is being watched with interest," the Kenora paper reported. "From Nova Scotia to British Columbia, the newspaper bulletin boards recorded the progress of [the] game."

The Wanderers hit the ice first while Kenora players lingered in their dressing room, "getting a preliminary rubdown." It was 8:35 when the Thistles hit the ice. They were given a tremendous ovation, with Art Ross receiving a particularly great reception from his Montreal friends. Both teams sported white sweaters with red collars, red cuffs, and red socks as they went about their warm-ups. The only noticeable difference was the logo on their chests: the Wanderers sported a broad red band and white W, while the Kenora sweaters featured two crossed thistles. When referee Bob Meldrum and judge-of-play Russell Bowie took the ice, the players from both teams shook hands at the side of the rink before Meldrum called them to centre. The Wanderers won the coin toss to determine ends, and chose to defend the southern goal. Meldrum then issued some final instructions before the teams lined up for the opening faceoff. Finally, at 8:55, the game began.

Kenora's Billy McGimsie beat Ernie Russell to the draw. The first rush carried the puck into the Wanderers end, but only for a moment before the Montrealers cleared their zone. Lester Patrick fed a pass to Moose Johnson, who fired the first shot at Thistles goalie Eddie Giroux, but the puck went wide. Several offsides in the early going slowed down the play, but the game generally raced from end to end in the early moments. Both Stuart and Kennedy of the Wanderers were rushing the puck as often as Ross and Griffis. The Wanderers had the best early chances, but Ross blocked a couple of shots before they got through to Giroux.

The first true scoring opportunity came when Kenora's Roxy Beaudro emerged from a scramble and sped for the Wanderers' end. He slipped past Hod Stuart and then rifled the puck across the ice to Tommy Phillips, who was "coming down the left wing like a whirlwind" and "shot as the disc struck his stick." Riley Hern had the short side covered, but Phillips's one-timer found the opposite corner. After four minutes of play, Kenora had a 1–0 lead. By halftime it was 2–2, with Phillips scoring both of Kenora's goals.

The Wanderers came out quickly in the second half. Ernie Russell had a chance to put his team ahead, but fired high and into the stands. The Montreal team kept up the early pressure, but then Beaudro stole the puck from Stuart and fed to Phillips whose third goal put the Thistles up 3–2 after just one minute's play.

Ross and Stuart took turns rushing as play resumed. "The Kenora point began now to cut loose, and his speedy sallies, skating and stick-handling drew each time wild applause from the crowd, who remembered him from old." The hometown fans had read about Ross's exploits in Brandon the previous winter, but reading was one thing. Seeing him now was believing.

The Wanderers worked hard for the equalizer, but luck seemed to be with the Thistles. Giroux turned aside a few hot shots and, after a particularly tense flurry around the net, Ross finally carried the puck to safety. There was a brief scuffle in the Wanderers' end before Phillips beat Hern for his fourth goal of the night. There was still more than 20 minutes to play, and the pace remained remarkably fast. Clearly, the Thistles were in proper shape now, and despite having to kill off a Ross penalty late in the game, the team held on for a 4–2 victory.

"Speed won," declared the *Montreal Star* the next morning. "It wasn't a question of superior hockey, superior courage, or superior combination, but it was simply a question of speed." The *Montreal Herald* reported that, "The Thistles are the fastest hockeyists seen on local ice in many seasons. Some of the work last night was simply marvelous." The *Gazette* agreed. "It was a ripping fast match. Fast, indeed, is not the word to describe the play. It seemed rather a series of sprints…. The visitors are simply great on skates. They move along beautifully. The term 'poetry of motion' has some meaning when an enthusiast watches the Thistle players glide along. They do not seem to be trying hard, but every man jack of them … is travelling some to say the least."

Tommy Phillips, having scored all his team's goals, was, of course, singled out for praise, but so were Si Griffis and Art Ross, who "formed as pretty a defence as has been seen on local ice for many a day…. They proved good checks, and speedy and excellent forwards…. Griffis played a beautiful game but he was not a whit more successful than Ross."

Summing up the play of the hometown boy's triumphant return, the *Gazette* noted that, "Ross is some miles above the Ross that played for

Westmount in the gone days, and his work at point last night was something to be remembered."

Game two in the series was played four nights later on January 21, 1907. The Thistles jumped out to a 5–2 lead by halftime, and were up 6–2 with about 14 minutes to play. The Wanderers refused to go down without a fight, and, amazingly, rallied for four goals to tie the game with less than four minutes to go.

Stuart and Patrick of the Wanderers and McGimsie and Phillips of Kenora were all in the penalty box near the end of the game when Roxy Beaudro jammed in a Si Griffis rebound with less than two minutes remaining. Thirty seconds later, Tom Hooper scored to clinch it. The Thistles had an 8–6 victory and the Stanley Cup.

Tommy Phillips, who scored twice, was once more hailed as the star of the game, but Griffis and Ross again shared honours with him. Griffis, according to Roxy Beaudro, "never played better hockey than he did at cover point," and Ross, "gave the Thistles excellent assistance." As the *Ottawa Citizen* noted after the game, "Wouldn't Montreal be proud to own Arthur Ross these days."

Montreal had a metropolitan population of over 400,000 in January of 1907. It was Canada's biggest, richest, and most important city. Kenora, with a population of about 6,000 people, was, and will likely forever be, the smallest city ever to win the Stanley Cup. It's a distinction the town remains proud of to this day. Art Ross only played these two games for the Thistles, but the memory of winning the Stanley Cup with the small-town team in the big city he grew up in remained with him always. When a plaque honouring the victory was unveiled in Kenora on August 24, 1960, Ross, with Billy McGimsie and James Link, were the only living members of the team. Ross couldn't be in Kenora that day, but telegraphed a message which was reported the next day in the *Winnipeg Free Press*:

> Regret exceedingly that I am unable to attend plaque unveiling ceremony honoring the greatest team in hockey history. My most cherished souvenir is a silver trophy presented to me in 1907 as a member of your Kenora Thistles.

And lest one think he was merely playing up the moment for an appreciative hometown audience, Ross had already offered similar sentiments to Tom Fitzgerald of the *Boston Globe* as the 50th anniversary approached late in 1956. He had reiterated it earlier in 1960 when WEEI sports director and Boston Bruins radio play-by-play man Fred Cusick asked him about his greatest thrills:

> I think possibly the first Stanley [Cup] game I won playing with the Kenora Thistles, and we beat the Montreal Wanderers in Montreal ... that was possibly the greatest thrill I ever had.

## 6

# A FIGHT TO
# THE FINISH

On January 23, 1907, two days after their win over the Wanderers, the Kenora Thistles visited Ottawa for an exhibition game. Art Ross remained at home in Montreal. Joe Hall wasn't in Ottawa either — the two players' contracts with the Thistles may only have been for the Stanley Cup games. Both Ross and Hall made their own way back to Brandon to rejoin that team while the Thistles continued playing in the East. Once they'd all returned west, Brandon gave Kenora a real run for its money as the season played out. So did Portage la Prairie. It was a fight to the finish in the Manitoba Hockey League.

The Thistles' eastern swing had turned troublesome after their Stanley Cup victory. A loss in Ottawa cost them Billy McGimsie, who suffered a career-ending shoulder injury, and Tom Hooper was hurt during a win in Toronto. All subsequent exhibitions were cancelled. When the Thistles returned home they added another future Hall of Famer to their roster in Fred Whitcroft, who'd been playing in Peterborough, Ontario.

The Thistles scored an easy 12–4 win over the Strathconas in their first game back in Kenora on February 11, but both Brandon and Portage beat them in their next two games. Kenora now had just one game left on its six-game schedule, and the Thistles' record was only 3–2. The combined nature of the scores for the games involving the other teams made it difficult to determine the standings, yet two things were certain: the Stathconas were hopelessly out of contention, and both Portage and Brandon had a real shot at topping Kenora. If either team unseated the Thistles for first place in the Manitoba Hockey League, the Stanley Cup would pass to them as the new league champion without the need of a challenge.

Reeling, and scrambling to find more healthy bodies as their injuries continued to pile up, the Thistles received permission to postpone their final game, which had originally been scheduled at home against Portage on February 25. That same night, Brandon romped to a 13–4 win over the Strathconas. Combined with their 10–2 victory at home earlier in the season, Brandon's 23–6 total-goal victory may have been overkill, but it certainly proved they were in it to win it. A 2–2 tie at Portage la Prairie followed on March 1. The Portage newspaper noted, "For the visitors, Ross was easily the star man. His rushes were hard to handle and he did some clever stickhandling." The *Brandon Daily Sun* called it, "the fastest game of hockey played in the west for some time," adding that, "the Stanley Cup games in Montreal could not have been faster nor have given more brilliant exhibitions of perfect hockey." Ross's end-to-end rush in the second half that put Brandon on the scoreboard was described as "one of the prettiest pieces of play seen during the whole game" and was said to have "carried the spectators off their seats with enthusiastic admiration" despite his being a visiting player. The paper also noted that Ross scored another goal for Brandon, which was not counted because Portage goalie Charlie Quinn fished the puck out of the net before the referee had seen it. A 3–2 win for Brandon wouldn't have made any difference, though. With their season-opening 8–5 defeat in Portage, Brandon suffered a 10–7 loss on aggregate and one more goal wouldn't have mattered. The key now was to hold on for a win in the rematch in Brandon one week later.

Brandon carried a one-goal lead from a 4–3 victory on February 15 into the big game with Portage la Prairie on March 8, which was the final home game of the season. The *Daily Sun* hyped the game with a bold headline: "Battle of the Giants on the Ice To-Night." The paper seemed to be writing off the Thistles, declaring that, "With what is now considered the two best teams in Western Canada facing each other … one of the most magnificent struggles in the annals of hockey should be offered the followers of the game at the Caledonian rink tonight."

If Brandon was defeated by more than one goal, it would officially mark the team's third loss of the season. That would mean the best they could do was tie for second place with the loser of the Kenora-Portage game, which had been rescheduled for March 12. Since only first-place teams had a chance to play for the Stanley Cup, the *Daily Sun* was justified in stating, "To-night's battle … carries with it that life or death feature, so far as Brandon is concerned."

There were 500 fans expected to arrive from Portage la Prairie for the game, and though the rink's full compliment of 2,000 tickets had been snapped up by the hometown fans, everyone was squeezed into the Caledonia rink like a "sardine box." The big game was late starting and didn't face off until 10:10 due to a delay to the train from Portage. When it finally got under way, the game certainly lived up to the hype. Play was fast, but the hitting was hard and the game was described as a little rough in spots. It was a tight defensive struggle in which Brandon trailed 1–0 as the clock wound down. Then, a late Portage penalty gave the hometown team a chance to tie it. "Two minutes, then one minute remained, and as the crowd watched the hands on the big clock crawl around, the excitement was intense." When the final gong sounded, it was still 1–0 Portage. The combined score now stood at 4–4 … and so the game headed for overtime.

After a few minutes to clear the ice of fans who had spilled out of the stands, the teams changed ends and went at it again. It was nearly 1:00 a.m., which likely explains why only a brief account of the overtime appears in newspaper reports of the game. "There was the swiftest kind of hockey for six minutes," reads the final sentence in the lengthy game story in the *Daily Sun*, "when on a Brandon rush A. Ross slipped in the winner."

Art Ross had helped Kenora win the Stanley Cup earlier in the year, and now he'd helped keep Brandon alive in its attempt to dethrone the champions. Essentially, the Thistles, Brandon, and Portage were all tied with a 3–2 record in the standings. With Portage to visit Kenora in three days' time, and Brandon to close out the season against the Strathconas on March 14, the race would come right down to the wire … and then some.

In the East, the Wanderers played their final game of the regular season on March 6. They scored a 16–5 win over the Montreal Shamrocks to complete the schedule with a perfect record of 10–0. Ottawa, hopelessly stuck in second place, had nothing to play for on the final night of the ECAHA season and dropped an 8–6 decision to the Montreal AAA. Two key members of the Ottawa team had skipped the game. Alf Smith and Harry Westwick had caught a westbound train at 12:45 that afternoon and were on their way to Kenora. The two veteran stars were expected to arrive in town on Monday, March 11 and they would play for Kenora in the game against Portage la Prairie the following night.

Smith and Westwick lined up at right wing and rover. Tom Hooper and Si Griffis played point and cover point in front of Eddie Giroux in goal. Fred Whitcroft was at centre and Tom Phillips was at left wing. With the Ottawa newcomers starring, the Thistles played better then they had at any point since their Stanley Cup victory in Montreal and romped to a 7–0 victory.

Kenora was still alive for the Manitoba championship. Portage was out, but Brandon could still tie the Thistles for top spot and force a play-off if the team held on to its two-goal lead in the season finale against the Strathconas in Winnipeg. Everyone expected they would. In fact, a best-of-three championship series had already been arranged to break the tie. It would be played on the neutral ice of the Winnipeg Arena beginning on Saturday, March 16. But the Strathconas gave Brandon a scare. In a see-saw contest that saw the lead change hands seven times, the teams battled through a rough game that ended in a 7–7 tie. Combined with their 5–3 win back on February 1, Brandon claimed a 12–10 victory. The *Daily Sun* thought Brandon's showing was "somewhat of a disappointment," but that "Art Ross was in fine form. He was both a defence man and a forward. Ross is surely a glutton for work, never seeming to tire."

Fans in Brandon were excited for the playoff against Kenora. Many of them went by train to Winnipeg for the series opener on Saturday night.

Those who stayed behind but couldn't wait for the Monday newspaper flocked in large numbers to the Imperial and Empire hotels, as well as to Taylor Hanna's barber shop, where bulletins were received by telegraph. Kenora won the game 8–6, but the general impression was that the Thistles were lucky. The *Daily Sun* referred to "Dame Fortune" playing a hand in three early Thistles goals, and to prove they weren't just being homers, the paper included a special report from the *Manitoba Free Press* in Winnipeg:

> The champions had to go to the limit even with [Smith and Westwick in the lineup] and with all the luck they managed to win the opening game by 2 goals. Had the Wheat City boys had the Kenora's luck the score would certainly have been reversed.

"Everyone thinks Brandon has a good chance yet," the *Daily Sun* assured its readers, "they had all the hard luck while horseshoes were with the Thistles."

The reporter from the *Winnipeg Telegram* saw things differently. He thought the game was only as close as it was because Kenora was weakened by yet another injury. Si Griffis had been hurt in the win over Portage, forcing Tom Hooper to go to cover point and Roxy Beaudro, who'd always been a forward, to play out of position at point. The *Telegram* believed, "the Thistles should win the series, for they showed plainly that they are the better team."

Kenora did indeed sweep the series in game two, scoring a 4–1 victory. Brandon may have been a little unlucky in this one too, especially when Joe Hall left the game with a broken thumb just before halftime. However, the score was already 3–1 Thistles by then, and the better team probably won. It had been a good season in Brandon, but it was over. Kenora would play on, facing the Montreal Wanderers once again, but this time without Art Ross in their lineup.

When the Wanderers submitted their Stanley Cup challenge, they specifically protested against the western champions using players not part of their usual lineup. William Foran was the acting trustee in charge of the Stanley Cup in March of 1907. Foran ruled in favour of the Wanderers, announcing that any player who had played for another team in the same league would be ineligible to play in defence of the Cup.

The issue of player eligibility would likely have ended with Foran's announcement — until Kenora signed Alf Smith and Harry Westwick. The Wanderers protested their eligibility, too. Foran indicated they would also be barred, but national opinion was against him this time as there didn't seem to be any hard-and-fast rule against importing player for big games as long as they hadn't already played in a Stanley Cup challenge during the same season. The Thistles added to the squabbling when they balked at playing in Winnipeg as the Wanderers requested. Officials from both teams finally met in Kenora to sort things out, but cooler heads did not prevail.

"At one stage," Alf Smith later remembered in a 1957 Stanley Cup publication for the NHL, "this Kenora club official picked up the Cup and prepared to leave the room with it. Asked what he intended to do, he replied that he was fully prepared to pay the bond [that was supposed to insure the Cup's safekeeping] for it. He was actually heading for the Lake of the Woods to throw it in. He would have done it too, if he hadn't been restrained, and it was no easy job in the humor he was in."

In the end — though Foran wasn't happy with the decision — the Wanderers agreed to let Kenora use Smith and Westwick and the Thistles agreed to play the games in Winnipeg, where the larger capacity and bigger gate receipts would help the Wanderers cover the cost of their trip. Game one on March 23 ended with a 7–2 win for the Montreal team, and though the Thistles scored a 6–5 win two nights later, the Wanderers won the total-goals series 12–8.

Kenora's championship reign had ended after just two months.

The Stanley Cup returned to Montreal.

Soon Art Ross would too.

# 7

## BACK TO THE
## BIG CITY

Hockey fans in 1907 didn't have dedicated cable TV channels, 24-hour talk radio, twitter accounts, or apps for their smartphones to keep them informed in real time on their favourite players and teams. They did have many more newspapers to read than fans do today, and though there was usually only a page or two of sports news, the amount of hockey gossip was as staggering then as it is today.

Almost immediately after Harry Westwick and Alf Smith arrived back in Ottawa on Saturday morning, March 30, rumours began circulating about the fate of other Kenora players. Some were said to be heading for the Canadian capital themselves, others to the IHL, or the West Coast. Most of the Thistles stars did end up leaving Kenora, and on September 24, the *Brandon Daily Sun* reported that Brandon might not have a pro team anymore, adding that "Art Ross, it is stated, is slated to play with the champion Wanderers of Montreal."

By the end of September, there were reports that Ross had signed a contract with the Montreal team. "The Wanderers officers refuse to confirm it," newspapers admitted, "but it is understood that the arrangements with Ross have already been made." In fact, the *Ottawa Citizen* on

September 30 reported that he would arrive in Montreal in early October and that there was "a possibility that he may be seen on the half-back line of the Montreal [AAA] football team." Two days later, the *Citizen* noted: "Arthur Ross is undoubtedly one of the best half-backs that ever punted a pigskin and if the Montreal team lands him the other star kickers in the Interprovincial [Rugby Football Union — the newly formed forerunner of Canadian Football League's eastern division, which was known for years at the Big Four] may expect to see their laurels flying."

According to a story out of Montreal on October 10 that was printed in the *Brandon Daily Sun* the following day, the Wanderers had been corresponding with Ross "for several months." It would be reasonable to assume that their interest in Ross began shortly after the biggest hockey story of the summer: the death of Hod Stuart in a swimming accident on June 23, 1907.

Replacing Stuart, who'd become a huge star during his one season in Montreal, was a high priority for the Wanderers. They also had to replace Lester Patrick, who'd moved out west to help run his father's new lumber business near Nelson, British Columbia. Even so, Art Ross didn't seem to be in any hurry to make up his mind during the fall of 1907. A decision had already been made not to field a rugby team in Brandon, and even when it began to look more and more likely that there wouldn't be a Brandon hockey team that winter either, Ross still didn't appear anxious to leave. He had his business interest in the flour mill and, even without rugby, there was hunting and fishing to satisfy his sporting needs. He'd also captained both a bankers' team and a Brandon city team in a pair of three-game basketball series versus the local YMCA team back in May. Regarding hockey, when asked where he expected to play this winter, Ross replied, "Undecided as to myself," in a telegram to a reporter in Montreal on October 10. He told a writer from the *Daily Sun* the next day that he "had not made any definite arrangements at present." Still, the Brandon reporter concluded that, "the probabilities are that he will this season be wearing the Wanderers' colors on Montreal ice."

On October 14, the Wanderers held their annual meeting at the Windsor Hotel in Montreal. Newspapers the next day reported that no new player signings had been announced, but "it is understood that the club is building on getting Art Ross from Brandon." However, in a story about Kenora in the *Manitoba Free Press* on October 16, the Winnipeg paper claimed: "It is understood … that a good offer has been made to Arthur Ross, of Brandon, to play with the Thistles this year, and it is not unlikely he will be found on the line of the Manitoba champions." The very next day, the same paper reported that although Ross had received an offer to play with the Canadian Soo in the IHL, both he and Joe Hall had finally stated they would play with the Wanderers.

But still the saga continued.

Throughout November, stories kept up about Ross going to the Wanderers. The team had not signed Hall, but were said to be after Fred Taylor from Portage Lake once it became clear that the IHL would cease operations. Clearly, though, Ross had not signed a contract. Even when the *Brandon Daily Sun* reported on Saturday, November 30, that "Mr. Arthur Ross leaves for Montreal on Monday morning" and that he was "slated to play point for the Wanderers this winter," and then confirmed in the paper on Monday, December 2, that he really had left, it still wasn't certain where he'd play. "According to a statement made by the big cover-point before leaving Brandon," the *Toronto Star* reported on December 3, "there is a likelihood that he will not appear on the line-up of the Wanderers, as a tempting offer has been made to him by the Montreals [aka the Montreal AAA]."

Yet one day later, this new piece of news was contradicted as well. "There is nothing in the story Art Ross, the former Westmount boy, may play with the Montreals instead of with Wanderers," the *Ottawa Citizen* reported. "Ross wrote officers of the Ottawas [who were obviously still hoping to sign him!] that he had signed with Wanderers and will join the Cup-holders.…" On December 7, a similar story appeared in the weekly *Westmount News*.

But it would seem that even then, Ross had not put his signature on paper, and that he still might not sign with the Wanderers.

On Sunday morning, December 8, 1907, Ross arrived in Montreal. As it so happened, he completed the final leg of his journey through Toronto and left that city in a train car with the Montreal AAA intermediate football team that had just been defeated by the Hamilton Tigers for the Canadian championship the day before. There were all sorts of questions as to whether he would play for the Wanderers or Montreal, and although Ross gave evasive answers, it was the general belief he would sign with the defending champions.

Finally, on December 9, 1907, fans learned which team Ross would play for:

> The chief item of news in hockey circles today was the announcement that late this afternoon Art Ross, who arrived from Brandon Sunday morning, had affixed his signature to a contract with the Wanderers. What the salary is is not stated. It is a high figure but the Wanderers' officials say they have paid higher.

Had Ross been holding out all along, trying to squeeze the Wanderers for the same $1,250 Hod Stuart had reportedly been paid? Perhaps, but the story of his signing also noted that, during the course of the day, Ross received offers from two other local clubs for salaries higher than what the Wanderers were offering but he turned them down.

"I came east to play for Wanderers," Ross explained, "and will do so."

Ironically, one of the first things Art Ross did once he'd finally signed with the Wanderers was to take a train back to Manitoba. After just a few days of practice in Montreal, the team left for Winnipeg on Friday night, December 20, 1907, for a barnstorming exhibition trip that saw them play five games over the span of eight days, a grueling stretch at any time, but especially so during this era of 60-minute men who were expected to play the entire contest.

The Wanderers arrived back in Montreal on the morning of January 1, 1908, having gone 2–2–1 on the Manitoba trip. That middling record was considered less important than the fact the trip had been a financial success and that the team had been treated well. The biggest surprise was that they hadn't brought anyone back with them. Speculation was that the Wanderers would sign Tom Hooper from Kenora. The *Brandon Daily Sun* had reported on December 24 that Hooper was offered a $1,200 contract, but he remained loyal to the Thistles, only jumping to the Wanderers when the undermanned team withdrew from the Manitoba league after suffering a 15–1 loss to the Winnipeg Strathconas in their season opener.

In talking to reporters about their western trip, the Wanderers all spoke highly of Art Ross, who had served as team captain. Probably because of his familiarity with Manitoba hockey, Ross was asked what he thought of the clubs the Wanderers had faced. "They are playing good hockey in the West," he said, "but I don't think that they will turn out a team strong enough to bring the [Stanley] Cup from the East." Expressing his thoughts further, Ross stated that the "[Winnipeg] Maple Leafs seem to be the strongest of the lot; they have a good team, but it is not one that I would back as a Cup winner." With this, he proved to be a fine prognosticator. The Winnipeg team went on to take the Manitoba title with ease before losing a one-sided Stanley Cup series to the Wanderers in March. But that was still a few months away.

# 8

## A WANDERER
## WHO WANDERS

The Wanderers had little time to rest after getting back to Montreal. The first order of business on home ice was scheduled for 8:30 p.m. the following evening. The Hod Stuart Memorial Match would pit the defending Stanley Cup champions against a team of all-stars made up from the other five clubs in what was still known, for one more season, as the Eastern Canada Amateur Hockey Association.

The all-stars featured future hall of famers Percy LeSueur, Jack Marshall, and Art Ross's friend Frank Patrick, but they were slow to blend as a team. The Wanderers jumped out to a 7–1 lead by halftime and hung on for a 10–7 victory. This was Ross's first home game in Montreal as a member of the Wanderers, and given that he was expected to fill Hod Stuart's spot, "his work was watched with great interest," said the *Montreal Gazette*. Unfortunately, "he did not show up to the form he displayed with the Kenora Thistles here last winter." He was suffering from a leg muscle strain suffered on the western trip and also seemed to be having trouble with his skates. Still, "in flashes he showed his best form, and fast skating and clever stick handling won him rounds of applause."

Of course, wins, losses, and individual performances were not the point of the evening. A crowd of more than 3,800 had paid ticket prices ranging from 25¢ and 50¢ for standing room and rush seats, to 75¢ for reserved seats and $1 for promenade seats. With even the ushers working for free that evening, a total of $2,010.65 was raised for Hod Stuart's widow and her two young children.

With their active pre-season schedule complete, the Wanderers had a few days off before beginning another busy stretch of games. Their regular season began against the Montreal AAA on January 8. Ross, however, was back in action a few nights before that when the Victorias faced the Shamrocks on January 4. He served as a referee that night, as he would several times throughout the season (every team in the ECAHA nominated a few players to form a referee pool) and in the years to come.

Tom Hooper arrived in time for the Wanderers' opener and lined up at cover point against the AAA. He appeared a little rusty, whereas Ross, at point, "was easily the star player of the game," according to the *Gazette*. "He showed his best form since he has joined the Wanderers; he was sure in getting the man or the disc in Montreal attacks and time and again he dashed down the ice on end to end runs." The Wanderers won the game 7–3.

The Wanderers were next scheduled to play in Ottawa on January 11 — a shocking 12–2 loss by an exhausted team to a revamped Senators lineup now featuring Tommy Phillips and Cyclone Taylor. The likely reason why the Wanderers were so flat that night was that Stanley Cup trustee William Foran had sanctioned a two-game series with the Ottawa Victorias for January 9 and 13. The Wanderers did not want to play an opponent they deemed far inferior, and newspapers came down harshly on Foran, as they had with his decision against Smith and Westwick. Regardless, Foran insisted the team face the Ottawa Vics or forfeit the Stanley Cup. Game one was a 9–3 romp for the Wanderers. "Art Ross Star Last Night" read a headline in the *Montreal Gazette* the following morning. With a six-goal lead heading into game two, fewer than 500 fans showed up. Maybe wishing to atone for their lopsided loss to the Senators two nights before, the Wanderers crushed the Victorias 13–1 and took the series by a margin of 18 goals.

Following the stretch of four games in six nights, the Wanderers had only one day off before their next scheduled ECAHA game against the Montreal Victorias on January 15. Perhaps it wasn't surprising that they fell behind 3–0 in the first half, but soon their superior conditioning from all those games paid off and the team rallied for a 7–5 victory. Art Ross's old Westmount friend Walter Smaill replaced Tom Hooper in this game and scored three goals in the final 30 minutes. Ross was only ordinary, but his reputation as a star was spreading. On January 18, 1908, the *Morning Leader* in Regina, Saskatchewan, picked up the following story from the *Ottawa Free Press*:

> Reports of Arthur Ross being the sensation of the year have not been exaggerated. He is another Hod Stuart and then some. Speed, magnificent stick handling, ability to dodge anything and everybody, backed up by a fine shooting arm, places the celebrated athlete on a pinnacle few may hope ever to attain. Ross has everything. The cool head is ever prevalent. He can work by himself or with his teammates, has no disposition to be selfish and is gifted with a powerful physique to round off his other accomplishments.

After the game against the Victorias, the schedule afforded the Wanderers some time to rest, as they were not slated to play again until January 22 when they would beat the Montreal Shamrocks 3–1. But Art Ross managed to keep himself busy and earn a few extra dollars too.

\* \* \*

On Thursday evening, January 16, two members of the Pembroke team in the Upper Ottawa Valley Hockey League were at the Montreal Arena watching the various local teams practice. Though they denied it, it was said that they were scouting for players. Pembroke had a big game coming up with their archrival Renfrew, which had a well-paid team of top talent that had already beaten Pembroke 8–1 in their first meeting of the season on January 8.

Betting on hockey was common — and quite in the open — in this era. Large amounts of money often changed hands, particularly when key rivals met. Supporters of teams in small towns like Pembroke and Renfrew were just as likely to throw their money around as those in the bigger cities of Ottawa and Montreal — maybe even more so. In his 1990 book *The Renfrew Millionaires: The Valley Boys of Winter 1910*, author Frank Cosentino sets the scene:

> There was a public fetish for gambling. Side-bets between Renfrew and Pembroke supporters were plentiful. Club owners would put up a money purse to go to the winner of the game or the bet. Almost any variety of bet was available: the number of goals scored, the difference between the teams in goals, the number scored in each half, the difference taking into account the handicap given. Thus there would be a lot of preliminary investigating and scouting done of the competition.... Before one agreed to a bet, one liked to think that there would be no surprises.

But there often were surprises, and when the fans and team from Renfrew finally arrived on a train delayed by a snowstorm for the game in Pembroke on the night of January 17, 1908, they got one. Waiting to face them in the local lineup were Art Ross, Tom Hooper, and Charlie Chipchase of the Wanderers.

Reporter Sean Chase, writing about the game in the *Pembroke Daily Observer* on March 18, 2010, notes that some Renfrew gamblers had as much as $300 or $400 riding on the game. When they realized the star power that Pemborke had acquired, they wanted those bets called off, which nearly sparked a riot. Bill O'Brien was the Renfrew trainer at the time (and later the trainer for the Montreal Maroons and Montreal Canadiens). In a conversation with John Kiernan of the *New York Times* in 1931, O'Brien recalled that several townsfolk from Renfrew who'd bet $5 or $10 on the game were also wondering how they could get those called off. Thomas Low, a wealthy Renfrew businessman (and future Canadian Minister of Trade) was president of the team and promised to cover the bets. He also gave his team a special pep talk about how to deal with the ringers: "Go out on the ice and don't give those fellows a glance. Pretend you don't see them. As soon as the whistle blows, start checking until something breaks."

The game finally got under way around 9:30. It was a rough one, with plenty of scoring. Renfrew led 4–1 at halftime, but Art Ross scored three for Pembroke after intermission to even it up. When Renfrew went ahead 6–4, Ross added two more goals to tie the game again. As play stretched on well past midnight, Renfrew broke on top with another pair of goals. It was around this time that Baldy Spittal of Renfrew was penalized for a hit on Pembroke's Oren Frood. It was, depending on the reports, either an elbow in the face that knocked him out or simply an innocent infraction. Pembroke failed to score with the man advantage and, according to Frank Cosentino's account, just as Spittal was about to be released from the penalty box, he was arrested by Constable Dickson of the Pembroke police and taken from the rink. Despite what was clearly a deliberate attempt to aid the local team by removing a key opponent, Renfrew held on for an 8–6 victory. Spittal was soon released on bail and the charges against him were dropped the next day.

Pembroke had lost, but with Ross's five goals — and the beating he took throughout the game — Bill O'Brien, according to an undated clipping in the Art Ross files at the Hockey Hall of Fame, always maintained that the star player's performance that night was the greatest display of courage and skill he ever saw. Still, the importing of players with no local ties for big games, and the violence it so often spawned, was among the chief complaints supporters of amateur sports had against professionalism. The Stanley Cup trustees continued to put up barriers to players who jumped from team to team, but there was nothing yet in the rules of most professional leagues to prevent such movement. Even so, the Wanderers hadn't been happy with the play of Tom Hooper since his arrival from Kenora and saw the Pembroke game as a chance to get rid of him.

Announcing that Hooper had broken the terms of his contract by playing for Pembroke, the Wanderers released him (after which, the Montreal AAA promptly signed him). Charlie Chipchase, who was only a bit player anyway, was also released and as it seemed there was no way of releasing those two without releasing Art Ross, he was let go as well. The Wanderers expected to re-sign him immediately under the terms of his old contract, but Ross, "was annoyed at the treatment meted out to Hooper [and] promptly accepted his release." He then told the Wanderers it would cost them an additional $400 to sign him again. As the *Montreal Gazette* noted, "Ross is the backbone of the Wanderers defence, and the executive had nothing to do but to accept the terms." The figure he received may have been even higher according to a *Gazette* story on Monday, January 27 reporting on the Wanderers' 13–8 win over Quebec on Saturday night. "There was a lot of brilliant playing in the game, but Arthur Ross was the particular star. His work has been a feature of the Wanderers' game, but with a $500 increase of salary, the former Westmount boy … looked better than ever."

\* \* \*

Four weeks into the ECAHA season, the Wanderers had a record of 4–1, which was good for first place. They were already halfway through their 10-game schedule, and with six weeks left to play their final five games, they'd have plenty of rest down the stretch. In reporting on their win over Quebec, the *Gazette* noted that despite their lopsided loss to Ottawa and the fact that the Senators were also playing well, "from now on, [the Wanderers] will probably be strong favorites for the championship."

After losing an exhibition game to Renfrew with three substitutes in their lineup on January 28 and dropping their next league game 6–5 in overtime to the Montreal Victorias on February 5, the Wanderers closed out the season with four straight wins, including the key 4–2 victory in their late-season rematch with Ottawa. The Wanderers retained the ECAHA title with a record of 8–2 and kept their hold on the Stanley Cup.

There was still plenty of action on tap for the Wanderers after the 1907–08 ECAHA season concluded, and the games were packed just as tightly as they'd been for most of the winter. After beating the Montreal Shamrocks 6–4 on March 4 to conclude their regular schedule, the

Wanderers had five days off before playing three Stanley Cup games as part of two separate challenges over the next five days. Their two-game, total-goals series with the Winnipeg Maple Leafs was played on March 10 and March 12, and saw the Wanderers emerge as easy winners with 11–5 and 9–3 victories. Next up was the Toronto Hockey Club, champions of the Ontario Professional Hockey League. Originally scheduled as another two-game series, this would instead be a one-game, sudden-death challenge played on March 14. The Winnipeg series had left the Wanderers pretty banged up, but most observers expected the one-game set with Toronto to be just as one-sided. Instead, the Wanderers got all they could handle.

Warm weather in Montreal turned the ice to slush with pools of water on the surface. Tempers became even hotter than the temperature. The game was slow and full of penalties. Midway through the second half, shortly after the Wanderers scored to go ahead 4–3 for their first lead of the game, Toronto star Bruce Ridpath — who had two of his team's goals — went down after taking a butt-end to the groin. There was a lengthy holdup before it was finally determined that Ridpath wouldn't be able to continue. During the delay, Wanderers goalie Riley Hern and his defencemen, Art Ross and Walter Smaill, passed the time chatting with three girls sitting at rinkside. Frank Patrick was working the game as referee, and when he blew his whistle to resume play, "that trio paid no attention to me." Frank whistled two or three times more, "but still the prima donnas kept right on talking to their girl friends. I guess Art Ross still saw me as the younger kid on the block and wasn't going to be pushed around by any young whippersnapper. I was annoyed."

With the faceoff deep in the Toronto end, Frank decided to drop the puck, figuring that "by the time the play got up near the Wanderer cage, Ross, Smaill and Hern would be in position."

They never got the chance.

Newsy Lalonde was the Toronto centre. "The minute I dropped the puck," Frank remembered, "he shot it for the Montreal net.... Of course, the crowd's shouts as they sensed Lalonde's move roused Ross et al out of their lethargy. But it was too late."

"Ross," reported the *Montreal Gazette*, "made an effort to reach out and stop the flying rubber, but Hern was yards away when it landed up against the twine."

"The play by Lalonde," Frank believed, "was the smartest bit of hockey I ever saw." It must have been hard to appreciate it at the time, though. "I was on the spot for [sure]," he admits. "The Wanderers clamored around me and insisted it was an illegal face-off. I stuck to my guns, however, and allowed the goal." Still, "you can rest assured that I breathed more easily when the Wanderers tallied two more goals to clinch a 6–4 victory."

Frank Patrick would also write that Ross, Hern, and Smaill later married the girls from that night. The story meshes nicely with the Ross family legend that Art was first introduced to his future wife, Muriel Kay of Montreal, at a hockey game. According to John Ross, Muriel was a friend of Walter Smaill and used to race sailboats with him. She and Ross would see each other until 1914, when he finally proposed, and were married in the Kay family home, at 41 Lorne Avenue in Montreal, on April 14, 1915. They remained together until Muriel's death at the age of 67 in 1953.

"She always had a smile to cheer me and sweet patience to comfort me," Ross would say of his wife many years later. "She could always convince me that tomorrow would be a wonderful day."

# MONEY
# MADNESS

Life must have seemed pretty wonderful for Art Ross in the spring of 1908. He was young (still just 23), strong, and in love. He was also being paid double, maybe even triple, what he'd recently received in a full year as a bank clerk to play hockey for just under four months. He was nationally famous too. And if his ego needed any more boosting, it got plenty during a post-season trip to the United States the Wanderers embarked on after beating Toronto.

The first stop was New York City on St. Patrick's Day, where the Wanderers defeated the Montreal Shamrocks 12–7. Ross received no mention in the extensive *New York Times* coverage of the game, other than his name in the lineup and one goal in the scoring summary, but he would be the centre of attention when the Wanderers arrived in Pittsburgh the next day.

Pittsburgh was the birthplace of professional hockey. With the collapse of the International Hockey League, the old Western Pennsylvania league, whose four teams were all based in Pittsburgh, had been revived. It was once again the top pro circuit in the United States. The champion Pittsburgh Bankers, bolstered by future hall of famer Tommy Smith from the Pittsburgh Lyceums and Harry McRobie of the Pittsburgh Pirates, took on the Wanderers in a best-of-three series that was billed as a fight for the Hockey Championship of the World.

Pittsburgh was the city where Hod Stuart had first come to prominence, so there was plenty of interest in seeing Art Ross. He scored two goals as the Wanderers defeated the Bankers 6–4 in game one on March 19, and the *Pittsburgh Press*, referencing his supposed contract amount, noted that, "Ross, the $2,000 beauty, is worth all he is being paid. He resembles the late Hod Stuart in appearance and build, but if anything is faster. As a stick-handler he is Hod's superior, but on the defence is not his equal." His play in his own end must have improved in the Wanderers' 8–1 win in game two on Saturday night, March 21. "Ross was a stone wall on defence," reported the *Press*, "the Banker forwards being unable to get past him." The paper added that Pittsburgh fans had begun calling him "The Great Ross."

Having clinched the Pittsburgh series, the Wanderers dropped the final game to the Bankers 6–3 on March 23. The next night, they were in Cleveland, where they scored an easy 9–4 win over an all-star team made up from clubs in Ohio. The Wanderers then returned to Montreal, although Ross went back to the eastern U.S. to visit his sister Sybil in Newark, New Jersey, and brother Alexander and his wife in Essex.

When the Wanderers got back to Montreal, team president William Jennings was asked if he'd made any arrangements with the players for next season. He told reporters it was too early yet to talk of anything like that. Given recent reports that baseball star Ty Cobb was holding out for a three-year contract at $5,000 per year, the Wanderers may soon have wished they'd locked up some of their stars with multiyear contracts.

By September, Ross was back in Montreal, but his attention had turned to his first sporting love. As a professional athlete who'd openly accepted money to play hockey, he was no longer allowed to play rugby, which had remained an amateur sport. Instead, Ross coached the Westmount AAA junior rugby team — featuring a young Odie Cleghorn — to the city championship in November of 1908. He also assisted Chaucer Elliott, an all-around sportsmen best known today as the one of the first referees elected to the Hockey Hall of Fame in 1961, in coaching the Montreal AAA team in the Interprovincial Rugby Football Union.

With Ross coaching the Montreal AAA halfbacks and Wanderers goalie Riley Hern taking an interest in the Montreal AAA lacrosse club, rumours soon had both men signing to play for that organization's hockey team in the upcoming season. Back on October 24, 1908, the *Montreal Gazette* reported that Hern had already signed and that Ross would likely follow. The paper also noted that Ross was looking into opening his own business in Montreal, and so was unlikely to sign with Ottawa. Six days later, the *Gazette* quoted Ross as saying he was "practically certain" he would not leave Montreal, but he wouldn't say if he'd play for the Wanderers or the AAA.

In early November, Ross confirmed his plan to open a sporting goods store in downtown Montreal. Working in partnership with Auguste Ernest Bregent, who'd been running a similar business in Montreal's East End for several years, Art Ross & Co. opened on St. Catherine Street West, near the corner of Peel, on November 21, 1908. Over the next 10 years, the store would move to a handful of different locations, but always near this downtown intersection.

Ross had obtained the exclusive rights for this part of Montreal to sell a wide range of goods from A.G. Spalding Bros., the largest sporting goods company in the United States. Walter Smaill would also have a part in the business, and another kid from the neighbourhood, Sprague Cleghorn, would work there too. Judging from advertisements of the time, it seems that Ross was soon selling "Art Ross Special" hockey equipment (skate blades, skate boots, sticks, gloves, knee and shin pads, and uniforms), which he designed himself. This is the earliest indication of Ross's inventive mind trying to find ways to improve the game ... and if he could make himself a few extra dollars at the same time, all the better.

By November 11, 1908, it had been widely reported that Ross had signed to play hockey with the Montreal AAA — for perhaps as much as $2,500, and certainly not less than $1,500 — but Ottawa still claimed to be after him. The Senators were said to have offered $1,600 plus a substantial off-ice job in a local sporting goods company that would be turned over to Ross after one year.

Come the annual meeting of the Eastern Canada Amateur Hockey Association on November 14, 1908, it was a known fact that both Ross and Hern had signed with the Montreal AAA, as had another future hall of famer, Didier Pitre, formerly of the Montreal Shamrocks. But the Wanderers and the Shamrocks were not pleased. Those clubs hoped to introduce a motion prohibiting players from leaving the teams they had played for the previous season. Not surprisingly, the Montreal AAA was against this. Though delegates proposed a compromise that might have allowed the AAA to keep both Ross and Hern, the club chose to quit the league instead. They returned to their amateur roots, joining a new league to be called the Interprovincial Amateur Hockey Union. When the Montreal Victorias also joined this new league, the ECAHA was left with only the Wanderers, Shamrocks, Ottawa, and Quebec. All four teams were committed to professionalism, so the league dropped the word "Amateur" from its title and became the Eastern Canada Hockey Association (ECHA).

Pitre soon signed with the Edmonton team that would play the Wanderers for the Stanley Cup at the start of the season in late December, but for the next few days, it seemed that the Montreal AAA might be forced to pay both Ross and Hern even though they wouldn't be able to play them. There was, apparently, some sort of release clause in the contracts they'd signed, but no one seemed willing to say what the terms were. It's not clear if any money ever changed hands, but soon both Ross and Hern agreed to walk away from their AAA contracts. They were now considered open to any club, and though it was expected they would re-sign with the Wanderers, neither seemed to be in a hurry to do so.

The *Montreal Gazette* reported that Ross was "up to his eyes in work fitting out his new store in the Bell building on St. Catherine Street." Stock was being brought in daily, "and the bright display of athletic outfits in the windows has attracted a lot of attention."

"I'm too busy to talk hockey for two weeks," Ross told reporters. He admitted that he'd received a good offer, but wouldn't say if it came from the Wanderers — although Ottawa was thought to have little chance of signing him, and Quebec and the Shamrocks never expressed any interest. "Perhaps I will not play at all," Ross added.

On November 25, the *Gazette* claimed Ross wanted $1,600 from the Wanderers, but that the team found his terms "pretty steep." On

December 3, the *Montreal Star* reported that Hern had been signed, but that, "The deal between Art Ross and the Wanderers does not seem to have come to a head yet." Ross told the paper that he was still not thinking about hockey. "It's all work with me just now," he admitted. He also said, "you never can tell what a fellow might do," but that if he stayed in Montreal, "he would probably play with the champions."

Ross apparently signed with the Wanderers that very afternoon, although he refused to confirm the report when questioned by the *Star* the next morning. Still, by now, all the newspapers were including Ross in the proposed lineups they printed for the upcoming Edmonton challenge, and when the team held its first informal workout at the Montreal Arena at 7:30 p.m. on December 10, Ross was there with them.

The Stanley Cup series with Edmonton was a two-game, totals-goals affair scheduled for December 28 and December 30, before the ECHA season kicked off on January 2. (The Wanderers would play their first regular-season game at home to the Senators on January 6.) The Wanderers had lost Cecil Blachford and Ernie Russell to temporary retirement, and had seen Bruce Stuart — Hod's younger brother — lured back to his hometown of Ottawa, but the team had re-acquired one-time Wanderers star Jimmy Gardner from the Shamrocks as a player-manager. They would also lure former Ottawa star Harry Smith (brother of Alf and Tommy) away from Pittsburgh in the first of many moves for the player that winter. Later in the season, the Wanderers signed Art Ross's old Brandon teammate Joe Hall as well.

Meanwhile, in preparation for the Stanley Cup games and the start of the new season, the Wanderers practised daily for an hour, either at 9:00 a.m. or 9:00 p.m. Beginning on December 22, they would practise every day at both of those times. Jimmy Gardner had hired John Duggan to get the team into shape. Duggan, who had previously trained the Portage Lake team of Houghton, Michigan, in the International Hockey League, was a former boxer and one-time sparring partner of Canada's World Heavyweight Champion Tommy Burns. Duggan would also serve as the referee in a boxing match on a busy night for Art Ross on December 16, 1908.

That night began after a full day at the sporting goods store, after which Ross attended the annual meeting of the Westmount Rugby Club at

Victoria Hall. As reported in the *Montreal Gazette* the next day, Ross was presented with a gold locket, engraved to commemorate the junior team's undefeated season, and made a short speech. Afterward, he hurried a few blocks to the Arena, where he was on the ice for the Wanderers' 9:00 p.m. practice. An hour later, he rushed off to the headquarters of the Bohemian Club in King's Hall at 591 St. Catherine Street West, not too far from his store. There, he boxed a three-round exhibition bout against noted local fighter and Montreal AAA boxing instructor Billy Armstrong.

Although the fight ended in a draw and Ross probably had a decent size advantage on Armstrong, boxing a perennial contender for the World Lightweight crown during training camp would probably be frowned on today. Then again, it seems boxing was fairly commonplace for hockey players at the time. Or at least it was for Art Ross.

Stories turn up repeatedly (though the original source is impossible to trace) of Ross going several rounds with a pro boxer in the dressing room of the rink in Brandon, knocking out the fighter, and collecting on bets he'd made with teammates. John Ross liked to tell a tale about the oft-staged boxing matches that teams would have in their dressing rooms after games. There was always a fair amount of betting involved, and, as John heard it, his father was "just about killing everybody they set up against him." So someone decided to find a ringer to teach the kid a lesson. They brought in a professional boxer from the United States, of whom, John says, it was later learned was "on the lam because he had killed somebody in Detroit." In John's telling, the boxer had also once fought to a draw for the Heavyweight Championship of the World, and as he stepped into the ring with Ross, told him: "Sonny, just go down quickly and I'll go easy on you." Ross answered, "Oh, is that right?" and then beat the boxer to a pulp. While there must be some truth to the story, no heavyweight title contender of the era appears to match John's description.

Almost every day, there was a new report of some hockey star being offered a contract to play for Edmonton. Among the ringers added to the lineup with Didier Pitre were goalie Bert Lindsay (father of future Detroit Red Wings superstar Ted Lindsay), and Lester Patrick, who had originally hoped to challenge for the Cup with the team in his new hometown of Nelson, British Columbia. Despite the money Edmonton was offering, Lester came on board as an amateur at his father's insistence. Tommy Phillips, who'd left Ottawa to pursue his off-ice career in Vancouver, was said to be receiving a guaranteed salary of $300 per game with a bonus of $200 more if Edmonton defeated the Wanderers.

Newspapers all across Canada mocked Edmonton's spending spree and predicted the demise of the Stanley Cup as a meaningful trophy if professional hockey continued to do business in such a reckless fashion. Writing in volume one of his seminal work *The Trail of the Stanley Cup* in 1964, Charles Coleman noted: "Considering all the fuss that was made over Kenora playing two imports in the 1907 series with the Wanderers, it was remarkable that the trustees did not protest the packed Edmonton team." Others have echoed that sentiment, but William Foran did offer his opinion on the events. No doubt having seen the difficulty teams were already having in re-signing their own players, Foran was quoted in the *Globe* in Toronto on December 16, 1908, saying,

> It is ridiculous and next to impossible to bind a challenging team down to the same players who went through the previous season and won the right to play for the cup.... A contract lasts for one year, and at the expiration of that period any club can sign up players for the succeeding season if it pays the money.... Professional hockey in Canada is now well organized.... The trustees have already instituted a ruling that covers everything relating to the eligibility of players on a challenging or defending team during the season. That is a period where it is practicable to bar out men imported specially for the cup matches. Had Edmonton played for the cup towards the close of last season they would have been compelled by the trustees to place the same men on the ice who helped the team win the championship of the league.

Despite all the fuss, Edmonton's team of ringers proved no match for the Wanderers in the series opener. A large crowd of more than 5,000 fans saw the hometown team score a 7–3 victory. Tommy Phillips played the entire game even after breaking a small bone in his right ankle with about 10 minutes to go. He was unable to play in game two, and Whitcroft decided to insert Edmonton regulars Harold Deeton and Hay Miller into the lineup. The team played much better, with Deeton scoring three times and Millar twice. Edmonton scored a 7–6 victory, but lost the total-goals series 13–10.

Although his team lost, Lester Patrick had enjoyed his return to Montreal and played well in the series. After game two, he confirmed reports that Ottawa had tried to sign him up for the new season, but was quoted in the *Gazette* as saying "I would not play hockey in the East again this season for $2,000." Then he left the Arena for a late supper with his old friend Art Ross.

Writing about that dinner in his 1980 biography of the Patrick family, author Eric Whitehead related an interesting conversation that Lester could still recall word-for-word many years later:

> "Lester," said Ross over coffee, "how much did they pay you for the series?"
>
> "Just expenses," said Lester. "Why?"
>
> "Why?" snorted Ross. "Do you know what kind of money we're getting now in the East to play hockey?"

At this point, Whitehead writes that while Ross had asked for $1,600 from the Wanderers, he'd actually signed for $1,200 — although the next exchange indicates that Ross had found a way to make up the difference.

> "I got four hundred dollars for this series," said Ross. "In advance."
>
> He reached into his pocket, pulled out a wad of bills and counted them out on the table.
>
> "And I was cheated, too. Phillips got six hundred from Edmonton.... Lester, you are a *dummkopf.*"

Whitehead writes that Ross allowed the *dummkopf* to pay for dinner. After all, he noted, Lester was getting expenses.

# 10

## HIGH PAY LEADS TO
## HARD KNOCKS

The Wanderers' Stanley Cup victory over Edmonton, followed by a 7–6 overtime win against Ottawa in the ECHA opener, marked the high point of a season that was good, but not good enough. The 1908–09 campaign was a particularly trying one for Art Ross. Maintaining his status among the best players in the game seemed a whole lot harder while trying to run his own business than it had been while working at jobs handed to him because of his on-ice skill.

With just four teams in the ECHA, each one played the other four times, twice at home and twice on the road, for a total of 12 games per team. After their opening win against Ottawa, the Wanderers rattled off a pair of wins against Quebec and another pair against the Shamrocks to run their record to 5–0. They finally suffered a loss in their first game at Ottawa, dropping a 5–4 decision to the Senators on Saturday night, January 30, 1909. For all the money he was making (whatever the total actually was), and the success the team was having, Ross was not playing well. Newspapers across the country were taking him to task. "He is the top notch man in regard to salary," reports from as far away as Saskatoon noted, "but so far this season has not displayed the form that was expected of him."

Ross took heat again when the Wanderers lost a return match at home against Ottawa 9–8 one week later. He'd taken a costly penalty late in the game that led to the winning goal and was criticized in the *Montreal Gazette* for failing to pass on three occasions when Ottawa goalie Percy LeSueur had cut off his angle, particularly on a play when the game was still tied 8–8 and a pass could have set up a go-ahead goal.

For their next game, on February 10 against the Shamrocks, the Wanderers made a decision that would have seemed unthinkable just a few weeks before. To use a modern term, they made Art Ross a healthy scratch. Speculation was that teammates Moose Johnson and Pud Glass had refused to play if Ross was in the lineup, but on the day of the game the *Gazette* said simply: "Ross has not been in the best of shape, and will rest up. The big point has been through a pretty hard winter of it, between hockey and his new enterprise in the sporting goods line, and has not yet struck his form of last winter."

After the Wanderers struggled to beat the Shamrocks 8–6 without Ross, the *Gazette* reported that his doctor had advised him he shouldn't play again that winter. "It is likely, however, that he will be out at practice again in a couple of days." Ross was back in action for the next game, on February 17, when the Wanderers faced the Shamrocks again and crushed them 12–2, but after the game he told friends that he was done for the season. Still, the *Gazette* doubted the Wanderers would let him go. "He has not yet struck his old form," the newspaper said, "but at his best he is one of the best defence men in the game."

The Wanderers had a 7–2 record with three games left to play. Ottawa was 7–1 with four to go. They would meet for the final time on the second-last night of the season, March 3, 1908. Everyone anticipated that both teams would continue to pound the Shamrocks and Quebec, so it was expected that the ECHA championship, and the Stanley Cup, would be decided that Wednesday night. The Wanderers might not need Art Ross for the upcoming home-and-away set with Quebec, but they had every intention of playing him in the big game at Ottawa. How he chose to prepare himself for that one was somewhat unusual, but he seems to have had the Wanderers' consent.

* * *

It was no secret in 1909 that there was big money to be made playing hockey in the mining towns on the shores of Lake Temiskaming in northern Ontario. There was even more money to be made betting on the games there.

The main towns in the Temiskaming region were Cobalt, Haileybury, Latchford, and New Liskeard. The area had only been lightly settled until 1902, but began to boom when silver was discovered near Cobalt during construction of the Temiskaming and Northern Ontario Railway in 1903. People flooded into the region, and as they did, the usual establishments associated with boom towns followed: bars, brothels, and casinos. In an attempt to channel men's interests into something more wholesome, sports clubs also sprang up. By the 1904–05 season, hockey had made its way to the region and with betting rampant, the main competition seemed to be mostly about which team could buy the best hockey talent from the south.

"Haileybury and Cobalt are having an exciting time of it to see which town can import the best aggregation of hockey players," noted the February 5, 1909, weekly edition of the *New Liskeard Leader*. Reporting on the recent 6–5 overtime win by Haileybury, the paper claimed that "Cobalt backers dropped in the neighborhood of $15,000 on the game, which would indicate that there was about $30,000 up on the matches." In other words, gamblers on both sides had wagered enough money to pay the wages of ten star hockey players for an entire season … or about as much as 15 average Canadians might earn in an entire year! A week later, the newspaper noted that the two teams had met for the fourth, and supposedly final, time that season, "and the result was a win by Haileybury with the score of 7–5, and the incidental gathering in of a sum of money anywhere between $10,000 and $15,000 from the Silver City."

Fortunately for Cobalt supporters, their team had already beaten Haileybury twice during the 1908–09 schedule, and when they downed New Liskeard 10–4 on February 13 to sweep their four-game season series against them, they finished the year with a 6–2 record. But when Haileybury also completed a season sweep of New Liskeard, they were 6–2 as well, so a two-game, total-goals playoff was arranged to determine the champion of the Temiskaming league. Haileybury had already enticed Harry Smith to jump his contract with the Wanderers and join them at the start of their local season, and had just recently signed his younger brother Tommy as well. Cobalt had brought in Bruce Ridpath from Toronto for its last two games of the regular season, but with a league championship, and the hopes of a Stanley Cup challenge, in the balance, something more had to be done.

On February 18, 1909, reports made the rounds that Ottawa captain Bruce Stuart had turned down an offer of $400 to play one playoff game with Cobalt. It was later reported as far away as Lethbridge, Alberta, that Ottawa management refused to give Dubbie Kerr permission to accept a $700 offer to play both games, but on February 19, *The Toronto Star* reported that Cobalt had sent telegrams to Art Ross and Walter Smaill stating: "Name your terms to finish the season here." The *Montreal Gazette* said the following day that Ross would remain in the city despite a $1,000 offer from Cobalt, but the two players were soon on their way north.

Ross and Smaill caught a train late Sunday night and arrived in Cobalt on Monday afternoon, February 22. The *Cobalt Daily Nugget* referred to them the following day as "ex-Wanderers," but that was not the case. The two players had left Montreal in the open, so it seems the Wanderers must have known about their plan to play for Cobalt and approved it. In fact, a few days later, the *Montreal Gazette* reported that the Wanderers tried to cash in on the series themselves. The team wired Haileybury an offer to send them their remaining starters for the second game of the series for $5,000. The offer called for the seven players to receive $300 apiece, with Haileybury also shelling out close to $1,000 for their travel expenses. The remaining $2,000 or so would go directly to the Wanderers' management. "It is made in all seriousness," said the Wanderers' new president Fred Strachan of the offer, but Haileybury turned it down; not because of the expense, but because they felt it was too late to make such a drastic change.

Ross and Smaill made much better deals for themselves than the amounts the Wanderers would have given the rest of the players. The *Ottawa Citizen* reported that they would receive $500 and $400 for the two games respectively, but Smaill would say years later that, "[Cobalt] offered Art Ross and me $1,000 each to come up and help them out in the Silver Country playoff with Haileybury." Ross would later say that he was paid $600 per game, which was a figure noted in the *New York Times* in a story about hockey salaries on January 30, 1910.

No matter how much money the players were paid, the gamblers who backed them were wagering more. Smaill recalled "thousands of dollars" being bet on the games. "That's why we were paid so much." Ross remembered seeing a hotel clerk handle $40,000 in bets in just 20 minutes. The heavy action ensured both sides went all-out. "That first game was a harrowing experience for me," Ross would remember. "I wouldn't go through it again for many times $1,200." Smaill had similar memories, saying: "It was the bloodiest game I ever saw."

Game one in the Cobalt-Haileybury playoff began at 8:37 p.m. on Tuesday, February 23, 1909. It was obvious from the very first minutes that Ross and Smaill were marked men. Ross's memories of the game don't always mesh perfectly with the reports from the time, though they're certainly close, and paint a vivid picture of a very violent game.

"I [didn't] know what happened," Ross admitted of an early hit that knocked him out, "but the next thing I did know was that I was lying on the ice surrounded by the players and my face swathed in bandages. They had held the game up 20 minutes while they gathered my nose together and plastered it up.

"The referee asked me if I could continue and I got up. Play started again and a few moments later I went behind the net to recover the puck and was jammed in the pit of the stomach by one of the players and went to the ice again. As I was down, another took a playful kick at my ribs with his skates, and, while he didn't break any, he cut me up considerably. That held the game up a few more minutes." Tommy Smith likely delivered either the spear or the kick, as he was penalized for five minutes.

"Once again I was knocked out before halftime from a rap in the stomach," Ross recalled. "Meanwhile, Smaill had been sent down and out three times, so we were even on that score." The first half ended with Cobalt in front 1–0, and when they scored twice more in quick succession after the intermission, the *Toronto Star* reported that, "the real dirty work commenced."

"The second half ... was not five minutes old when a kick came crashing down on my head from behind and again the lights went out for me," Ross recalled. "More bandages and plaster, and I was off again to get another smash later on in the half. They scored two more wallops on Smaill as well."

All the Haileybury violence was to little avail. Ross scored the sixth goal in a 7–1 win for Cobalt and the team took a six-goal lead into game two at their rink on Friday night, February 26.

After game one, Ross and Smaill were rushed to the hotel where the Cobalt team had made arrangements for them to stay. "The next day," (Ross remembered it as a Sunday, but it would have been Wednesday), "the fans came up to my room and every other one would toss a nugget into the corner ... where a respectable pile had began to accumulate."

On Thursday evening, the night before game two, Cobalt manager Tommy Hare put the two Wanderers on the train back to Montreal, "and all thought we were out of it," Ross related. Even the Cobalt newspaper reported their return in their Friday edition, noting that they would probably not get all the money they had been promised since they had only played one game. "However," Ross continued, "we got off at North Bay and remained there for the balance of the week [in fact, they would have been in North Bay for less than 24 hours], while Haileybury was advancing plenty of backing on the next game." When the two players returned to Cobalt just before game time, "There was much consternation."

Ross admitted that he was "still pretty sore and out for revenge," but he never got it. Cobalt captain and league scoring leader Herb Clarke urged his teammates to avoid dirty play. Ross, Smaill, and the others abided by their captain's wish, and game two was surprisingly peaceful. Cobalt took no penalties at all against six for Haileybury and though the home side let a 5–1 lead slip away in the second half, the 5–5 final still gave them the league championship by the combined score of 12–6.

"More nuggets came piling into me," Ross remembered, "ranging in size from a marble to great chunks of pure, virgin silver that took two hands to hold."

Because of the ringers they'd brought in, Cobalt's challenge for the Stanley Cup would be denied at the end of the 1908–09 season, though they hoped to get a chance to play for it before the start of the 1909–10 season. Meanwhile, Ross and Smaill headed back to Montreal to help the Wanderers try and hang on to the Cup.

Ross and Smaill began their train ride back to Montreal almost immediately after the Friday night win in Cobalt. The Wanderers were scheduled to play their final home game of the season against Quebec the next day. It's unlikely the two would have played in any case, but they arrived in Montreal a little too late for game time. They watched from the stands as the Wanderers took an early 4–0 lead and held on for a nerve-wracking 7–6 victory. The team needed the win to have any chance at the ECHA title in their final game at Ottawa because the Senators crushed the Shamrocks 11–2 that night.

The Senators now had a 9–1 record to the Wanderers' 9–2. Ottawa's lopsided win over the Shamrocks marked the fifth time in 10 games the team had scored in double digits, including a high of 18 goals in an 18–4 win over Quebec on January 23. Senators stars Marty Walsh and Bruce Stuart both scored six that night, yet the biggest star — as he was all season — was Cyclone Taylor.

Playing Bobby Orr to Walsh's Phil Esposito (Bruce Stuart would be Johnny Bucyk in this analogy), Taylor provided strong defence in front of Percy LeSueur, and though assists were not tabulated as official statistics in this era, his puck-rushing abilities were said by some to have accounted for nearly half the goals Ottawa scored that season. The Senators were certainly favoured as the home team in the big game with the Wanderers on March 3, but unfortunately for Ottawa, Taylor was injured in the win over the Shamrocks. He'd suffered a deep, three-inch cut between the heel and ankle of his right foot that went right down to the bone. He was considered doubtful for the Wanderers' game, but after a few days in bed, Taylor pronounced himself fit to play. The Ottawa doctor treating him agreed, and Taylor took to the ice with his injured foot tightly wrapped and wearing a specially reinforced skate boot.

As for the Wanderers, Smaill skipped the team's final practice on March 1 to rest up from the battering he'd taken from Haileybury, but Ross took to the ice that night. Both would be in the lineup for the big game, and both played well but Cyclone and the Senators got the better of them. The game was close until the final minutes, then three quick goals gave Ottawa an 8–3 victory and clinched the 1908–09 ECHA title for the Senators.

"I must concede that the Ottawa hockey team, which has just won the Stanley Cup, was the greatest and strongest bunch of hockey players that I have ever played against," Ross admitted in an interview that ran in the *Ottawa Journal* on March 19, 1909. "Their great speed, with combination plays, have placed them without a doubt so far ahead of any former puck chasers that there is no comparison."

The Senators' dominant season had moved Cyclone Taylor to the top of the list as the biggest star in hockey. He would be rewarded for his new status when salaries exploded the following winter — though Art Ross didn't do badly either.

# 11

## MORE MONEY
## MADNESS

By the summer of 1909, Art Ross found his own place to live at 96 Stanley Street, between Cypress and St. Catherine Streets, not far from his sporting goods store. He lived either above the dance studio, or in the former residence of gymnastics and dancing instructor Frederick W. Norman, whose name appears at that address in the street listings. Ross was also fighting a lawsuit at the time. The case was summarized in the *Montreal Gazette* on July 24, 1909.

The owners of the property that housed his sporting goods store were looking to evict Ross and his business partner, who had originally signed a six-month lease. Terms of their lease agreement stated that any extension had to be arranged prior to February 1, 1909, and it was proven in court that Ross and Bregent had met the terms in a letter before the deadline asking to extend the lease for three more years, beginning on May 1, for $7,000 payable at $2,333.33 per year. Though they won the case, Ross would move the store to 172 Peel Street the following summer, and later relocate to 751 St. Catherine Street West in 1913, and then to 532-534 St. Catherine in 1916. (Ross would turn to the courts again in October of 1913, suing the millionaire executives of the Cobalt hockey club, whom he claimed owed him $320.25 for providing the team with skates, sticks, and other supplies during the winter of 1910–11.)

Once the lawsuit was behind him, it was time once again for Ross to think about his own sporting pursuits. He didn't attend the meeting at the end of August where Westmount made its rugby plans for the coming fall, but it was announced that he would again serve as coach. By early October, Ross was putting the junior team through its paces in preparation for another season in the Montreal and District League. He also coached the Grand Trunk Railway's rugby team in the intermediate division of the Interprovincial League.

In early November, thoughts turned once again to hockey, but it was soon clear that something was up with the Wanderers and the ECHA.

A significant shakeup had taken place among the Wanderers executive during the 1908–09 season. The most visible change had seen Fred Strachan assume the presidency from William Jennings. The bigger move came behind the scenes, when Patrick J. Doran bought control of the team. Doran owned the new Jubilee rink in the East End of Montreal and it was now clear that he'd bought the Wanderers in order to move them into his arena. Given that the Jubilee had less than half the capacity of the Montreal Arena, and that smaller crowds would mean smaller gate receipts for visiting teams, fellow ECHA owners — most vocally in Ottawa — were not pleased with Doran's plan.

As early as November 5, 1909, there was word that the former Wanderers executives planned to organize a new team. A few days later came a report that the Montreal Arena was prepared to back them. In its Monday paper on November 15, the *Gazette* confirmed that a new club, backed by former members of the Wanderers executive, headed up by William Jennings and headquartered in the Arena, had definitely been formed. This new club planned to press its claim for admission to the ECHA, and Art Ross would be its player-manager. Later that day, Ross announced that the new team would be called the All-Montreal Hockey Club.

There had been talk for weeks that the ECHA planned to freeze out Doran's Wanderers, and at a meeting on November 25, that's exactly what happened. After just a few minutes of discussion, the ECHA ceased to be.

Ottawa, the Shamrocks, and Quebec, followed by the Wanderers, all re-signed from the league. The first three teams then formed a new league they called the Canadian Hockey Association (CHA), and began reviewing applications for new members. Teams from Cornwall and Renfrew had both hoped to join the ECHA, but were quickly rejected by the CHA.

Young businessman John Ambrose O'Brien, son of millionaire railroad builder and mining tycoon Michael John O'Brien, had hoped to represent his hometown of Renfrew at the meeting. He had spoken to the Ottawa executives already, and knew they had very little inter-est in admitting Renfrew. They didn't even invite him in to speak. As told in Scott and Astrid Young's 1967 book *O'Brien: From Water Boy to One Million a Year*, Ambrose O'Brien recalled: "I was sitting there later outside the meeting and I guess it was a pretty hot one. They turned down our application without much discussion [Cornwall was dismissed just as quickly], and then came the big surprise: they threw out the Wanderers entirely." Art Ross's All-Montreal was voted in to replace them, as well as the Montreal-based National club from the French-Canadian sports organization of the same name that had operated its own hockey teams for several years.

Almost as soon as the CHA meeting ended, newspapers speculat-ed that the Wanderers and other rejected applicants would form their own league. As Ambrose O'Brien remembered it, the idea came to one of those spurned representatives almost immediately.

"Out of the meeting came Jimmy Gardner of the Wanderers swear-ing like a trooper... Gardner came out and he sat down in a chair near me. He was so mad he could hardly do anything but swear — and then he turned to me and said, 'Say, you O'Briens have other hockey teams up North haven't you? In Haileybury and Cobalt?' I said we had; at least we helped support the teams up there. And he said, 'Ambrose, why don't you and I form our own league? You've got Haileybury, Cobalt and Renfrew. We have the Wanderers....'" O'Brien also remembered it as Gardner who suggested that he bankroll another French-Canadian team for their new league, which they started up a week later on December 2, 1909, and called the National Hockey Association (NHA). Two days after that, the NHA unveiled its French team, which the *Montreal Gazette* said would be called *Le Canadien*, although the *Ottawa Citizen* correctly labeled *Les Canadiens*.

The CHA and the NHA quickly went to war over the best players, driving salaries higher than they'd ever been before. With wealthy backers in Ambrose and M.J. O'Brien, as well as fellow father-and-son Renfrew millionaires Alexander and James G. Barnett, plus mining magnates Noah Timmins and Thomas Hare up in silver country, the NHA easily outbid the CHA owners. The O'Briens spent lavishly on their hometown team, which was officially named the Renfrew Creamery Kings, but came to be known as the Renfrew Millionaires.

The large salaries offered by Renfrew have been passed down as fact for more than 100 years, but there's plenty of confusion upon closer investigation. Lester Patrick wrote that he received $3,000 plus expenses to play in Renfrew, and that his less-experienced brother Frank received $2,000. Frank's salary is consistent with a post-season story in the *Renfrew Mercury* of March 25, 1910, but Lester is reported by the local paper to have earned $2,700. Renfrew's biggest coup was luring Cyclone Taylor from Ottawa for what Taylor forever maintained was a salary of $5,250.

Sprague Cleghorn and his brother Odie signed with the Millionaires in 1910–11 and had fond memories of their one winter in Renfrew. "You couldn't help liking Renfrew," Sprague related in the second of a four-part series about his life that appeared on December 1, 1934, in *Maclean's* magazine. "For one thing, the men behind the club believed that money was for spending — and they spent it…. The story is that M.J. O'Brien paid $5,000 for Cyclone Taylor's jump from Ottawa. I never saw the documents, but if Renfrew wanted Taylor and Taylor wanted $5,000, that is what was paid." Interestingly, Ambrose O'Brien always maintained Taylor's salary was only $2,000.

Regardless of what salaries were actually paid, it was clear the NHA was winning the bidding war for players. For its part, the CHA tried to win the fans by setting an earlier start to its season. Ross's All-Montreal team kicked off the schedule with a game against its new local rivals the Nationals on December 30, 1909.

When All-Montreal was formed, it was reported that Ross would have himself, Walter Smaill, and Riley Hern in the lineup, while the Wanderers would retain their top forwards for themselves. However, Hern re-signed with the "Jubilee Wanderers" on November 17 and Smaill — despite being employed by Art Ross & Co. — received a tempting offer to return to Cobalt and left Montreal for the silver district on December 12. Ross also announced that he hoped to have a couple of star amateurs, by which it was expected he meant his friends Sprague and Odie Cleghorn who'd played for Westmount as intermediates in the Canadian Amateur Hockey League the winter before. However, the brothers were working in New York City, where they would play hockey as well that winter.

Ross was able to lure future Hall of Fame goalie Paddy Moran from Quebec to All-Montreal for what *The Daily Telegraph* in Quebec City reported on December 16, 1909 was just $50 up front, but a salary of more than $2,000 for the season, plus a $200 bonus if the team won the league championship. However, the rest of the roster was made up of unknowns and itinerant pros, the best of whom was Jack Marks — a decent goal-scorer, but no superstar. Marks scored four goals in All-Montreal's 7–2 win over the Nationals, but the most impressive feat of the night was that the game actually drew 1,800 fans — although that was only about a quarter of the Montreal Arena's capacity. Only about 1,500 were on hand when the Shamrocks surprised Ross's team with a 6–3 win on January 4. All-Montreal bounced back with a 5–1 win in Quebec four nights later, but the Nationals drew just 500 fans for their home game with Ottawa, and were trounced 14–4. Meanwhile, 3,000 fans packed the Jubilee rink to see the Wanderers beat Cobalt that same night, and a similar crowd had seen the Canadiens defeat Cobalt 7–6 in overtime on January 5, 1910. When only 1,500 fans showed up at the Arena on January 13 to see All-Montreal take on the Stanley Cup–champion Senators and lose 15–5, the writing was on the wall for the CHA. After the game, Ross announced that he and Paddy Moran "were going to jump the Canadian league" and sign with Haileybury.

A series of meetings was then set up for the weekend of January 15–16, 1910. It was expected an amalgamation of the two leagues would result, but what happened instead was that Ottawa and the Shamrocks jumped to the NHA, which restarted with a new schedule beginning that Saturday. The CHA went out of business. The Nationals were offered a chance to take over the Canadiens franchise, but declined in bitterness at the turn of events. Quebec also must have been angry, but All-Montreal went quietly. The team had virtually disbanded by the Saturday meeting and didn't even send a delegate on Sunday. The club was said to have run up a deficit of $1,800 during its short career according to a story about the meetings in the *Ottawa Citizen* on January 17.

Ross and Moran did, indeed, sign with Haileybury, as did All-Montreal teammate Fred Povey. Although there is no record of what Ross was paid for his two months or so running All-Montreal and for the four games he played with them, there is no guesswork needed when it comes to his deal in Haileybury. A copy of his contract is part of the collection of the Hockey Hall of Fame. It states that Ross was paid $2,700. Of that sum, he received $1,000 up front followed by payments of $170 a week for the next 10 weeks.

Despite earning the highest salary he'd ever been paid, the winter spent in Haileybury couldn't have been Art Ross's favourite. Though they were now in the big leagues, the Cobalt-Haileybury rivalry was not what it had been in recent years, and both teams struggled to 4–8 records. The highlight of the season came early, on January 22, 1910, when Ross led Haileybury to a 4–2 win over the Wanderers, who still boasted many of his former teammates. It was the only loss the Wanderers suffered during the NHA schedule, as they went on to post a record of 11–1 to take the new league championship and win back the Stanley Cup from Ottawa.

For Ross in Haileybury, it was a winter marked by long road trips and cold home games, as Frank Patrick would recall of Renfrew's visit on February 22. "It was 25 below zero," Frank remembered, "with a bitter wind that made it seem much colder than that." Frank said the players wore mittens under their gloves "to keep our hands from dropping off," and recalled Ross being decked out with a pair of fur gloves and a woolen toque rolled down over his face with peepholes cut out for the eyes. "He looked like the very devil himself, and played as mean as he looked."

Frank wrote of Ross attacking his brother Lester with his stick at one point, clubbing him on the jaw. "I think he was just looking for a good scrap to keep from freezing to death," Frank said, and when Lester retaliated, Ross took off his gloves and threw them down on the ice. "He made a few gestures with his fists," Frank remembered, "and then suddenly turned and scrambled to retrieve his gloves and get them back on again. Lester burst out laughing, and the fight was called off. Called on account of cold."

# 12

## FIGHTING THE
## SALARY CAP

The free-spending ways of 1909–10 would not continue. "The time has come," claimed one hockey executive, "when hockey salaries … must be cut down. If the game is ever to be [returned] from its present state to a businesslike era, the clubs must now secure control of the situation."

NHL Commissioner Gary Bettman voiced similar sentiments in 1994, 2004, and 2012, but it was Ottawa Senators secretary Martin Rosenthal who issued this statement on November 23, 1910, according to the next day's *Ottawa Citizen*. By then, the hockey world was nearly two weeks into its very first salary cap dispute.

With no major rival to contend with as they headed into the winter of 1910–11, executives with the National Hockey Association made no secret about the fact that salaries were going to come down. The rumours became public knowledge on November 9, 1910. The night before, T. Emmet Quinn, president and secretary of the NHA; Eddie McCafferty, the business manager of the Montreal Baseball Club who had recently purchased the Wanderers from P.J. Doran; and Dickie Boon, the former player and long-time Wanderers executive, completed a lengthy draft of a new league constitution to be discussed at the upcoming NHA annual meeting. The *Montreal Gazette* ran the entire proposal, which filled nearly a whole page of the newspaper. "To Place Hockey on Better Basis," the headline explained. Only one small item, which was found in Section 21, nearly three-quarters of the way through the document, was thought worthy of highlighting in its own sub-headline: "Salary Limit of $5,000." Lest anyone think that was $5,000 per player, the text of the document made the true intent very clear: "No club shall be permitted to pay more than $5,000 as salaries for entire club."

The *Gazette* clearly favoured the idea of a salary cap — as most newspapers and sportswriters seemed to. On the morning of November 12, 1910, the *Gazette* wrote:

> If the amateurs are to threaten the popularity of the pros, who have been in the spot light for a couple of seasons, the pros are going the right way about preparing for the fight by considering the new scheme of organization to be submitted at the National Association meeting in the Windsor [Hotel] this afternoon. Many look on the coming winter to decide the fate of professional hockey. If it is run as recklessly as it was last winter, that will be the finish, think many good judges. The players may kick over the proposed reduction of salaries, but unless a definite step is taken to reduce and control them by the salary limit proposal, there may be no one to pay salaries the winter of 1912.

At the NHA meeting, the new constitution was adopted with only a few minor changes. As expected, the league also lost its Haileybury and Cobalt franchises, which were too far away from the others to be viable. The Shamrocks would also pull out a week later with plans to return to their amateur roots, but replacements for the two Northern clubs had already been lined up. The Quebec Bulldogs, who'd been dropped the year before when the CHA folded, were welcomed back into business, and Le Club Athlétique Canadien would also be given a franchise. Though these new Canadiens officially replaced Cobalt, they would take over many of the same players from the Canadiens team set up by Ambrose O'Brien, whose original club would technically remain in the league, though it would be inactive. It was expected that O'Brien's franchise would be sold to Toronto interests, which it was a year later. The team became the Toronto Hockey Club — more commonly referred to as the Blue Shirts — and was formally admitted to the NHA on October 11, 1911, although construction delays in building the Arena Gardens on Mutual Street meant the team would not actually play until the winter of 1912–13. There would be talk of adding another new team to the NHA for the 1910–11 season, but the league would play with just five clubs that winter.

In addition to adopting the new constitution and sorting out the new teams, the NHA executive also approved new playing rules for 1910–11, changing the game from two 30-minute halves to three 20-minute periods. The additional rest provided was one reason why the NHA decided to drop the rover the following winter, reducing the game to the six positions still in use to this day. (Art Ross became a big fan of the new alignment. "Just wait until you see the six-man game," he'd be quoted in the *Manitoba Free Press* while in Winnipeg on March 21, 1913. "It has the old style beat a thousand different ways.") Still, it was the salary cap that made the biggest news coming out of the NHA meeting.

"Now that the association has been reorganized … with the salary limit of $5,000 adopted," opined the *Gazette* on November 14, "the next business will be whipping the players into line. There will, without a doubt, be a strenuous kick all along the line at the salary reductions from the ridiculous figures of last season, but if the league sits tight it can control the situation."

Other newspapers weren't as sure. "The clause calling for a $5,000 salary limit is certain to cause trouble as it would necessitate cutting each man down to about $500," said the *Ottawa Citizen* that same day. "None of the puckchasers who have been drawing twice or three times that amount will consent to play for a paltry half thousand."

Ottawa players were the most vocal in their opposition to the salary cap, which none at first believed would truly come to pass. Senators star Marty Walsh joked in a story that appeared in the *Citizen* on November 16 that $500 wouldn't pay his beefsteak bill during the season. "I'm not going to play hockey at all this winter," added team captain Bruce Stuart with a laugh. "I am going up the bush for the winter. There's more money in shantying."

A day later, the situation took a more serious turn. "The Ottawa players had some kind of conference [yesterday]," reported the *Gazette* on November 17. "Bruce Stuart and Albert Kerr stated … that they would never accept the salary which the clubs now propose to offer and that rather they would proceed to organize another league." It was thought this was merely a bluff designed to raise the salary cap higher, and that Ottawa management, whose delegates had been absent from the November 12 NHA meeting, would push for a $10,000 cap. However, at the team's own annual meeting on November 18 the Ottawa executive agreed to abide by the NHA's decision. Senators president D'Arcy McGee announced that the $5,000 cap was necessary to "rescue the famous sport from a disastrous finish." A few days later, Martin Rosenthal suggested that NHA clubs should "drop hockey for two or three seasons" if the players didn't fall in line.

The players believed they had fan sympathy on their side. "They pay their money to see good hockey," an unnamed player said in the *Citizen* on November 26, "and will certainly not get it unless the salary limit clause is wiped out." On the other hand, "Talk to the man on the street," the paper reported on December 3, "and he will tell you that the players have in the past been given altogether too much money for their services." Then again, the article continued, "The next hockey enthusiast will emphasize his feelings in favor of the stickhandlers and convince you that he would rather see his money go into their pockets than into the hands of the promoters."

NHA president Emmett Quinn seemed to feel the public was behind the owners. And besides, he didn't agree that a salary limit of $5,000 meant stars had to settle for $500. "It would be possible," he was widely reported as saying, "to pay a player of particularly high class as much as $900, allow $700 or $800 for two other men, and complete the team within the salary limit." He further pointed out that teams were not compelled to carry 10 players, noting that the Wanderers had won the Stanley Cup in 1909–10 with just eight regulars.

But if the public was split over which side to support in the salary dispute, the newspapers — particularly in Montreal — clearly sided with the owners. So much so that on November 25, 1910, Art Ross had been moved to take matters into his own hands by way of a letter to the sports editor of the *Montreal Herald:*

> For some little time now the newspapers, especially the Herald, have been handing it to the hockey player. It seems to me about time somebody took up the cudgels on behalf of the players, who, after all are not asking for any princely salaries, but who do object to doing all the work and getting a small portion of the gain, as they will likely do if they go into the clubs on the $5,000 salary limit basis. Hockey players have been compared to professional baseball players, but the comparison is unjust. The hockey season is comparatively short, and the majority of players engaged as professional players hold other positions also. While playing hockey they run the risk of injury and probable loss of time, in addition to suffering a certain amount of distraction, which is almost bound to effect the prospects of advancement in business. All these things have to be taken into consideration in assessing the value of a professional hockey player. Hockey isn't a gentle pastime — not as it is played among the big teams. If it were, people wouldn't go to see it and there wouldn't be any need for salary limits, because there would be no paid players. With the possible exception of football, which after all only lasts one month, hockey is the most strenuous game I know.
>
> The promoters, I see, claim that they will uncover a lot of stars from the bushes if the older players insist on standing out. To do this the promoters will have to go into the amateur field. Do they think they will get many of the amateurs to abandon their good standing, to cut themselves off from any other game except lacrosse, for a paltry $500 or less? And remember these bush stars might not make good at that, but their amateur standing would be gone just the same.

During a period of four years my own salary as a professional hockey player has varied from $1,000 to $2,700, the amount I got from Haileybury last season. But I would gladly give back all I have made as a professional player to regain my amateur standing and there are a good many other professionals who feel the same way I do.

But once a man has become a professional, he naturally places the highest value he can on his skill. The pros of today who are standing out against the salary limit aren't asking for any princely salaries, but merely what their skill is worth as revenue producers.

The contention of the promoter is that a $5,000 salary limit is necessary to make both ends meet. Now the Wanderers have paid on the average from $10,000 to $14,000 a year in salaries since they first started in the pro game. Ottawa has paid from $10,000 to $25,000 and yet Wanderers and Ottawa have never been in the hole. As a matter of fact, they have or should have made money.

All the players want is a fair deal. Personally, I am taking no active part in the matter just now, but if necessary will do what I can for the cause. The players are not trying to bulldoze the NHA, but we want to know where we get off at.

Ross's letter, or segments of it, was reported in newspapers all across Canada the following day. It hardly seemed to earn much support for the players' cause. In the *Ottawa Citizen*, for example, an unnamed sportswriter acknowledged that Ross had been "probably the greatest halfback that ever played in Canada and has often regretted the step he took in jumping to the professional ranks," but still got in his sarcastic digs by reporting that Ross had "taken up his pen in defence of the poor, downtrodden hockey players." Elsewhere on the same sports page, it was mockingly reported that, "Art Ross announces he has received an offer of $1.33 per week to play for Chicoutimi in the Shantyman's League."

Soon, though, more and more players were speaking out. Walter Smaill had left Cobalt for Ottawa midway through the 1909–10 season, and was now expected to remain in Ottawa, but he considered himself a free agent and said that he objected to being called "property" of any club. Moose Johnson of the Wanderers stated that he'd had his "nose broken, teeth knocked out and head and face cut many times," and "that rather than play for what the National association offers, I will quit hockey altogether." Other Wanderers made similar declarations. Ross himself added, "Unless I get an adequate salary I will not play, and there are a number of others who will not." Then, in a statement that would be echoed somewhat by Wayne Gretzky and his Ninety-Nine All Stars, who barnstormed through Europe during the 1994–95 NHL lockout, Ross added: "If the worst comes to worst, we might easily get up a professional team to tour the United States and leave Canadian hockey alone."

Meanwhile, Bruce Stuart was moving ahead with plans to organize a new league, working in tandem with Dr. David H. Baird, an Ottawa dentist and president of the Ottawa Football Club (the Rough Riders). There was also interest from moneymen in nearby Brockville who'd recently been denied entry into the NHA. In Montreal, the Wanderers' holdouts were said to have the support of former club officials James Strachan and George Gales. Art Ross, it was reported, would head up a second Montreal team.

Progress on the new league was slow, but promising enough that players continued to hold out. "We are all suffering from writers' cramp and cannot sign up," said Stuart sarcastically on December 1. A day later, he offered to turn the tables on the NHA owners. "We'll make up five thousand and give it to the Ottawa club if they will allow us to take charge of their gate receipts this season and split them up on an equal percentage." Stuart figured the Ottawa players could earn about $2,000 apiece that way.

Conflicting reports on the labour situation continued to dominate headlines in Ottawa, Montreal, and elsewhere. As late as December 12, the *Toronto Star* reported that Stuart felt the new "outlaw league," as the newspapers insisted on calling it, was a certainty, that Art Ross would be found at the head of one of the Montreal teams, and that Ross believed he could sign Walter Smaill, as well as Newsy Lalonde, Didier Pitre, and Jack Laviolette of the Canadiens. Yet just one day later, it was clear that Stuart and his gang of rebels would not succeed. Unable to convince the operators of the Montreal Arena to back the players over the NHA owners, the new league was abandoned and players began signing with their old teams. The salary cap dispute had lasted one month, but the NHA season would start as scheduled on December 31.

A disappointed Bruce Stuart was said to have retired, but eventually signed with the Senators, who inked only their top eight stars and reportedly paid them all between $600 and $700, likely an even $625 a piece. Ottawa went on to win back the Stanley Cup from the Wanderers in 1910–11, and their players were allowed to earn a few extra dollars by splitting up the receipts from the two Stanley Cup games they played, as well as from a post-season trip with the Wanderers to New York and Boston.

For Stuart, champagne sipped from the Stanley Cup didn't wash the bad taste from his mouth. After the Senators used him in just three of their 18 league and playoff games, he walked away for good. Stuart turned his full attention to the shoe store he owned on Bank Street, and would manage it until 1952. He died at the age of 79 on October 28, 1961 — two months after his induction into the Hockey Hall of Fame, where his brother Hod had been among the first inductees in 1945.

Like Bruce Stuart, Art Ross appeared to walk away from the game at the start of the 1910–11 season, but his so-called retirement wouldn't last. Ross's fight for players' rights would also continue in the years to come, although it would not survive into his later life as a National Hockey League executive with the Boston Bruins — but those days were a long way off.

## 13

## A NEW
## HOCKEY WAR

It's never been clear how strictly the NHA enforced its salary cap. When writing about it before the 1911–12 season began, the *Montreal Gazette* stated: "For the present, the old salary limit stands, at least, nominally, and if not changed later individual clubs may feel as free to disregard it as they did last year." Canadiens owner George Kennedy openly admitted to playing out $8,000 in salaries. Yet as the dispute lingered on in the early winter of 1910–11, Art Ross really did appear ready to walk away from the game because of it. In an interview with the *Ottawa Journal* that appeared in the paper on January 11, 1911, Ross maintained that he would not return to the NHA for the salaries being offered. His sporting goods business kept him busy, and he certainly had lots of other things going on.

During the summer of 1910, and then again in 1911 (when he also served as honorary president), Ross helped the Montreal Stars baseball team win the Independent Championship of Montreal and the province of Quebec as a heavy-hitting first baseman. The ball club also featured Sprague and Odie Cleghorn, and was run by Cecil Hart — a future coach of the Montreal Canadiens and son of Dr. David Hart, who would donate an MVP trophy to the NHL in 1924.

As well, in the fall of 1911, and again in 1912, Ross coached the Montreal Football Club in the senior division of the Interprovincial Rugby Football Union. Unfortunately, despite his former prowess as a player and his previous success coaching Westmount juniors, Montreal finished last in both seasons under Ross, posting a record of 1–5 in 1911 and 0–6 in 1912.

Meanwhile, in November of 1910 while the salary cap dispute was heating up, the Montreal Stars entered a team in the new, amateur, Montreal City Hockey League. Ross was reportedly named coach of the Stars, but it's unclear whether he actually held the job or not. However, records from McGill University show that Ross spent a lone season as their hockey coach in 1910–11. Sports Information Officer Earl Zukerman of McGill says the school didn't pay salaries to coaches in this era, and the position was considered honorary, but Ross did accompany the team to Boston when McGill defeated Harvard 5–3 on January 7, 1911. As for his involvement with the Montreal City League, Ross definitely refereed some games during the winter, but made his most important contribution by donating the Art Ross Cup.

In the beginning, the Art Ross Cup was one of two championship trophies (along with the Jubilee Cup) competed for by the teams in the Montreal City League. By 1913, when the league moved its games from the Jubilee rink to the Montreal Arena, the Jubilee Cup was dropped. The Jubilee Cup had always been a challenge trophy, available also to the teams in other Montreal-based amateur leagues, but now the Art Ross Cup assumed that. Soon, it became available to teams all across the province of Quebec, and was later opened up to challenges from the northeastern United States.

Beyond donating the trophy, Ross actually had little involvement with the Art Ross Cup, as trustees Cecil Hart and Eddie St. Pierre oversaw its competition. He did, however, take an active role in other endeavours bearing his name. In the fall of 1913, he organized the Art Ross Hockey League. It featured divisions across the city of Montreal with teams for all ages, including a junior league for children. A cartoon in the *Montreal Standard* on Saturday January 3, 1914, depicts Ross as a "modern pied piper of Hamelin" leading a parade of small children with hockey sticks.

There was also an Art Ross Baseball League, and though he didn't always serve as president of these two namesake organizations, annual meetings were always held in the sales rooms of Art Ross & Co.

No doubt a sportsman such as Ross believed in the good these leagues provided in and of themselves, but they certainly benefited his sporting goods business as well. "Through his connection with athletic clubs and his reputation as an athlete, he has built up the largest business in that line in the Dominion," boasted a Montreal city guide. "His trade, which is large in Montreal, is augmented by a mail order business that extends throughout Canada, where the name of Art Ross is a synonym for high quality goods."

Still, Art Ross was a competitor, and despite his unhappiness with the way things played out in November and December of 1910, he couldn't keep off the ice. In January of 1911 he began to referee games in Montreal. Near the end of the month, he turned out for practice with the Wanderers, but was said to be out of shape. He didn't suit up on January 28 when the Senators romped to an 8–2 victory, but was out with the team for practice again the following Monday and was expected to sign with the Wanderers the next day. Given the salary cap dispute, it's interesting to note that newspapers seemed much more concerned with Ross's physical condition than how much money he signed for — his salary doesn't seem to have been reported.

Ross finally returned to action on February 1, 1911, in a 6–3 victory over the Canadiens. He played the remaining 10 games with the Wanderers after that. It was a poor season for the team, however. Ottawa romped to the NHA championship with a record of 13–3, comfortably ahead of the Canadiens and Renfrew, who both finished the season 8–8. The Wanderers were fourth at 7–9, ahead of only the 4–12 Quebec Bulldogs. The highlight of the season for Ross, or, more accurately, the lowlight, occurred in a rough game against Quebec in Montreal on February 25.

As Quebec desperately hung on to a 3–2 lead, Walter Smaill bumped the Bulldogs' Eddie Oatman with his knee and received a penalty. Oatman was then thrown against the boards by Ross and responded with a wicked slash to Ross's head. Ross was prevented from striking back, but with only two minutes remaining, all three players were sent off for the remainder of the game. As they approached the penalty timer's box, Oatman began to climb over the boards but Ross removed his glove and struck the Quebec player with a solid punch over the eye. With that, some 50 fans jumped onto the ice, followed quickly by several members of the Westmount police who managed to restore order. When the game finished, policemen were sent to guard the dressing room doors. It was expected that charges would be laid, but neither man was arrested. NHA President Emmett Quinn took quick action, though, announcing that Oatman and Ross would be fined $25 apiece. With both players likely earning little more than $1,000 for the season (and possibly less), this would be comparable to a fine of $14,375 to a modern player making the current NHL minimum salary of $575,000 … even without allowing for inflation.

Some reports have Art Ross retiring again once the 1910–11 season ended, but he was induced to return to the Wanderers for a pair of postseason series against Renfrew and Ottawa in New York and Boston. Serving as a referee during the games in Boston was his old friend Lester Patrick. There had been plenty of rumours — particularly about Frank returning to Renfrew — but the reduction in salaries had not made it financially viable for the Patricks to come east to play hockey during the winter of 1910–11. Instead, they had stayed, and played, out west in Nelson. Now, financed by their father's sale of the family lumber business, they planned to set up a new professional league on Canada's West Coast. In fact, though Lester was in Boston on his honeymoon, he was also researching the equipment at the Boston Arena for the new artificial ice rinks the family planned to build in Vancouver and Victoria.

Frank and Lester Patrick formally announced the launch of the Pacific Coast Hockey Association on December 7, 1911. Construction on their rinks had begun in August, as had their attempts to lure eastern stars out west. There were plenty of naysayers. Eddie McCafferty had brought in Montreal Baseball Club owner Sam Lichtenhein as majority stockholder and president of the Montreal Wanderers in December of 1910, and Lichtenhein expressed the opinion of most eastern hockey men when he was quoted in the *Westmount News* on August 11, saying that he doubted the Patrick brothers' aspirations were going to amount to anything. In fact, he was willing to bet $50, "to be given to any charity in Montreal," that the brothers wouldn't pull it off. But just in case they did, Lichtenhein threatened that if any Wanderers did go west, "they will virtually cut their own throats, for both myself and the NHA will make it as hard as possible for players who jump and want to jump back again."

Still, money talked, and the Patricks were offering more than was available in the NHA. As owners of their own buildings, they didn't have to pay rent to arena managers the way NHA owners did, so there was a bigger pool of money for salaries. In the era of 60-minute men, the Patricks didn't need a lot of players. Although they held fast to seven-man hockey even after the NHA eliminated the rover position, the Patricks signed only 21 men in addition to themselves to fill out the rosters of their three teams. Of those 21, 11 came directly off of NHA rosters. The biggest name was Newsy Lalonde, who left the Canadiens. Moose Johnson, Walter Smaill, Harry Hyland, and Jimmy Gardner all left the Wanderers. Cyclone Taylor would jump the following year.

Given Art Ross's close friendship with the Patricks, it's not surprising to learn that they were after him too. Ross admitted to reporters that he was offered "a fat sum to make the trip," but that he preferred to stay in the East. There were rumours that the new Toronto Hockey Club was interested in Ross and that there was a good chance he would join them. "Stranger things have happened," he said, but the Wanderers wanted to keep him happy. He was given the opportunity to become a stockholder in the club and a place on the team's executive. On the ice, he would serve as team captain.

New faces with the Wanderers in 1911–12 included Sprague and Odie Cleghorn, who both enjoyed strong seasons. The Cleghorns were as rough as anyone who ever played the game, and Sprague may have been the meanest man in hockey history. "Sprague was as wild as they came," remembered Newsy Lalonde, who had more than his share of run-ins with him. He told Stan Fischler in a 1970 interview that Cleghorn "once said he had counted the number of stretcher-case fights he had been in and the grand total was fifty. Imagine that! Fifty!"

The most vivid description came from Red Dutton and was published in Trent Frayne's *The Mad Men of Hockey* in 1974: "If some of the
longhairs I see on the ice these days met Sprague Cleghorn, he'd shave
them to the skull. Jesus, he was mean. If you fell down in front of Cleg
he'd kick your balls off."

Sprague split his time between forward and defence in his first year
with the Wanderers, beginning the season playing left wing across the
ice from his brother Odie at right wing, but later moving to cover point
in front of Art Ross at point. Ross enjoyed the best offensive season of
his career this year, leading all NHA defencemen with 16 goals in the 19
games he played.

The races were tight in both the four-team NHA and the three-team
PCHA that season, with the understanding that the winner of the PCHA
might challenge the NHA winner for the Stanley Cup. The Quebec
Bulldogs emerged as surprise champions in the East, finishing 10–8,
including a key overtime victory against Ottawa in their last game of
the season on March 2. The Senators and Wanderers both ended at 9–9,
while the Canadiens were 8–10.

Out west, New Westminster won the PCHA championship, but the
March 19 conclusion of the season, plus the week it would take to cross
the country by train, meant it was too late for a Stanley Cup challenge
on the natural ice in Quebec City. Instead, the Patrick brothers planned
an East versus West all-star game on the coast, where their artificial ice
surfaces meant warm spring weather was not a problem.

"Everyone considered this to be an excellent idea," wrote Eric
Whitehead in his biography *The Patricks*. "Everyone that is except the
directors of the National Hockey Association. And especially Sam
Lichtenhein." But with the Patricks guaranteeing the eastern team either
$5,000 or $6,000 to make the trip, according to various newspaper reports, the players weren't about to pass up the chance. Art Ross wired
Frank Patrick that he would pick the team himself, and after the NHA
clubs returned from a barnstorming trip to New York and Boston, the
all-stars boarded the Canadian Pacific Railway's Transcontinental for
Vancouver on the night of Monday, March 25. Reports out of Montreal

now claimed: "Not only are the All-Stars going west with the full consent of the National Hockey association, but their leader, Art Ross, has been informally commissioned to bring about an understanding with the British Columbia league, which will be better for the game in general." Ross himself confirmed this version of events upon arrival on the coast, telling the *Vancouver Sun* that the eastern media had made up the story about the NHA owners' opposition.

The all-star series was a big success, with large turnouts for the games in Vancouver and Victoria. The PCHA stars took the series, winning the first two games under seven-man rules before the NHA won the finale playing the six-man game without a rover. Still, it did little to lessen the battle between the two leagues.

In the fall of 1912, the athletes once again played the owners against each other, with Newsy Lalonde and Harry Hyland among the biggest names to return east, while Lester Patrick lured Goldie Prodger, Eddie Oatman, and Jack McDonald West from the Stanley Cup-champion Bulldogs. Both leagues threatened lawsuits, with the Wanderers' Sam Lichtenhein once again making the loudest noise. Meanwhile, Art Ross remained a favourite of the fans in Montreal as witnessed by his landslide victory in the vote for most popular player on the Wanderers which was reported in the *Montreal Tribune* on November 28, 1912. Ross unseated Harry Hyland, who was returning to the team from New Westminster, by nearly a million votes. He was presented with a sizeable silver loving Cup before the Wanderers' game with Quebec on New Year's Eve 1912.

The NHA and PCHA were still fussing by the end of the 1912–13 season, and though Lichtenhein really did appear to be threatening to ban any players that took part, Art Ross once again led an eastern all-star team west for a series against the western stars. In addition, the Quebec Bulldogs — who had hung on to their title despite the defections — also defied their fellow NHA clubs by agreeing to come west for a non-Stanley Cup championship series against Victoria, who'd won the PCHA title. Ross served as a referee in one of those games as Victoria took the series two games to one.

With the NHA losing both the best-of-five all-star series and the best-of-three championship series, combined with the fact that attendance was down at their own league games, it was apparent the PCHA was winning the new hockey war. By the end of the summer of 1913, the two leagues finally agreed to make peace, but the deal they signed would create its own problems.

Lester Patrick first brought up talk of a hockey commission to oversee the professional game in Canada in the early fall of 1912. Given that he was doing his best to raid players from the NHA at that time, club owners in the East were not particularly inclined to listen to his one-sided terms. Nearly a year later, in August of 1913, Frank Patrick came to Montreal. He was recuperating from a recent surgery in New York and was said to be taking things easy for a few days. Still, "the chances are that he will take a few of the Eastern hockey players with him for next season," reported the *Ottawa Citizen* on August 11. As for any talk of a hockey commission, "he says that the chances for [that] are as far away as ever." However, just two days later, the *Citizen* reported that Lester would be in Montreal by the end of the month, and that the Patrick brothers "will then be in a position to make or break any hockey commission that is broached by the Eastern magnates."

On August 23, a *Citizen* headline read "Commision Assured." Then, on September 3, under a story headlined "Peace in Sight," the paper confirmed that a meeting would be held the following evening. That Thursday night in Montreal, Frank and Lester Patrick sat down with NHA president Emmett Quinn. With the exception of Ottawa, all the NHA clubs were represented at the meeting. Sitting in on behalf of the Wanderers was Sam Lichtenhein, Dickie Boon, Odie Cleghorn, and Art Ross. Together, they reached a working agreement, based on the National Commission established several years earlier by baseball's National and American leagues, to govern the conduct of the two leagues. In early November, the NHA reached a similar agreement with the Maritime Professional Hockey Association, but this rival league that had also started in 1911–12 would wobble through its third season in 1913–14 and then go out of business.

The agreement reached between the leagues contained 15 points. Most of them dealt with honouring the terms of each other's contracts, which league would have the rights to which players, and how the teams could buy, sell, or trade them. Three of the terms also dealt with rules for a best-of-five post-season playoff between the league champions. When the trustees of the Stanley Cup later agreed to make their prize available for this annual series, the original challenge era of the trophy ended and the Cup competition became a World Series of Hockey between the game's top professional leagues.

Problems between the two leagues continued despite the Hockey Commission, and the biggest change to the game in 1913–14 actually had little to do with the agreement; it was the decision reached by the Patrick brothers to paint blue lines on the ice surface and allow forward passing in the neutral zone. Frank and Lester urged their eastern rival to adopt this new rule too, but it would not happen until the 1918–19 season — a year after the National Hockey Association was reorganized as the National Hockey *League*.

# 14

## PEACE, WAR ...
## AND A REAL WAR

In 1913, at the age of 28, Art Ross was certainly still at the height of his skills. At the end of the 1912–13 season, sportswriter John F. McMahon called Ross, "the perfect hockey player," adding that he, "shows one a big athlete with the nerve of an aviator, the grit of a boxer, the head of a quarterback and lungs like the best of the long and short distance runners.... All Canada knows of the deeds of Ross and others prominent in the ice sport as we do of [baseball star Ty] Cobb."

In talking to McMahon, Ross espoused the importance of staying in shape year-round. "The one big danger [young players] have to steer clear of is rest in the summer time and the taking on of flesh." However, Ross admitted that all the sports he played had taken a toll on him. He told McMahon he was only 27, but "he acknowledged when the question was put to him that everyone took him for 35" and that he suspected his time in the game was nearing an end. "Youth is necessary to professional hockey material," he said. "Every star sticks for but little over three years at the big salary limit. New men continually arise."

Given that Ross felt this way, and knowing his history of fighting for the highest contract possible, it's difficult to believe he was happy with the Hockey Commission he'd help to forge. As a businessman, his quotes at the time clearly show that he understood the benefit of running the game in a more business-like manner. Yet he seems to have underestimated just how much the end of the bidding wars would allow the eastern owners to once again decrease salaries — which they certainly did. There was nothing as drastic as the $5,000 salary limit of 1910–11, but the new contracts offered by NHA owners as the 1913–14 season approached called for big pay cuts … and newspapers warned of a possible hockey strike.

On October 24, 1913, the *Daily Telegraph* in Montreal claimed the players "were up in arms" and "will not stand" for the proposed cuts. Ross is not mentioned by name in the story, and it's unlikely that he was the one described as "one of the most prominent local players" who had discussed the situation with the newspaper. Even so, it would soon be clear that Ross was in sympathy with the views expressed:

> They are trying to bottle the men up by their new peace contracts with the other governing hockey bodies in Canada. The owners appear to be of the opinion that they can cut our salaries, treat us like a bunch of animals and shove us into what section of the country they wished, but they have been mistaken. There are many players who would rather drop out of the game altogether than be sold and traded like so much goods…. The owners only think to shove us out on the ice to amuse the public, so as to draw a crowd and give them a more difficult task in counting the gate returns. They do not understand what treatment a player undergoes when he carries through his contract. We are shoved into two games a week, during which we get battered and slashed until we are so weak that we can hardly stand up, and yet the owners think we get too much cash for our services. It is well seen that none of them played professional hockey. They don't appear to consider the fact that during the course of any game we might possibly receive such injuries as to maim us for the rest of our lives.

It is a cut-throat hold-up on the part of the hockey club owners but we will give them their share of troubles before the season is over.

Throughout November, there were reports that players who'd received between $1,200 and $3,000 in recent years were now receiving offers in the area of $750 to $1,000. On November 13, 1913, the *Montreal Gazette* reported that Ross had been paid $1,500 the season before but was now being offered only $1,000 for 1913–14. "Ross is credited with stating that he will not play for less than $1,500," the newspaper said, "and will not state how much more he wants for the season." By then, most of the other Wanderers had already signed new contracts, but Ross was holding out.

At the Wanderers' annual meeting on November 24, the club showed an $800 deficit, but the *Gazette* the next day reported, "prospects were of the brightest" for the coming season. In a shuffle of team executives, Ross was promoted to the position of second vice president, but he still hadn't signed a contract to play for the team. Harry Hyland was also holding out against an offer of $1,000.

By December 1, Ross was said to be devoting all of his time to looking after his sporting goods business and organizing the startup of the Art Ross Hockey League. He admitted that there was "a strong probability" he would be out of hockey as a player. Sam Lichtenhein agreed. "It is quite likely he will not play," said the Wanderers president and principal owner. "Not that there are any differences between us, other than the salary question [but] I think you will more likely see him on the bench cheering for the team than playing his old position."

There was also talk that Ross was organizing a players' fraternity league, in which star holdouts from other teams were said to be interested, but the fact that it was only the top stars whose salaries were threatened meant average players weren't interested. Still, when eight members of the Wanderers reported for a pre-season workout at the gymnasium of the St. Patrick's Amateur Athletic Association from noon to 1:00 p.m. on December 8, Ross and Hyland were absent. A week later, 14 men were under contract and working out, but still no Ross or Hyland. The two were reported as suspended by the team on December 18, but one day later, when the team held its first on-ice workout, Art Ross was on hand … watching his teammates from rinkside. Perhaps that was a mistake, because once he was there, the competitive instincts seemed to take over. On December 22, 1913, Ross and Hyland announced to the press that they would turn out for practice that afternoon. Details of their contracts weren't reported, but they'd come to terms with Lichtenhein and the holdout was over.

Regardless of finally signing their stars, the 1913–14 season was a bad one for the Wanderers. The team was an offensive powerhouse, but poor play from four different goaltenders resulted in the league's worst defensive record. Things were so bad the Wanderers had Ross practising in the net at one point. The team finished the season with a 7–13 record and were fifth in the six-team NHA.

The Wanderers now found themselves in the hole, financially. The deficit from the 1913–14 season was reported as $3,987. Sam Lichtenhein himself was apparently still doing fine. He'd announced his intentions of selling his 51-percent stake in the Montreal baseball club, but on November 18, 1914, he instead paid out $30,000 to buy the remaining 49 percent. Still, Lichtenhein planned to introduce steeper pay cuts for his hockey team in 1914–15. The reason likely had less to do with his personal finances or the Wanderers' growing deficit, and more with a much more serious issue. On June 28, 1914, Archduke Franz Ferdinand, heir to the Austro-Hungarian throne, and his wife were assassinated in Sarajevo, which would ultimately lead to the outbreak of the First World War in early August.

Amateur athletes from every sport were encouraged to enlist after England (and therefore, Canada) declared war on Germany on August 4, 1914. Many did so willingly, and many amateur sports organizations shut down for the duration of the War. Most pro athletes — perhaps because they tended to be older, family men with off-ice careers as well — didn't rush to follow the lead of their amateur colleagues.

"I had no illusions about war, and I was not the soldiering type," Cyclone Taylor told biographer Eric Whitehead. Taylor had just recently been married, and he was not anxious to serve overseas. "But if they wanted me and needed me, I was willing and ready to go." Whitehead writes that the choice to enlist was taken out of Taylor's hands when his off-ice job as an immigration officer was declared vital to national interests.

Ross would also soon be married, and as the owner of his own business (although not an essential service), he was not a prime candidate for the military. His brother George would later join the Royal Canadian Medical Army Corps, while his soon-to-be wife Muriel saw her brother Stuart Kay become an artillery officer, and her sister Bea serve overseas as a nurse. Still, Ross seems not to have been the soldiering type either. As the years went by, he made his war contributions in his own way on the home front.

Meantime, it was known in the hockey world even before the end of August in 1914 that Sam Lichtenhein planned to offer Wanderers players no more than $600 per man for the upcoming season. The Canadiens would offer the same to their players, with Ottawa said to be establishing a $700 limit. In the United States — which wouldn't enter the global conflict until 1917 — the war was given as the cause for "the remarkable tumble" in hockey salaries.

"Canada is hard hit in a money way," read a report that ran in many American newspapers in advance of the 1914–15 hockey season, "and, according to indications, this coming winter will be a real rough one. Citizens won't feel like handing real money over to the hockey magnates, and the latter will, under no circumstances, dish out fat stipends to their star players."

Summer games such as baseball, lacrosse, and horse racing had not suffered after the outbreak of war, but by November, there was a noticeable effect on sports, particularly in eastern Canada. Numerous events were cancelled in several different sports and those that continued suffered at the box office. The situation for Art Ross could be considered worse than that of most of his fellow players, since sporting goods dealers were also said to be feeling the pinch. But despite all the obvious strains, a brand new hockey war was heating up. It began almost as soon as the plan for pay cuts became known in August and continued throughout September and October.

A.L. Caron led the new battle. He was president of the National Club, the French-Canadian sports organization that was once again looking for a way into top-level hockey. Some saw Caron's plan merely as a way to force his team into the NHA, but he insisted otherwise. Like the Federal League in baseball, which had nearly managed to lure star pitcher Walter Johnson away from the Washington Senators and had operated in open defiance of the National and American League in 1914 (and would again in 1915), Caron had a larger vision. He spoke of a new international hockey league with teams playing in New York's St. Nicholas Rink and the Boston Arena. He hoped to sign Newsy Lalonde — who played lacrosse for the Nationals — to lead a new Nationals hockey club, and planned to put a team in Quebec City or Ottawa, or perhaps install a second, English, team in Montreal.

Art Ross had merely laughed when talk of the $600 salary restriction first came up. He wasn't worried, he explained, because (once again) he was through with hockey. "I am getting too old for such strenuous work, and intend to drop out of the game this winter," he told a reporter. But soon Ross's name was front and centre in the plans for Caron's new league.

Players in Montreal and Ottawa held tight throughout October of 1914, refusing to sign with their NHA teams for reduced wages. "I have not signed a hockey contract for the coming season as yet," Ross told reporters on October 27, "and do not know with what club I will play." His Wanderers teammates Sprague and Odie Cleghorn, Gord Roberts, and Harry Hyland all declared they would stay out of hockey this winter rather than play for just $600. The Canadiens were said to be offering Didier Pitre $1,000, but even that wasn't enough to tempt him.

Everyone was waiting to see if the new international league would actually come to be. NHA owners insisted that talk of a new league was nothing more than a joke, but President A.L. Caron told reporters on the night of November 3, 1914, that he was confident he could pull it off. "We will be there when the time comes," reported the next day's *Montreal Daily Mail.*

Caron was now focusing on two teams in Montreal, his own Nationals for the French Canadian fans, and an English team. "The Nationals will have a strong line-up while the English team will be composed of many stars of the NHA," he said. "Many people believe that we have not the backing for the two local teams but I want to say right here that both the local teams will be well backed. In fact, the English team will be backed by half a dozen very prominent Montreal financial men." As for the league's proposed American involvement, "We are also confident that New York will enter a team in the league while I have received a very favorable letter from the magnates in Boston." Regarding players, Caron said that he had received promises from the best players of both the Canadiens and the Wanderers.

Sam Lichtenhein was having none of it. "The new league will never start," he said, and this time he was willing to back his words with ten times the amount he'd offered when betting that the PCHA would never take to the ice. Lichtenhein offered to deposit a check for $500 in any bank to be paid out to charity under the following terms:

- $200 if the new league ran all season in 1914–15;
- $200 if the new league started and had four regular players off the Wanderers roster;
- $100 if the Boston and New York team actually joined and lived out the season.

He agreed to pay out the money to any charity named by Caron, provided that the he put up a similar amount to go to any charity named by Lichtenhein if the proposed new league fell through.

Amid the trash talk between Caron and Lichtenhein that newspapers all across Canada jumped on so gleefully was another interesting story, also reported in the *Montreal Daily Mail*, on November 4, 1914:

> That Arthur Ross, long famous as a defence player on the Wanderer Hockey team has resigned from the Wanderer Club and directorate and has worn a Red Band uniform for the last time, is the startling rumor which is persistent, although unconfirmed, among hockey players and close followers of the game yesterday. While the Wanderer management refuses to either deny or confirm the rumor, which states that Ross's resignation is already in the hands of the directorate, and that he has sold out his holdings in the club, the statement in view of recent developments bears all the earmarks of a well authenticated fact.

Those recent developments, as the *Daily Mail* reminded its readers, included the fact that Ross's name was repeatedly coming up in stories relating to the management of the English team to enter the National's "new scheme" and that he was also believed to have been negotiating with players from both the Wanderers and Canadiens on behalf of the new league. While those were also just rumours, "Ross, as is well known, has been at outs with the Wanderer management since the first intimation of a coming cut in salaries was published. Ross has urged at first, that there be no cut made at all, and later that the cut be much less than management anticipated."

As he had been when rumours of his involvement with the new league first came up in October, Ross was out of town and couldn't be reached for comment. Meanwhile, Sam Lichtenhein issued a statement saying: "The Wanderer management has nothing to say in regard to this rumor." He then added that, "A special meeting of the directors of the club, has, however, been called and will be held at my office at noon today." That evening, November 4, 1914, Lichtenhein confirmed that Ross had resigned from the Wanderers. The club had accepted his resignation, and Ross's stock was sold back to the directors. He had not been offered a new playing contract, "and he is therefore no longer connected with the club."

Newspapers from coast to coast in Canada reported the story the following day, noting that Ross was now a free agent and that he was currently in New York, where it was believed he was meeting with prospective owners of the team for Caron's new league. Caron refused to make a statement to this effect, but he wouldn't deny the rumour either.

# 15

## BANNED FOR LIFE ...
## FOR A WHILE

When he got back home, Art Ross denied his trip to New York had anything to do with Caron's new league. He did admit that he'd been offered the management of an English team in Montreal, but had not yet made up his mind. "If the proposition is sufficiently attractive," he confessed to a reporter, "it is just possible that I will accept."

Ross was being coy and claimed he had no authority to negotiate with players — on November 6, the *Daily Mail* had reported that members of the Ottawa Senators were negotiating with Ross. Additional players were also curious about the new league. That night, Jimmy Gardner, who joined the Canadiens as a player-coach in 1913–14 after two seasons in the PCHA, stated that he wouldn't re-sign for reduced wages, and the next day's *Daily Mail* noted: "It will likely be some time before the players start sending in their contracts. They all appear to be anxious to wait and see just how the proposed new hockey league will plan out. They figure that if the new league is launched with success they will get more money by making the owners of the various clubs bid for their services." The paper also noted that Caron had "nothing new" to report, "but that things were going along smoothly." But that probably wasn't true. Things were apparently rough, and getting rougher.

According to the *New York Times*, both Caron and the NHA were wooing New York and Boston for their leagues. On November 5, the *Times* reported that Cornelius Fellowes, manager of the St. Nicholas Rink in New York, had announced the city would be represented in one of the Canadian professional leagues — but not until the following winter. This news, however, didn't appear to make the Canadian papers until November 12. Two days later, the *Montreal Daily Mail* reported that Caron "did not appear to be at all cheerful over the prospect of launching a rival organization," while the *Ottawa Citizen* reported on rumours of a shakeup in ownership of various NHA clubs that would result in Caron's Nationals entering that league. The latter case never came to pass, and though Caron fought for his league a little while longer, he appeared to give up completely by November 24. That same day, the Wanderers announced that the Cleghorns and Gord Roberts had re-signed. Those three and Harry Hyland apparently received $800 apiece. Goalie Georges Vezina also re-signed with the Canadiens, who had signed Didier Pitre a few days earlier. George Kennedy wouldn't confirm the prices, but it was "stated on good authority," the *Daily Mail* had noted on November 20, "that [Pitre] will receive nearly $2,000 for his services during the coming winter." Newsy Lalonde and Jack Laviolette were still reported as holdouts.

As for Art Ross, he appeared ready to move on, but the question was to where? On November 18, 1914, the *Daily Mail* said that Ross had received an offer from his friend Frank Patrick to act as the player-manager for the PCHA team that had been moved from New Westminster, British Columbia to Portland, Oregon. "The local star," the paper said, "is seriously considering the offer." In fact, "the only thing that prevents Ross from accepting the offer at once is his sporting business which at this season of the year needs his personal attention." Even so, "the offer made by Patrick is said to be one that is very tempting, and if the former is willing to wait until the first of the year, the chances are that Ross will play out west, where he has a great reputation."

A week later, however, Frank "Shag" Shaughnessy, who served as coach of the McGill football team in Montreal and business manager of the Senators hockey team in Ottawa, met with Ross to talk terms. "Ross has not yet decided what he will do," newspapers reported, "but [he] will await word from Ottawa before dealing with any other clubs."

"It would not be surprising to see Art Ross on the Ottawas this winter," said the *Ottawa Citizen* on November 27. But before going into a serious recap of Ross's career, the paper had a bit of fun with his team-hopping reputation. "[I]t wouldn't be astonishing to see Ross playing for Rotterdam, Petrograd or any other club. Ross is one of the champion tourists of the professional game." The *Citizen* also reported that, "Sam Lichtenhein declares that Art has shot his bolt," but the paper pointed out that, "there are many who believe the big fellow due for a comeback."

Ross had reportedly signified his willingness to come to Ottawa, and it was said that he would ride the train up from Montreal on the afternoon of each game and return home afterwards. Another headline in the *Citizen* that day stated that he, "Wants Steep Price for Coming Season," but the story mentioned only that he had "named his terms" — which were not reported — and that he would be signed, "if they are not extraordinarily large." In Ross's favour, Senators president Llewellyn Bate was "determined to strengthen the Ottawa defence," and as the *Citizen* pointed out, by signing Ross, "he would be killing two birds with one stone as he would be landing a drawing card as well."

Ross as a drawing card was something the *Citizen* talked about again the following day when addressing what must have been a rumour that was making the rounds:

> There is nothing in the NHA constitution that would bar Ross on account of his association with the proposed new league. There is no danger, in fact, of a man of his ability being kept out of the game. It is 10 to 1 that if the Ottawas do not sign the big fellow he will be found with one of the Montreal teams. Ross is a powerful drawing card and that is what the NHA appreciates just now.

And yet, just two days later, word came that Ross had indeed been barred from organized hockey because of his involvement with Caron's new league. The story didn't break until November 30, but Ross had been informed of the decision in a letter from NHA president Emmett Quinn, which had been written on November 22. In it, Quinn states that Ross had endevoured to "disrupt" the NHA and that Ross's conduct was "prejudicial to the interests of the National Hockey Association of Canada, Limited," and that it was his duty as president to "expel [Ross] from organized hockey and am advising my directors and affiliated associations of my ruling thereon." However, the door for an appeal was left open. Officials of the Ottawa club were notified to break off negotiations with Ross on November 30, and felt they had no alternative but to do so.

"It is learned on good authority," the *Ottawa Citizen* reported the next day, "that Ross, Hyland, the Cleghorn boys and Gordon Roberts had signed with President Caron. Didier Pitre, Newsy Lalonde, and Jack Laviolette are also said to have given them options on their services for the coming winter. Ross, however, has been indicted as the ringleader."

Still, the opinion of the press, and likely the public — as well as most of the NHA owners — seemed to be that Quinn had overstepped his bounds. Regardless of what Ross may or may not have done, what right did Quinn have to expel someone who was not under contract to any team in the league and had resigned his position as a club director? And if Ross was expelled, shouldn't some of the other players face suspensions as well?

It was speculated that Ross would take the NHA to court, but he denied he would even make an appeal. In fact, as he pointed out in a return letter he wrote to Quinn that was printed in the *Montreal Daily Mail* on December 11, he felt that he was "unable to utilize the opportunity" that Section 9 of the NHA Constitution afforded because he was not currently affiliated with any NHA club in any way. (Section 9 allowed for appeals from any player or manager who had been expelled, suspended, or disciplined; Ross was none of those.) He wouldn't name names, but he didn't deny what he had done, admitting that he'd signed four Wanderers players to options with the new league, but pointing out that the options were only for 10 days, and that since they had expired without being taken up, "I do not see how any club in your association has been affected in any manner." His actions, he explained, "were purely a matter of business" and inspired because the contracts the Wanderers were offering the players "called for amounts approximately one-half of what they received last year and they could hardly be censured for obtaining a legitimate remuneration of their services." Ross concluded by saying, "My expulsion appears extremely severe, and though unable to exercise the right of appeal, the facts stated above should warrant a reconsideration of your decision."

Quinn must have agreed, or was pressured to act, because he called the NHA owners and executives together to discuss the matter further on December 18. Ross was invited to appear that night via another letter from Quinn and he informed newspaper reporters — who'd also been invited to the meeting — that he planned to attend. "Sure I will be at the meeting," said Ross. "I will be there bright and early and with some pretty interesting facts.... When I first received the letter from President Quinn in which he notified me that I was expelled from organized hockey, I thought that I had several men to go up against in my fight but it now appears that Mr. Lichtenhein is the only opponent I have. Well, he will have to hustle some at the meeting tonight to keep me out of hockey."

The *Daily Mail* expected that "some very interesting details are likely to come out," but in reporting on the meeting the next day, the *Ottawa Citizen* claimed, "the evidence offered in the case was practically a re-hash of the letters which have already appeared in print." Ross would still not name names, but Lichtenhein tried to establish that he had signed Roberts, Hyland, and the Cleghorns to options for the new league while he was still a member of the Wanderers' executive.

Lichtenhein read from correspondence he had with Ross and the dates of these letters did make it clear that Ross had advised several players not to sign contracts for $600 while he was still with the Wanderers. Ross admitted this was true, but added that when he told the players they should get more than $600 for their services he was, "speaking as a player and not an officer." He then explained that he had not had any dealings with the proposed new league until November 10, and that by that time he had already resigned from the Wanderers and sold his stock back to Lichtenhein.

Once Ross and Lichtenhein had argued for a while, President Quinn asked the rest of the delegates to either uphold his decision or overrule him with regard to Ross's expulsion. Several club magnates had already expressed their belief that Ross deserved some sort of punishment, but that Quinn's action was too drastic. Before expressing themselves further, they asked that the newspapermen be removed from the room. Shortly thereafter, it was announced that Ross's expulsion had been lifted. He would not be barred from organized hockey, but merely suspended. He wouldn't be allowed to play in the charity exhibition game on December 19 for the benefit of Montreal hospitals, nor in any league games from the start of the NHA season a week later on December 26 through to January 7.

For his part, Ross was required to give his word "that he would remain loyal to the National Hockey Association," but the question now was to which NHA team would he give that loyalty?

# 16

## MEMORABLE
## MOMENTS

Even before the meeting on December 18, Art Ross wasn't acting like someone who believed his career was in jeopardy. Neither was the NHA.

On December 13, 1914, Ross was back on the ice. He turned out at the Jubilee rink for the morning practice of the Montreal Stars. Over 200 fans were at the rink that morning according to the next day's *Montreal Daily Mail*, and Ross "was watched closely by the large number of onlookers." He didn't extend himself much, but "he would cut loose now and again with one of his famous zig-zag rushes from end to end."

The next day the Canadiens held their first practice of the season at the Montreal Arena. "Art Ross Will Likely Turn out with the Flying Frenchmen," read a headline in the *Gazette*. Later that day, in the French-Canadian newspaper *La Patrie*, he was clearly visible in a photograph, and identified in the caption, from the practice. A story in the next day's *Ottawa Citizen*, datelined Montreal on December 14, stated: "The surprise of the practice was the appearance of Art Ross." However, it was noted elsewhere on the same page that: "The announcement that Art Ross had signed with Canadiens provisionally, did not come as a surprise to the Ottawas. When he asked them to relieve him of his promise last week they surmised there was something in the air."

Lest one think the Montreal team was trying to pull a fast one under the nose of the NHA, it was also reported that George Kennedy, manager of the Canadiens, and league president Emmett Quinn had gotten together during the practice. "[T]he club manager was given permission to write to the other teams in the league, requesting them to waive on the rule which limits Canadiens to using only two English players." This piece of news, according to the *Citizen*, was "taken as an indication that Ross is to be reinstated to good standing with the National Association."

Ross continued to work out with the Canadiens prior to the December 18 meeting, and the day after his expulsion was lifted the *Gazette* noted: "Art Ross never played in better form than he is doing at practice and only has to continue in league fixtures to show himself one of the best defencemen in the game this winter." Other reports in the week that followed weren't quite as glowing, but it was clear that Ross was rounding into fine shape.

Jack Laviolette had re-signed with the Canadiens by then, though dental work kept him off the ice until December 21. Newsy Lalonde had been at practice since the beginning, but he had yet to agree to a contract. Lalonde didn't play when the season got under way, and when the Canadiens dropped their first three games without him, the *Daily Mail* reported on Tuesday, January 5, 1915, that Kennedy "expected to have both Newsy Lalonde and Art Ross signed up before the end of the week."

According to family stories, Art Ross won a contest to design the sweaters for the Montreal Canadiens by submitting the famous CH (*club du hockey*) design still worn by the team today on their famous *bleu, blanc, et rouge* colours. The Canadiens began wearing the CH in 1916–17, but the logo was only a slight variation on the CA (*club d'athlétique*) the team had worn with the same colour scheme since 1913. Ross designed and sold hockey sweaters at his Montreal sporting goods store, and may have sold the Canadiens the sweaters they wore, but there doesn't appear to be any proof that he designed the uniforms. Nor did he ever wear one in an actual game.

The Canadiens signed Lalonde for undisclosed terms in time to face the Wanderers on January 9. With his suspension over, Art Ross made his season debut that night as well. Only, it wasn't as a Canadien.

When George Kennedy declined to meet his terms — which no newspaper seems to have published — Ross made his debut in Ottawa for the Senators in a game against the Toronto Blue Shirts.

Despite the cost-cutting measures in other NHA cities, Ottawa had reportedly signed up the most expensive roster in the league. "They had to have a winner," read a report that appeared after the season in the *Brandon Daily Sun* on April 14, 1915, "and they realized this: hence their heavy investment for Art Ross."

Ottawa had been after Ross since the fall of 1905. Now that they finally had him, his debut in the Canadian capital got off to an embarrassing start.

"As the team came out to go on the ice, I was given a big ovation," Ross still remembered for a story that appeared in a Boston Bruins program during the 1949–50 season. "I smiled and sort of waved as I was about to step down about a foot from the stands to the ice. Then on the ice, I was about to stride when I went down on my seat. And I couldn't get up. Imagine my embarrassment when I looked at my skates and saw they both were taped with the same stuff we used on the sticks. I hadn't even bothered to look at them in my excitement while getting dressed. And I had to sit there on the ice, my face as red as a beet, while I unwound the tape."

Ross began his first game for Ottawa sitting on the bench. Clint Benedict, a future hall of famer in his first full season with the Senators, was in goal, with Horace Merrill and Hamby Shore lined up in front of him. Substituting for players was becoming more common, and was a policy Art Ross had supported since at least the fall of 1912 when he wrote about his views on hockey rules for a story that ran in the *Winnipeg Tribune* on September 7 of that year. Though starters still saw the bulk of action, Ross got plenty of ice time in relief of the two starting defencemen this night. When the Senators won 2–1 after 18 minutes of overtime, Ross and Benedict were lauded as the stars of the game. A headline in the *Toronto World* read, "A. Ross Big Factor in Ottawa Victory." The hometown fans were certainly appreciative according to Montreal's *Daily Mail*, as "the crowd applauded him to the echo."

Not everyone was happy to see Ross in Ottawa. A few years earlier, he'd knocked out a few of Horace Merrill's teeth in a fight, and Merrill was refusing to speak to his new teammate. Ross put up with the silent treatment for a few games, but, as Merrill later told Elmer Ferguson, "One night, Ross said to me: 'We can't go on like this. So let's go out in the alley and fight it out. If I win, you speak to me on the ice. If you win, don't speak.' Now what can you do with a guy like that? We shook hands and were pretty good friends except when I thought of my teeth."

Ross's first game with the Senators was generally considered a sensational one, but it was marred somewhat by rough play that left several players on both teams nursing injuries. Ross himself required several stitches above his left eye. Much of the blame for the violence was placed on Blue Shirts bad boy Roy "Minnie" McGiffin.

Usually listed as 5'8" and 160 pounds, Minnie McGiffin was only slightly on the small side of average for a player of this era, but he may still have been hockey's first goon. Whereas many of the tough guys of his time were also talented players, McGiffin seemed only to have a knack for piling up penalty minutes. He and Ross had been engaged in a simmering feud since McGiffin entered the NHA with Toronto in 1912, and it was about to boil over.

The Blue Shirts and Senators next met in Ottawa on February 3, 1915, and with the Senators pulling away in the third period towards a 7–2 victory, McGiffin went after Ross. Hockey has always been a rough sport, and there was plenty of slashing, spearing, butt-ends, and high sticks in this era, but actual fistfights were rare. The *Montreal Gazette* would later report that McGiffin had three teeth knocked out from a cross check by Ross during the game, although the *Daily Mail* in recapping events the next day said Ross "asked McGiffin to lay down his stick" and then "threw off his gloves, sailed into the Toronto forward and used his fists with such speed and effect that McGiffin hung limp in the arms of referee [Cooper] Smeaton after the smoke of the battle cleared away."

There was no more trouble between the two that night, but Ross and McGiffin were at it again when the teams met for the final time that season in Toronto on February 17. Ottawa was leading 2–1 through forty minutes en route to a 3–1 victory. "Everything went well for two periods," according to the *Toronto World*, "but the final round saw the high-feeling break loose, and it ended in a boxing affair." Several fights broke out, including one in the dressing room after the game when a fan attacked referee Cooper Smeaton and was pummelled for his trouble. But the bout that started it all was the one between Ross and McGiffin.

"The fun started when McGiffin and Ross bumped, and dire threats were made. The next collision resulted in a stand-up battle," the *World* continued. The fight broke out near the Ottawa net, where "the men first tried to get at each other with their sticks but finally dropped them and went to it with their fists." When the fight was finally broken up, the two players each received major penalties. That was apparently not enough punishment for Toronto police inspector Langford R. "Bob" Geddes, who arrested both men as soon as they got off the ice. After the game, Geddes explained his actions to the press, which was reported in Toronto's *Globe* the next day:

> In my opinion the game was free from rough play until ten minutes from the finish, when McGiffin and Ross seemed to meet by mutual consent. None of those present attempted to part the pair, until McGiffin had been knocked down. I then thought that it was time to take action, more so when I considered that warnings had been previously given regarding rough play.
>
> After I had placed these men under arrest and they had cooled down, they were willing to shake hands. That is not fair to the public who attend these games. Last night there were three hundred women in the audience of fifteen hundred. Professional hockey has been fairly clean this winter, but it is time that players should learn that no rowdyism will be tolerated. There can be no use in allowing it to continue. Such exhibitions will kill the sport.

Once they'd changed into street clothes, Ross and McGiffin were hustled off to Toronto's Police Station No. 2, just a few blocks from the Arena Gardens, which was located on Mutual Street near present-day Dundas and Jarvis. They were charged with being disorderly in a public place. Lol Solman, managing director of the Arena Gardens (among his many Toronto business interests), put up the $100 bail for both men who were required to report to police court at City Hall at 9:15 the following morning.

Fortunately for the two players, Police Magistrate Peter Ellis was known as a hockey fan. Thomas C. Robinette, of Robinette, Godfrey, Phelan & Lawson in Toronto, represented Ross and McGiffin in front of Ellis and entered an apologetic guilty plea on behalf of the players. Still, he wondered: "Don't the crowd want hot stuff?" Ellis ordered 15 days in jail ... or a fine of $1 apiece plus court costs. Ross and McGiffin flipped a coin to see who'd pay. McGiffin lost again and handed over a total of $8. The case was closed, but would live on forever in hockey lore.

Ottawa's toughest physical battles in 1914–15 may have been with Toronto, but the Senators' key battle in the standings was their fight with the Wanderers for first place in the NHA. Sam Lichtenhein's Montreal club was a high-scoring juggernaut whose 127 goals during the season worked out to 6.35 per game over the 20-game schedule. Ottawa scored just 74 times, but the Senators' 65 goals against were by far the lowest total in the NHA. The race between these two old rivals went right down to the wire, and when both teams won on the final night of the season they finished in a dead heat, each with a record of 14–6. A two-game, total-goals playoff was arranged to decide the championship of the NHA and the right to defend the Stanley Cup in the West, where Frank Patrick's Vancouver Millionaires had romped to the PCHA title.

In an age where top-scoring players routinely averaged two goals per game (they had averaged three or more just a few years earlier) and shutouts were rare, offense trumped defence, so the Wanderers were favoured over the Senators when their playoff series opened on March 10, 1915. Even in Ottawa, betting favoured the Wanderers to take the series, though odds ranged from even to 3–2 on the Senators to take the opener at home, which they did by a score of 4–0. Benedict's shutout for Ottawa that night was the first in the NHA all season as Senators' coach Alf Smith instructed his team to shoot as often as possible but to limit the number of players making offensive attacks in order to ensure there were always enough men back to guard against the dangerous rushes of the Montreal team. Ross scored the first goal for Ottawa and the *Montreal Gazette* noted that he outplayed Sprague Cleghorn, adding that he and Senators centre Angus Duford, "were the mainstays of the locals at all times."

"We were played off our feet," admitted Wanderers captain Harry Hyland after the game. Sam Licthenhein, manager Dickie Boon, and other members of the team's executive preferred to blame the loss on warm weather and soft ice, although the *Gazette* noted in a headline that: "The Montreal Team Was Outplayed Before and After Ice Became Slushy." Still, with the recently installed artificial ice plant at the Montreal Arena guaranteeing a hard surface for game two on March 13, the Wanderers and their fans were confident they'd wipe out the four-goal deficit. After all, they'd beaten Ottawa 15–6 and 8–1 in their two regular-season meetings in Montreal.

Tickets for Saturday's second game went on sale on Friday morning and fans began lining up Thursday night to get them. The biggest crowd of the season was expected, and there was plenty of talk about what kind of game they'd see. In a special to the *Montreal Daily Mail* from Ottawa on Saturday, coach Alf Smith refused to divulge his game plan, "but it is believed that the Ottawas will follow Wednesday's style and force the play from the start." A similar story in the *Gazette* was even more definitive. "Will Not Play Defence," read the headline, with the main text stating: "the Ottawas will go right after the home team from the start, probably in an effort to get a couple more goals and thus clinch the outcome. Smith had the players up in the club rooms for a talk tonight, and it is certain that they will not start on the defensive."

Whether the speculation was just wishful thinking on the part of the writers or a deliberate attempt to mislead them by Ottawa, the Senators' intentions became clear from the opening faceoff: "As the players lined up, [Punch] Broadbent and [Angus] Duford went up on the line against [Odie] Cleghorn, [Harry] Hyland and [Gord] Roberts. Art Ross, [Horace] Merrill and [left winger] Eddie Gerard played on the defence, forming a straight line across the ice." Ottawa never varied its strategy, always keeping three men back and whenever a defenceman did join the offensive attack (they were said to have "alternated in doing the rushing, which enabled them to get frequent resting spells") a forward always dropped back. The result was a rough, dull game. The Wanderers scored a 1–0 victory, but Ottawa took the series by a combined score of 4–1 to win the NHA championship and a trip to Vancouver to face the PCHA champs.

Over the years, Ottawa's tactics in game two have often been noted as the beginning of the defence-first strategy in hockey that would flourish in the 1920s. Even those writing about the neutral-zone trap and left wing lock in modern hockey have been known to invoke this game. Odie Cleghorn told reporters a few weeks after the game that it was, "the coolness and headwork of Ross that paralyzed the Wanderer scoring machine," but based on what had been written before and after the game, it seems that the defensive strategy should be attributed to Alf Smith. And yet, though his Boston Bruins teams in the years to come would feature many of the best offensive performers of their time, and he would take an active role in creating new rules to help the National Hockey League combat defensive hockey, Art Ross has long been considered the man who conceived the Ottawa system.

"On the train to Montreal, we got together and devised our kitty-bar-the-door style of hockey," Ross recalled for the Bruins program in 1949–50. "I was the only man to move, I played right defence and if a Wanderer came down their right wing I'd move up and crash him while the other fellows shifted over to cover my position. If the puck-carrier came down on my side I'd go up to check him as I would have naturally." With no forward passing or dumping the puck for wingers to chase, "we stopped them cold."

Ross doesn't say that he devised the system, only that "we got together" on the train. Interestingly, the *Ottawa Journal* on the day of the game indicated that Ross was already in Montreal at the time and didn't travel with the rest of the team when they left via the Grand Trunk Railway at 3:15 that afternoon! On the Monday after Ottawa's Saturday night victory, the *Journal* reported that the team was, "acting under the instructions of Coach Alf Smith," in playing three men on defence and that, "Coach Smith could be heard all over the rink yelling his instructions." Still, the story that Ross was responsible for the defensive strategy has taken on a life of its own. Elmer Ferguson would seem to be the source of that. He wrote at length about the kitty-bar-the-door strategy used that night in his nationally syndicated newspaper column, "Inside Hockey," on January, 30 1933, noting: "Crafty Art Ross ... was credited with devising the play."

Ferguson would revisit the topic often in articles over the years. Baz O'Meara would too, and he was likely the source of the *Ottawa Journal*'s flip-flop in a story on December 8, 1917, that credited Ross with the "neat bit of ice-generalship." Regardless of who actually came up with the system, beating the Wanderers was sweet revenge for Ross. "That's what I've been working for all winter," the *Journal* quoted him in the dressing room after the game. "I'd like to see Sammy [Lichtenhein] now."

Kitty barred the door in Montreal that night, but Ottawa's defensive skill couldn't stop the PCHA champions when the Senators faced the Vancouver Millionaires in their best-of-five Stanley Cup series beginning March 19. The games matched Ross against his old rival Cyclone Taylor, who'd been moved up to forward in Vancouver where he played centre and rover and was coming off his second straight PCHA scoring title. Alf Smith vowed the Senators would wear down Taylor with heavy hits, but PCHA rules didn't allow players to be checked into the boards. Only open-ice hitting was allowed, and Taylor was tough to catch in open ice. Ross hunted him throughout the series, but there was little he or his teammates could do to slow down the Cyclone even when the rules (which alternated by league for each game) allowed for the NHA style of play. Taylor scored seven goals in three games as Vancouver swept Ottawa by the one-sided scores of 6–2, 8–3, and 12–3.

This likely wasn't the ending Art Ross envisioned when he announced following the playoff victory in Montreal that he'd retire after Ottawa's Stanley Cup trip.

# 17

## END OF
## THE LINE

While most of his Ottawa teammates salvaged something from their West Coast visit with an enjoyable trip to the Panama Pacific International Exposition in San Francisco, Art Ross hurried home from Vancouver. On April 14, 1915 — less than three weeks after the Senators' lopsided Stanley Cup loss to the Millionaires, and nearly seven years since the empty-net goal in 1908 — Ross married Muriel Kay.

While it hardly ranks with the wedding of Wayne Gretzky and Janet Jones, Montreal newspapers dedicated most of the space in their social columns the following day to the Ross-Kay marriage. The groom is identified only as "Mr. Arthur H. Ross, of Westmount," and the "son of Mrs. Peter Mackenzie [sic]" and much of the space is dedicated to describing what the women wore, but it seems unlikely that such coverage would be given to the daughter of a widowed grocery and fruit merchant if she weren't marrying a hockey star.

Ross's gift to his new bride was a fitted travelling case. To her attendants he gave pearl brooches. The youngest of his older brothers, Dr. Colin Ross, was the best man and received a gold-tipped cane. Toward the end of the evening, Mr. and Mrs. Ross departed for their honeymoon at an undisclosed location "down south." Ross had recently been living with Colin at 4914 Sherbrooke Street West, but when the newlyweds returned to Montreal, they took up residence at 4934 Western Avenue (de Maisonneuve Blvd today), where they soon began to raise a family.

In writing about his "Granny Ross" who was known to the family as "Murey," Art Ross III recalls her as "an affable Grande Dame" who was "generous, energetic," though "perhaps a bit of a fussbudget." Art describes her as "very much a 'high style' lady of the times." She wore a mink stole, drove a Cadillac, and had a maid and a chauffeur after some years of marriage and her husband's success. "She was the kind of person you couldn't envision in jeans or slacks," says Art, although a 1942 feature on her in the *Boston Traveler* says, "she prefers sports clothes." Old family photos support that claim. There are pictures of her looking every inch the tomboy — albeit an elegant one! — fishing, hunting, and boating. John Ross maintained that she was also a good golfer, although the *Traveler* story says she favoured winter sports. "It's no wonder," says Art, "she caught the eye and heart of a great sportsman."

By the fall of 1915, this great sportsman was 30 years old. He was a married man, and it seemed he really might make good on his claim to retire from hockey. However, while the First World War hadn't hurt pro hockey too badly just yet (it soon would), the war with the Patrick brothers and the PCHA had heated up again.

A story from Ottawa dated October 31, 1915, claimed the Senators were after Cyclone Taylor, who, it was reported, was being sent back to the Canadian capital from Vancouver by the Department of the Interior, his government employer off the ice. The same report stated that Ross had been in Ottawa the day before, and that although "he declares he has played his last hockey," he was said to have met with team president Llewellyn Bate and coach Alf Smith and promised he would "assist the Ottawas if they needed his services." Senators business manager Shag Shaughnessy kept after Ross throughout the latter part of November and finally got his name on a contract on Thursday night, December 2.

Ross spent the majority of the 1915–16 season living at home in Montreal with his new wife and tending to his sporting goods business while travelling on the train to Ottawa for Senators home games. Like Lester Patrick for Westmount back in 1904–05, Ross wasn't there to practise with his team (which, according to several reports, had likely been the case the year before as well), but he was still able to maintain his status among the greats of the game. He suited up for 21 of the 24 scheduled contests and ranked among the top-scoring defencemen with eight goals and eight assists. However, the Senators slipped to second place behind the Montreal Canadiens, who went on to defeat the PCHA's Portland Rosebuds to win the first Stanley Cup championship in club history.

Despite a solid season, Ross seemed unwilling to undergo the same routine yet again the following winter. On July 6, 1916, the *Quebec Telegraph* reported: "It's a long way to the hockey season, but rumors and advanced dope has started. The latest is that Art Ross, who has been playing with Ottawa for the past two seasons, will return to his old colors and will manage the Wanderers." Ross had recently journeyed to Ottawa and asked the directors of the Senators to sell or trade him to a Montreal team. He was told to "go ahead and make whatever arrangements he could towards negotiating a sale."

It would not prove to be as simple as that.

In his history of the Ottawa Senators, *Win, Tie or Wrangle*, Paul Kitchen writes that the War had begun to impinge on the conscience of Canadians shortly after the Senators' unsuccessful Stanley Cup trip of 1915. Canadian troops entered the fight in April of that year and were on the battlefield at Ypres when the Germans first unleashed their newest weapon, poison gas. Reports of the horrors made their way home in letters and newspapers over the next few weeks, hurting recruitment, which had already dropped off considerably since the initial crush of some 32,000 volunteers in the late summer of 1914.

By the spring of 1915, Frank Patrick had looked into forming a Sportsman's Battalion to recruit athletes from British Columbia, but apparently received a letter from the Canadian government informing him that the PCHA was considered vital to morale in the shipyard and naval-base communities of Vancouver and Victoria. Presumably the NHA was just as important to morale in the East. Not everybody felt that way. Ottawa's Punch Broadbent had enlisted in July of 1915 and a few other pro players would enlist during the summer of 1916. Many pros were more likely to take jobs in essential services, and as the war dragged on, resentment grew towards well-trained athletes playing games at home while others fought and died overseas. Attendance fell and so did revenue.

Kitchen writes that by the end of the 1915–16 season, the directors of the Senators were losing their appetite for running the team. President Bate made it known that Ottawa wanted out of the NHA until the war was over, but the league refused his request to suspend operations. Instead, management of the team was turned over to Ted Dey, who owned the arena the Senators played in. It appears there'd been no transactions involving Ross to this point, but the new management told him on November 20, 1916, they would be unable to pay him the high salary he formerly received.

On December 4, 1916, the *Ottawa Journal* reported that Ross had written to Senators secretary Martin Rosenthal, one of the few holdovers from the old regime, saying he realized that hockey players could no longer expect the same large salary he'd been used to. Ross, who'd kept in shape playing amateur baseball in Montreal during the summer, wrote that if he had to play hockey for a lesser figure, he preferred to play in Montreal where he could do so without neglecting his sporting goods business. By then, it had already been reported in newspapers across Canada that Ottawa had given Ross his unconditional release and told him he was free to sign with a Montreal team, but three weeks later, the Senators changed their minds.

It seems that Ottawa was worried about losing a proven gate attraction. "[Ross] had a big following in the Capital" reported the *Montreal Daily Mail* on December 14, "and always played so determined at home and away that he became an idol with the local patrons." Secretary Rosenthal contacted Ross, but he clearly wanted to stay in Montreal. There was no longer any talk of Ross managing the Wanderers, but he was on the ice at practice with his former team when it was reported in the *Daily Mail* five days later that "if Ross can secure his release from the Ottawa Club, it is likely that he will figure on the Wanderers team once again."

Any lingering problems with Sam Lichtenhein had been resolved, and on Christmas day the *Daily Mail* made it clear that Lichtenhein had recently been in touch with Rosenthal about Ross. Lichtenhein believed that since he'd released former Wanderer Carl Kendall to sign with Ottawa, the Senators should now return the favour. As this was hardly a fair trade, the *Daily Mail* speculated that, "there may be a cash consideration."

Still, as late as the morning of December 27, the date on which the NHA season began, the newspaper could only report that the Wanderers still hoped to sign Ross. In the lineups the *Daily Mail* printed for the game that night, Sprague and Odie Cleghorn were listed as the starters on defence, while a blank spot was left next to the number 4 (which Ross had worn for his two years in Ottawa) among the list of spares. That same day reports in the *Ottawa Journal* and the *Vancouver Daily Word* claimed that Ross had purchased his own release from the Ottawa club for $400. That night he suited up for the Wanderers. They lost 6–2 in Quebec City, but the game story in the *Daily Mail* the next day stated that Ross "was far and away the best of the visitors."

Despite the return of the prodigal son, the 6–2 loss on opening night set the tone for a difficult season. The Wanderers finished the first half of the split schedule with a record of 3–7. They were just 2–8 in the second half. Ross, however, was still thought to be at the peak of his powers. "He has been in the professional ranks for many years," read a caption under his photograph in the *Calgary Herald* on February 5, 1917, "and is still considered to be the most formidable defence man in the game." A story in the *Winnipeg Tribune* on February 24 noted that he was still someone all of hockey's toughest players knew to watch out for. "Art is one of those exponents of the great ice game that never seeks trouble, but if anyone invites it he is present in full regalia. It is only natural that in his long career as a senior hockeyist, Ross should have figured in a few 'jams' but in no single instance, so far as history records, did he provoke a fracas, nor come out second best."

The 1916–17 season was not just a difficult one for the Wanderers, but for the NHA as well. The league had admitted a military team from the 228th Battalion, which had recruited a number of star hockey players from northern Ontario. Playing out of Toronto, the team drew big crowds and played good hockey, battling Ottawa and the Canadiens for top spot in the first-half standings. However, shortly after the second half started, the 228th Battalion was called overseas and the team had to withdraw. In trying to determine how best to complete the season, the other NHA owners used the loss of the army team as an opportunity to rid themselves of Toronto Blue Shirts owner Eddie Livingstone, who had been a quarrelsome member of their fraternity since 1914. With the Battalion team gone, the other NHA teams voted to drop Toronto from the league completely at a meeting in Montreal on February 11, 1917. They distributed Livingstone's players among the remaining clubs, and played out the second half as a four-team league.

Though it simplifies the situation greatly, the decision reached by the NHA owners in February, combined with the passing of the Military Service Act in Canada, which introduced Conscription in the summer of 1917 and caused a greater shortage in available hockey talent, led to the suspension of the National Hockey Association on November 10, 1917. It was followed by the formation of the National Hockey League at meetings held in Montreal on November 22 and November 26, 1917. The NHL was to operate with only four teams, and if Quebec had been able to recruit more players, the Bulldogs would likely have stayed in. When they didn't, the fourth franchise was given to Toronto, whose players were now returned. Despite the protests of Eddie Livingstone, operation of the team was given to those who ran the Arena Gardens. But even with all the changes, the NHL still faced many problems. Among the biggest was what to do about the Wanderers.

At the Wanderers' annual meeting on November 7, 1917, Art Ross was elected manager. The club's financial statement was described in newspapers all across Canada as "not very rosy," but Ross stated that some of the players had already agreed to play on a percentage basis. (He also said that some of that percentage would be donated to the Red Cross on behalf of each player.) Even so, the *Montreal Herald*, in reporting on his appointment as manager joked: "Art Ross will lead the Wanderers, and so will all the other teams on the NHA circuit unless the redhoops improve considerably over last season."

On the day the NHL was formed, the players from Quebec were dispersed throughout the league. The Wanderers hoped the four new players they selected would ease their problems, yet on or about that very same day came word that Sprague Cleghorn had slipped on an icy sidewalk in Montreal and suffered a badly broken leg. He would not play hockey that winter. News of this came only days after the club learned that a military exemption granted to Odie Cleghorn, excusing him from service until March, was granted strictly for business purposes and that his temporary exemption would become null and void if he played hockey. Making matters worse, when the Wanderers held their first full practice on December 3, 1917, Jack McDonald was the only one of the four players acquired from Quebec that turned out. Ross watched, and coached, the players from the sidelines, but even though there were reports throughout November and December that he'd retire as a player to concentrate on coaching, the player shortage soon saw him back in action.

No doubt Ross had lost some of the skill from his younger days, but many knowledgeable observers felt he was still a player to be reckoned with. "Art Ross is one of the greatest players the winter game has ever produced," read a story in the *Ottawa Journal* on December 8, 1917. "That battered title has been tossed about a bit, conferred on first one, and then another, but when they've all been rattled through the sifter, Ross stands out as the brainiest, most consistently brilliant player, over a long period of years, the game has ever known." The story continued to lavish the praise:

> Six feet in height, perfectly proportioned, always in the pink of condition, Ross in his hey-day added to these assets terrific speed, and a stick-wizardry that was little short of marvelous. In later days, he has lost his high flight of speed, but the ability to puzzle opponents with sheer trick-skill has not deserted the big sportsman. Although he doesn't flash and circle about the ice with that meteoric dash of yore, opposing defence still find it a difficult task to get the puck off Ross' elusive twisting stick. Add to this a hockey brain of far more than average keenness which stored up the experience of many years, and Ross is still today a formidable addition to any team.

As much as Ross might aid the Wanderers on the ice, both he and Lichtenhein had been telling the press that unless they received help in the form of players from the other NHL teams, they would not be able to play. Their pleas were met with surprise, and even anger, from other teams and league officials, who said no help would be forthcoming. Ross and Licthenhein went silent for a while, and even permitted their players to take part in an exhibition game with Canadiens players on December 15, 1917, to raise money for victims of the Halifax Explosion, which had killed nearly 2,000 people.

Four nights after the benefit game, the first games in NHL history were staged on December 19, 1917. The Wanderers scored a surprising 10–9 victory over Toronto in a game that attracted just 700 fans to the Westmount (Montreal) Arena. A Saturday night crowd of about 1,000 saw the Canadiens crush the Wanderers 11–2 in their next game on December 22. Ross played only one period, leaving after the first with his team down 6–0. He may have been injured that night, as the reports of the Wanderers' 9–2 loss in Ottawa on December 29 note that, "Art Ross, whose back was injured recently, did not get into uniform." However, he had seen action three nights earlier in a 6–2 home loss to Ottawa and could have suffered the injury in that one. The 6–2 loss to Ottawa on December 26, 1917, would be the last real hockey game Art Ross ever played. Even with all the stories of his retirement over the years, this was likely an ending no one saw coming.

Ross and Lichtenstein were still actively involved in trying to drum up players for the Wanderers when, on the afternoon of January 2, 1918, the Westmount Arena burned to the ground in a spectacular fire. The Canadiens quickly relocated to the Jubilee rink in the East End — the same rink that had sparked so much trouble back in 1909. Sam Lichtenhein was not convinced that Wanderers fans, mainly English Montrealers from the west side of the city, would follow the team across town. "I will ask the other teams to sell me three players," Lichtenhein stated prior to an emergency NHL meeting on January 3. "… but if they are not forthcoming then there is no use in our continuing." Ross agreed. "We are badly in need of players and unless we receive help from the other clubs we cannot make a race in the showing for the title." When the other teams refused to sell them any players, the Wanderers withdrew from the NHL, ending the brief but stormy life of one of early hockey's greatest teams.

Despite the sad saga of the demise of the Wanderers, Art Ross made an important contribution to the NHL rules this season. Credit is often given to goalie Clint Benedict's habit of "accidentally" falling to the ice for the change that was introduced on January 9, 1918, but Ross had been in favour for at least a year of striking the long-standing rule that required goalies to remain standing at all times. Frank and Lester Patrick had passed legislation in the PCHA for the 1916–17 season allowing goalies to drop to the ice, and the *Ottawa Journal* reported on November 29, 1916, that the Art Ross Hockey League in Montreal would adopt the rule as well. A year later, on December 17, 1917, under the headline "Art Ross Wants the Hockey Rules Changed," the *Journal* noted that he was proposing that the NHL "allow the goal-tender to take any position he wishes in stopping a shot — to bite the puck, if necessary." Ross, the paper continued, "points out that while the goal-tender is compelled to stand any other player can go into the nets and get down on his knees or elsewhere so far as the rules are concerned." He also favoured allowing players to kick the puck at any point on the ice, though presumably not into the net.

After the withdrawal of the Wanderers, the three remaining NHL clubs quickly scooped up the team's best players. Art Ross didn't go anywhere at first, but apparently notified Ottawa that he would be ready if they needed him. However, when a report made the rounds on February 15, 1918, that Ross would join the Senators for their game with the Canadiens the following night, the man who had prided himself on year-round fitness said he couldn't take the ice on such short notice because he was not in proper condition to play defence. The only thing he could stop, he admitted, "was a streetcar."

Ross returned to the ice in March of 1918, doing a favour for his friend Frank Patrick by serving as a referee for the two Stanley Cup games in Toronto that were played under PCHA rules. Ross angered Toronto fans when he told local reporters after game two that, "the Blues gave a most brutal exhibition" and that unless the Vancouver team was protected by the referees, "they'll all be killed." He then made matters worse by adding, "I thought the Jubilee rink fans were pretty one-sided, but they have nothing on the Toronto bunch." Toronto team boss Charlie Querrie fired back that Ross and fellow referee George Irving were to blame and that Ross had admitted he didn't know the PCHA rules well enough. Toronto fans gave Ross a rough ride when he returned a few nights later to work game four.

This was not the first time Ross had angered fans as a referee. Working an exhibition game between Vancouver and Quebec after the 1913–14 season, Ross's calls proved unpopular. He was jeered from the stands throughout the game and was even punched by a fan after it. Ross sparked a brawl by ruling off Harry Mummery of the Bulldogs for rough play near the end of the game, and then blamed Quebec management for the problem, stating that team officials ordered Mummery to ignore his ruling and return to play.

But come July of 1918, no one had anything but kind words to say about Art Ross. Of course, it was considered impolite to speak ill of the dead.

# 18

## LIFE
## GOES ON

In addition to his many other sporting pursuits, Art Ross loved motorcycles. Ross didn't just ride motorbikes; he raced them. He was considered one of Canada's leading experts in the field of sidecar motorcycle racing. He wasn't alone among the hockey fraternity in this pursuit. Jack Laviolette and Sprague Cleghorn raced professionally for Harley Davidson. Both were on hand for a three-day motorcycle and automobile meet Ross promoted in Montreal over the Labour Day weekend in 1917. Muriel Ross was fully nine months pregnant at the time. Almost exactly nine months after the birth of the couple's first child, Ross was riding his motorcycle for pleasure when tragedy struck. The report ran in newspapers all across North America, similar to this story from the *Evening Tribune* in Providence, Rhode Island on July 6, 1918:

> Art Ross, the Canadian hockey star, and his nephew, Hugh Ross, died this morning as the result of a motorcycle accident at Bethlehem last evening. They were riding at a moderate speed, but ran into a carriage owned by H. Easton of Littleton, which had no rear light, and both were thrown many feet.

They landed on the macadam road. Hugh passed away at the
Littleton Hospital and Art ... died three hours later.....

Out on the West Coast, Frank and Lester Patrick learned about
the death of their friend in the newspaper that same Saturday. Both
were contacted for comments, and both expressed their deep shock. A
telegram of condolence was sent to Ross's relatives. A similar telegram
was received the same day from Newsy Lalonde, who was in Quebec
City at the time. Undoubtedly, others must have arrived too, and even
more likely would have ... if not for the fact that the stories weren't
completely true.

Even today, when news breaks suddenly it can be hard to make sense
of the conflicting initial reports. This was even truer when newspapers
were the only real source of news and so many of them were competing
in the same market. In Toronto on July 6, the *Toronto World* reported
among its sports news on page nine that Ross had died, but also noted
on page two that he'd sustained no injuries whatsoever. Meanwhile, the
*Globe* in the same city reported him as "near death."

In Montreal, at least, where Ross's family lived, they had the right
story by that same Saturday morning. Hugh Ross, the son of eldest Ross
brother Simon, had indeed died of a fractured skull, but Art and another
riding companion, W.G. McIntyre, were uninjured. Even so, there were
still papers reporting Ross's death on Monday, July 8, and others that
didn't have the correct story until as late as Thursday, July 11.

Despite his brush with death, Art Ross didn't give up his infatuation
with motorcycles. He continued racing them, and increasingly made
them a part of his business. Some time around 1918 or 1919, he switched
the name of his store from Art Ross & Co. Sporting Goods to the Art
Ross Sales Co. Ltd. He continued to sell "*articles necessaires du hockey*,"
but had added accessories for cars as well. Soon after, he dropped the
other sporting goods entirely, as the Lovell's Montreal street directory
for 1921–22 shows his business as president and manager of Harley
Davidson Motor Cycles, while the listing for the Sales Co. Ltd. notes
"motorcycles and side cars" after the name. (Son John Ross claimed his
father was the largest Harley Davidson dealer in Canada.)

Ross, who had long enjoyed hunting, was also becoming more and more active — and increasingly competitive — as a trap shooter with the Montreal Gun Club. After retiring as a player, he also got involved for a time with the committee that oversaw boxing in his hometown, and in 1921 he'd turned his attention back to his first sporting love: football. As in 1911 and 1912, it didn't go well. More modern rules and changes to the way the game of Canadian football was played didn't suit the style Ross had played 20 years earlier. Under his watch Montreal went 0–6, losing all of their games by large margins.

During all this time, Ross kept up at least some involvement with hockey. In September of 1918, there'd been rumours that he would revive the Wanderers. These rumours were part of a larger story stating that the hockey owners planned to start up the NHA once again and that the NHL would go out of existence. However, when an NHA meeting was held in Montreal on September 28, 1918, the owners — over the objections of Eddie Livingstone — voted to suspend operations once again. The NHA was out of business forever, and the NHL would carry on, aided by the end of the First World War on November 11.

There was more talk that Ross might play again during the winter of 1918–19, but upon returning from his annual hunting trip in mid-November he told reporters that he was "out of hockey for all time." However, when George Kennedy put Ross's name forward as a prospective referee at an NHL meeting on December 14, 1918, he must have either cleared it with Ross already, or convinced him soon after, because Ross did serve as a referee in 1918–19, starting with the league's opening game one week later. He worked for the NHL as a referee through the 1921–22 season.

It took a few more days after the 1918 NHL meeting for this story to come out, but there was another piece of news involving Art Ross on December 14: The directors of the NHL decided that the Art Ross puck would officially replace the Spalding puck for the 1918–19 season. The Spalding puck had been adopted by the NHA before the 1913–14 season, and it seems the NHL would use both the Ross and Spalding pucks until 1940, when Ross obtained a United States patent for his puck design.

It's unclear how much, if at all, Ross's puck design changed over the years, but in his 1940 patent application, he explains that: "Heretofore, the type of standard and official hockey puck or disc was made of rubber of desired diametre, thickness, weight, and resiliency in the form of a round disc, with the top and bottom surfaces parallel and with the edge portion perpendicular thereto and flat throughout the circumference of same, producing sharp corners at both the top and bottom disc surfaces." He further explained that these sharp edges constituted a danger to players, "cutting faces, wrists, legs, and also the clothing of players." Furthermore, these old-style pucks were more prone to rolling on their sharp edges. "This is highly objectionable," Ross writes, "as a rolling puck cannot be readily controlled by a player...."

Ross's solution was to design a puck "formed with the edge or rim portion of a distinctive and predetermined contour so as to eliminate any sharp corners between the top and bottom surfaces of the disc and edge portion." He carried this out by "providing the edge portion of a hockey puck with a predetermined corner bevel either as a straight bevelled surface or in an arc."

The 1940 version of the Art Ross Puck, made by Henry G. Tyer of the Tyer Rubber Company of Andover, Massachusetts, would be the official puck of the NHL until 1968 when the patent expired. Since then, other companies have been making pucks for the NHL, but the basic design has never changed.

*  *  *

In the spring of 1920, there were stories that several Montreal sportsmen were angling for a second NHL franchise in the city, and that a group of them were urging Art Ross to run the team for them. Nothing came of it. When he finally did take an off-ice position with an NHL club, newspapers reported on November 15, 1922, that Ross had signed to coach the Hamilton Tigers.

Hamilton had entered the NHL in 1920–21, taking the place of the Quebec franchise that joined the league in 1919–20 but withdrew after winning only four of 24 games. The team fared little better in Ontario's Steel City, winning just six and seven games over the next two seasons, so the news of a new coach was reason for optimism. Ross's first order of business was to whip his team into shape. "Ross is giving them physical training and a lot of new conditioning stunts," reported Toronto's *Globe* on December 6, 1922. "So far the players have not been allowed to use their sticks." In reporting on the team's first practice, the *Hamilton Herald* said: "Coach Ross' novel training methods, which consist of a 'stop and go' order and oodles of physical training, told on Bert Corbeau yesterday. The big blond defence player found the going rather stiff for the starter and finally was forced to give up what he ate for dinner." Other out-of-shape players found the going rough as well, but in their book *Hamilton's Hockey Tigers*, authors Sam and David Wesley write that Hamilton fans were happy with the reports and were buying advanced tickets in greater numbers than any previous year.

Two days before the season opener at home to Ottawa on December 16, Ross made the short trip to Grimsby, Ontario, where the Montreal Canadiens were working out prior to their season opener in Toronto. He proved himself to be a fine judge of talent when he told Leo Dandurand that he thought young Aurel Joliat, whom the Canadiens had obtained from Saskatoon of the Western Canada Hockey League in a controversial deal for Newsy Lalonde, "was a find and would make a name for himself in the National Hockey League." Ross and Dandurand also joked about suiting up themselves if their two teams met for an exhibition game in Grimsby. By then, Ross hadn't played in five years, but the Tigers were thought to be short of capable substitutes and the joke got people thinking. "What if you saw Art Ross do some subbing for the Hams this winter on defence?" wondered the *Quebec Daily Telegraph* on December 15. "It is more than likely that he will."

Hamilton's rink only had capacity for 5,000 people, but almost 6,000 fans filled the Barton Street Arena for the opener and saw the Tigers score a 4–3 win over Ottawa in overtime. Hundreds more were turned away at the door. Ross's team remained respectable throughout the first half of the 24-game season, posting 5 wins against 7 losses. A tight, 5–4 loss to the Canadiens on January 31 drew the following comments from a Montreal newspaper: "Those Hamilton Tigers are the peskiest tailenders we ever heard of occupying the cellar of any organized branch of sports." The paper also provided perhaps the first instance in print of the fact that Ross had an affinity for swear words when it speculated on whether or not the team's feisty play was due to its coach "applying the caustic language of which he is a master." Still, Hamilton won just once over the final 12 games and the team limped to another last-place finish with a record of 6–18.

His professional coaching debut hadn't gone well, but Ross had much more success with the amateur Hamilton Tigers in the senior division of the Ontario Hockey Association. After that team dropped three of its first five games, the OHA squad turned to Ross for help near the end of January. "The pros' mentor will not be allowed to sit on the amateurs' bench, according to the new OHA regulations," reported the *Hamilton Herald*, "but he will be able to teach them a lot in their practice." Under Ross, the OHA Tigers rattled off seven straight wins to finish the season with a 9– 3 record and tie for top spot with the Toronto Granites, defending Allan Cup champions as Canada's best amateur team. Unfortunately for Hamilton fans, the Granites defeated the Tigers 6–4 in a total-goals tiebreaking playoff en route to winning the Allan Cup again, and then an Olympic gold medal in 1924.

Another highlight of the 1922–23 season occurred in an exhibition game between the NHL Tigers and Toronto St. Pats on February 22, 1923. A fundraiser was held in Kitchener that evening for Frank Trushinski of the OHA's Kitchener Greenshirts, who had lost partial sight in his left eye after suffering a fractured skull in a game in 1921 and had been blinded in his right when he was hit by a puck on January 11, 1923. The game raised $2,400 for the Trushinski Fund, which included $175 from a stick signed by the players of both teams and auctioned off by Ross. Ross was also one of the players that night as he started on defence for Hamilton in a game that ended in a 4–4 tie. The Trushinski game marked his only appearance as a player for the Tigers and the closest he ever came to making a comeback.

For Art Ross, the summer of 1923 marked a return to motorcycle racing, and when the 1923–24 NHL season got under way in December he was once again working as a referee. But behind the scenes, negotiations that would launch him on a brand new hockey career were already well under way.

# PART 2:

Building the Bruins

# 19

## ON TO
## BOSTON

The lengthy trail that eventually led Art Ross to Boston began with an arena fire in Montreal. Not the one that destroyed the Westmount Arena in January of 1918, but one that saw the Jubilee rink burn down in June of 1919.

Thomas Duggan, whose background was in horseracing, quickly put together a group of investors to build a new rink for the Montreal Canadiens. The Mount Royal Arena on Mount Royal Avenue between Clark and St. Urbain Street opened slightly behind schedule, and not quite completed, on January 10, 1920, after the Canadiens had begun the 1919–20 season with four straight road games.

Tom Duggan was in partnership with George Kennedy on events at the Mount Royal Arena, but he hadn't built the new rink solely to house the Canadiens. Duggan wanted to see the return of an English team to Montreal and applied for a club at the NHL's fall meeting in November of 1919. He was turned down, as he would be again in 1920. Duggan later tried to buy the Quebec Bulldogs and move them to Montreal. Then, after Kennedy died on October 19, 1921, Duggan made an offer on the Canadiens. At an auction for the club on November 3, 1921, he placed $10,000 on the table, but refused to get into a bidding war with another horseracing man, Leo Dandurand and his partners, Joseph Cattarinich and Louis Letourneau. Art Ross's old friend Cecil Hart represented the Dandurand group at the auction, and he won the day with an $11,000 offer.

Soon, Duggan changed tactics. He looked south to the United States, and in February of 1923, he made a deal with NHL president Frank Calder whereby he paid $2,000 for options on teams to be based in two of Boston, New York, or Brooklyn.

Within days of his deal with Calder, Duggan had approached George Brown, the manager of the recently rebuilt Boston Arena, which had opened on January 1, 1921. Brown also ran the Boston Athletic Association hockey club and was a prominent figure in the United States Amateur Hockey Association (USAHA). He wasn't much interested in the professional game, but one of the new directors of the rebuilt Arena was.

Charles Francis Adams had grown up poor in Vermont but prospered through hard work. He had become a multi-millionaire in Boston, most notably as a grocery store magnate. According to some stories, Adams had managed a Boston hockey team known as the Irish Americans and remained a fan of the game. He was intrigued by Duggan's proposal to put a professional team in Boston.

Adams and Colonel John Hammond (of Madison Square Garden) went to Montreal for a meeting and to attend a Stanley Cup semifinal playoff game between the Canadiens and Vancouver Maroons (formerly the Millionaires) on March 18, 1924. The results were encouraging, but even so, Adams may never have convinced the Boston Arena to give him ice time if not for a scandal that erupted in the USAHA a short time later. Apparently, the Pittsburgh Yellow Jackets threw a playoff game against George Brown's Boston AA club at the Boston Arena in order to ensure a lucrative gate back home in Pittsburgh at the Duquesne Gardens. This black eye for amateur hockey was good news for the professionals, and by the end of September Adams was all but assured of a franchise.

The story broke on September 26, 1924, and a day later, it was in newspapers everywhere. "The Montreal Star yesterday declared that the National Hockey League will shortly be turned into a six-club circuit, and that Boston will operate under a franchise bought by Tom Duggan some time ago. The Star says that Art Ross and Tom Duggan are said to be on their way to Boston for final arrangements, and that Ross is slated for the position of manager." Ironically, given all of Duggan's past efforts, the other team slated to join the NHL was a new English team for Montreal that became known as the Maroons.

By September 30, the deal in Boston was done. Adams would be majority owner and president of the team, and the Arena had agreed to give him ice time. Art Ross agreed to serve as Adams's vice president as well as coach and manager of the team. But Ross had been reluctant to join Boston at first.

Adams had seen Ross play during his visit to Boston with the Wanderers in either 1911 or 1912, and had been impressed by the way Ross handled the game as a referee when Adams was in Montreal earlier in 1924. Adams claimed he wanted a fighter for the Boston job, and so likely knew (or had been told) about Ross's reputation when it came to dealing with owners. But, "[Ross] was lukewarm to the proposition," Adams told A. Linde Fowler of the *Boston Transcript* some years later. "There was a special reason at that time for his attitude, but we need not go into that now. Suffice it that before our second conference the stumbling block was removed; it was not a matter of salary."

What it was, it seems, is that while Duggan had endorsed him to Adams wholeheartedly, Ross — for reasons that never seem to have been reported — wanted no part of the Boston job if Duggan had a financial stake in the team. Ross was assured that Duggan didn't, although it would take a court to decide that for certain during a lawsuit in 1929 and 1930. As to salary, Ross testified during that court case that he had wanted $5,000 to manage the club. "Duggan said it was too much," Ross remembered, but "Adams said he liked to have a high-priced man."

Ross's first contract with the Bruins is dated November 29, 1924, and shows a salary of "not less than $4,500" for five seasons through 1928–29. Ross also received 50 shares of common stock in the team each year. The stock was included as an option by Adams on the services of Ross for another five years, beginning October 1, 1929, for not less than $6,750 and 75 shares of stock. Ross would own 10 percent of the Bruins by the mid-1930s, but would still return to Montreal each spring and summer, where he continued to work for himself for many years. He was no longer associated with Harley Davidson, but was listed as an insurance broker in city directories from 1925–26 to 1930–31. The Montreal directories didn't begin listing him as "vice pres & mgr Boston Hockey Club" until 1931–32. He finally moved to Boston in either 1933 or 1934, but was still listed as the owner of the house at 4934 Western Avenue until 1937.

News of Ross's hiring by Adams was well received. "Boston surely will have a noted man as manager of the combination in Art Ross," reported the *Boston Globe* on October 4, 1924. "[He] is one of the best-known, all-around sportsmen in Canada." The paper mentioned his early notoriety in rugby before giving the highlights of his hockey career, and ended by saying: "Ross also is a fine baseball player and hunter, while his hobby now is golf, he having been captain of the Country Club at St. Lambert, a fashionable club, just outside of Montreal, for some years."

The NHL was slated to approve Adams's purchase of the team at a meeting in Hamilton the day after the *Boston Globe* story appeared, but that meeting was postponed a week. It was not until October 12 in Montreal that league directors approved both Boston and the new Montreal club. The Boston Professional Hockey Association, Inc. was officially formed on October 23, and formal approval came at the NHL's annual meeting, again in Montreal, on November 1, 1924. It's usually said that Adams paid $15,000 for the franchise, but testimony during Duggan's lawsuit indicates that Adams only paid $13,000 because Duggan had already paid the $2,000 option. Adams also agreed to settle a couple of personal debts for Duggan.

The business of building the Boston hockey club began almost as soon as Art Ross agreed to come on board on September 30, 1924. Many newspapers reported the next day that Adams would buy the Seattle Metropolitans of the PCHA and bring the entire team to Boston. It was already known that Seattle had dropped out of the league and that Vancouver and Victoria were going to join Calgary, Edmonton, Saskatoon, and Regina in a six-team Western Canada Hockey League. However, Frank Patrick, who the papers all noted was a life-long friend of Ross, immediately set the record straight. He was willing to assist Ross in putting together a major league hockey team, and admitted that the Seattle players gave him and his brother a surplus of talent, but the Patricks planned to keep the best players for themselves as they entered the new league.

Ross soon acquired past-their-prime PCHA veterans Bobby Benson, Lloyd Cook, Bernie Morris, Bobby Rowe, Alf Skinner, and goalie Norman "Hec" Fowler, but he also had his eye on the future as he built his team. Ross wanted talented amateurs, and had a pretty good idea where to look. In early October, he was in Hamilton, where his former OHA Tigers of 1922–23 had romped to the title in Group 1 play in the senior circuit of the Ontario Hockey Association in 1923–24. Hamilton had then defeated Stratford for the provincial title before losing the Eastern Canada final to the eventual Allan Cup champions, the Greyhounds of Sault Ste. Marie — which was Ross's next stop. From his trip to Hamilton, he would sign forwards George Redding, Herb Mitchell, and Carson Cooper, who had all played for him in 1922–23. He was unable to land defencemen Stan Brown and Babe Donnelly on his trip north to the Soo, but then headed west to Eveleth, Minnesota, where he locked up another of his old Tigers: Jim "Sailor" Herbert.

Back in southern Ontario after his northwest jaunt, Ross signed Werner Schnarr of Kitchener and made it known he wanted Charles Dinsmore of Toronto's Aura Lee hockey club as well, but Dinsmore would sign with the Maroons instead. The *Montreal Gazette* on November 4, 1924, picked up a story from Toronto saying that Ross was also after the prized catch of all of amateur hockey, Toronto Granites scoring sensation Harry Watson. Watson, however, would never agree to turn pro.

By the second week of November, Ross was home in Montreal. The big news there was that the artificial ice surface would soon be in at the brand new Forum, which had been built to house the Maroons. Meanwhile, the Canadiens were preparing for their third annual trip to Grimsby where they would hold training camp on the artificial ice rink in that tiny Ontario town. The Saskatoon Sheiks of the Western Canada League would also be training there, and before their player-coach Newsy Lalonde left for

Grimsby from his home in Montreal, he and Ross arranged for the Sheiks to travel to Boston to inaugurate pro hockey in the city with an exhibition game on Thanksgiving night, Thursday, November 27.

Ross told reporters he felt the Saskatoon team was, in many respects, stronger than many of the NHL teams. In addition to Lalonde, they boasted future hall of famers Bill Cook, Bun Cook, Harry Cameron, and George Hainsworth. "If the new Boston team … can overcome this Saskatoon outfit," reported the *Boston Globe* on November 11, "the Hub may well feel assured that this city will carry formidable representation in the big professional circuit."

Ross had asked most of his new players to assemble in Montreal, and the evening edition of the *Globe* on Friday, November 14, reported that the squad had arrived in Boston by train that morning. All were taken to Putnam's Hotel, which would be their home in the city. It was also reported that the Boston Professional Hockey Association, Inc. now had uniforms and a nickname. The uniforms would be brown with gold stripes on the sleeves and socks. (Black wouldn't replace brown in the uniforms until 1934–35.) The colour scheme surprised no one.

"An interesting item is connected with Pres. Adams' partiality towards brown as the team color. The pro magnate's four thoroughbreds are brown; his 50 stores are brown, his Guernsey cows are of the same color; brown is the predominating color among his Durco pigs on his Framingham estate, and the Rhode Island hens are brown, although Pres. Adams wouldn't say whether or not the eggs they lay are of a brown color." Adams had also considered Browns as the team's nickname, but the *Globe* noted his concern that people would call them the Brownies, which struck him as childish. Instead, the team would be called the Boston Bruins.

Stories surrounding the Bruins name are all pretty much the same. Charles Adams held a contest, but had very definite ideas about what kind of name he wanted. He wanted the name to relate to "an untamed animal." He wanted the animal to be big, strong, ferocious, and smart. (Of course, it wouldn't hurt if that animal happened to be brown!) A secretary in the team office is usually credited for coming up with Bruins — which comes from an old English term for a brown bear first used in a medieval children's fable. It's sometimes said to be Adams's secretary who coined the name, and sometimes Ross's secretary, or sometimes even Ross himself. In his book *The Bruins*, Brian McFarlane specifically names Bessie Moss, who he says was a transplanted Canadian working for Ross.

Whoever came up with the name, the Bruins hit the ice for the first time in a practice at the Boston Arena on Saturday, November 15, 1924. "Nothing of a strenuous nature was attempted," said the *Boston Globe*. "Ross worked his men easily, just enough to furnish him with a line on the character of their style of play." The *Globe* was impressed that he donned skates himself to demonstrate how he wanted various plays executed, but cautioned that he knew he would have to work fast with so many players fresh from the amateur ranks.

Seven amateur teams in addition to the Bruins were vying for ice time at the Boston Arena, and the pro club was given noon to 1:00 p.m. each day the following week to practise. A large crowd was on hand for the Monday workout, and were said to be pleased by the sturdy physiques of the players. Ross had them going all out at times, and reporters were impressed with their speed. Ross pushed them harder the following week, as the game with Saskatoon approached. "He demands that players be in the best physical condition," reported the *Globe,* and with two men at every position, except for Hec Fowler alone in net, "this double shift of men in good condition means hockey of the thrilling type." Ross had one line featuring Fred "Smokey" Harris, Fern Headley, whom the *Globe* called "Gopher" (and who is usually listed as a defenceman), and Carson Cooper, dubbed "Bullet." The other line was made up of Herb "Silent" Mitchell, Werner "Kid" Schnarr, and Alf "Dutch" Skinner. On defence were George Redding, Lloyd Cook, Sailor Herbert (who's usually listed as a centre), and Bobby Rowe.

*Toronto Star* sportswriter and longtime referee Lou Marsh would handle the exhibition game with Saskatoon. In sizing up the six NHL teams in the *Star* on November 26, Marsh found the relative strengths and weaknesses of Boston and the new Montreal team to be of the greatest interest. "Right now, Boston seems to look by far the best. Art Ross ... is a wise old canary. He has gathered together a combination of amateur stars and experienced pros who are still good for several years service. [M]ost of the amateurs seem to be of the right caliber, and the vets should hold them together until they find their feet. The Boston club on paper looks like an outfit that will have to be reckoned with before the flags are handed out."

The Bruins might have looked good on paper, but on the ice, it soon became apparent they were anything but.

There were a few empty seats in the most expensive areas of the Boston Arena for the game against Saskatoon, and the play was not particularly sharp, but nobody seemed too disappointed by the Bruins' 2–1 loss. When play opened for real against their Montreal expansion cousins four nights later on December 1, 1924, the crowd was once again slightly less than capacity. Despite Ross pushing them, the players weren't in peak condition, though no one had really expected they would be yet. Montreal jumped into a 1–0 lead midway through the first period, but then the Bruins began throwing their somewhat heavier weight around in the second period. The result was Carson Cooper setting up a goal for Smokey Harris before notching another one himself.

There was no scoring in the third period as Boston held on for a 2–1 victory, but it all went downhill from there.

# 20

## GROWING
## PAINS '

The Bruins' second game of the 1924–25 season was their first road game, and the home opener for the Toronto St. Pats. Toronto won 5–3. It was the first of 10 straight Boston losses. The Bruins didn't win again until January 10, 1925, in Montreal. Seven straight losses followed before win number three, again on a Saturday night in Montreal, this time against the Maroons. Four more losses then dropped Boston to 3–22–0 with five games remaining in the newly extended 30-game schedule.

Boston managed to double its win total during the final give games, posting three victories against two defeats to finish the season 6–24–0. Only a complete collapse by the Maroons, who lost 13 of their final 14 games to finish 9–19–2, kept the Bruins from being completely buried in the cellar. Meanwhile, Hamilton (19–10–1), Toronto (19–11–0), the Canadiens (17–11–2), and Ottawa (17–12–1) waged a tight battle for the three playoff spots with just four points separating those four teams.

The Bruins had been casting about all season, trying to find the right roster combination. They never really did. Boston used 22 players, whereas most other teams used between 12 and 14. Only Toronto dressed as many as 17. "I kept them coming and kept them going," Art Ross told Bruins radioman Fred Cusick in 1960. "You actually had three teams then," said Cusick, setting up an old joke. "That's right," Ross replied with a chuckle. "One [playing], one coming, one going."

With the losses piling up at the start of the season, Canadian newspapers strongly hinted that Ross would cut his ties with the team, but Charles Adams declared himself to be perfectly satisfied with Ross's work and believed him capable of turning the Bruins into an NHL power. Not everyone was convinced. In far off Brandon, Manitoba, where he'd first become a star nearly 20 years before, Ross was taken to task in the *Daily Sun* late in the season. "Montreal made a better showing than expected in the pro race," noted an unnamed reporter in a sport gossip column on February 19, 1925, "and yet the man who organized the team [old friend Cecil Hart] was fired. At Boston Art Ross is still in charge and no one takes the team seriously."

As with many modern expansion teams, publicity during Boston's first season focused on visiting stars. The team's fan base in the area may have been greater than it appeared inside the Arena, since Adams had arranged to have all Bruins home games broadcast in their entirety over Boston/Springfield radio station WBZ, announced by Frank Ryan of the *Boston Traveler*. Still, attendance failed to meet expectations, even when ticket prices were slashed.

Keeping the turnstiles clicking with such a terrible team was a constant struggle. It wasn't so much that Ross was trying to sell an unknown sport to a new audience, as is often written, but that he was selling an apparently hopeless outfit of Canadian professionals to a city used to top-ranked American amateurs. "The Arena put out the programs for all the games," Ross would later recall, and though the Bruins were tenants, paying rent, "the programs would carry the line-ups, and then there would be an article knocking us as a lousy team."

Ross was always trying to promote the Bruins, and never refused a speaking engagement. "No group was too small for his talks," remembered *Globe* writer Arthur Siegel, "and he was at his best at men's gatherings, where his stories could be earthy."

Ross's talks would not be politically correct today, but in the 1920s, they were a hit. Ross, with his ability to speak English, French, and two First Nations languages, made up a bevy of colourful Quebecois characters to help sell Boston on Canada and the Canadian game. "He had the broken-English dialect of the French-Canadian down to its entertaining best," wrote Siegel, and "Bostonians soon knew about Joe LaPorte and Joe's wife, Marie, and Jeannine who was the wife of Pierre, Joe's friend. There was the village judge, always counselling the clerk at the trials, 'Be sure to took the good note.'" There was never any definite locale, but Ross created a vivid scene. "His listeners could see the picturesque village somewhere in Quebec, with a canal and its drawbridge.... And everybody knew that the judge [which, according to other Siegel stories, was pronounced *Zhoosh*, in an exaggerated French-Canadian accent] not only wore glasses, but looked over the rims when he asked kindly questions of the litigants or passed his judgments."

"We sold tickets," said Ross of his offbeat promotional technique. "Later, of course, we bought and developed our players and the games sold the tickets."

The lowest point during the inaugural season of 1924–25 came in a 10–1 loss to Toronto on December 22, the sixth-straight loss during the Bruins' 10-game slide. Boston papers had already commented on the growing dissatisfaction of goalie Hec Fowler. "Fowler is displeased with the way he and the other players are handled," wrote John J. Hallahan of the *Boston Globe* on December 20. (Ross was said to be issuing a steady stream of fines as a way of maintaining discipline.) Fowler was also unhappy that Bobby Rowe and Lloyd Cook had been released, and there were rumours — correct, as it turned out — that Smokey Harris would get a ticket out of town as well. "It would look as if trouble is 'Bruin' among the Boston Pro Club," Hallahan concluded. It boiled over during the lopsided loss to the St. Pats.

Reports from that game the following day note only that Fowler was replaced after the ninth Toronto goal at 9:11 of the third period. Spare forward George Redding donned the pads for the rest of the game, allowing only one final goal. According to Ross, he hadn't been the one who decided to replace Fowler. "In the middle of the third period," Ross explained years later to Arthur Siegel, "he just left the ice. He went into the dressing room, changed into street clothes and left the Arena."

Ross more or less confirms the old story that Fowler had begun giving up goals on purpose, saying that he called him into his office the following afternoon along with Charles Adams and that he said: "That was a terrible thing to do, Hec, but I guess you gave it the best you had."

"'Like hell I did," came the reply.

"That ended his hockey career," Ross remembered.

The next day, Fowler was suspended and fined $200. He never played for the Bruins again, though he did play in a few more pro games in other leagues.

A few days after the Fowler incident, another Toronto hockey team visited Boston. The University of Toronto arrived for a four-game set against Boston College, Dartmouth, Harvard, and Boston College again beginning on December 29, 1924. Future Maple Leaf boss Conn Smythe was the U of T coach. "On our trip there that season," he recalled in his autobiography, "I managed to start what became nearly a lifelong feud with Art Ross."

In Smythe's telling of it, "When I arrived with the Varsity team, somebody asked what I thought of the Bruins. I said my Varsity team could handle them anytime, anywhere." Smythe admits that if someone had done the same thing to him in Toronto, he'd be mad too, adding: "Ross was furious. He never got over it."

As Smythe says, this incident is often portrayed as the start of a legendary feud. It was certainly a long and bitter one, and though it later helped to sell tickets in Boston and Toronto, it certainly wasn't a staged dispute. By all accounts, it was true hatred. "Yes, we detest each other," Smythe told Boston sportswriter George C. Carens in 1933. "The feeling is mutual."

But did it start this simply? Art Ross's son John believed it actually started when Ross convinced New York Rangers president John Hammond to dump Smythe as coach in favour of his friend Lester Patrick. This happened shortly after Smythe had been hired to head up the team when they joined the NHL in 1926–27. In his 1933 interview with Carens, Smythe doesn't say that Ross was behind his ouster in New

York, but does say that: "When I joined the National Hockey League, Ross told me a college coach would not last in big league company. He said he'd run me out of the league in a year and a half." Other stories claim the feud began when Ross convinced Smythe to buy a washed up Sailor Herbert from him during the 1927–28 season.

However it started, Smythe was grudgingly willing to admit that Ross, "along with his stubborn, insulting, devious way of dealing with people," did have "unlimited courage." And yet, "every place Ross and I met, we fought."

Despite Smythe's digs, the Fowler incident, and the .200 winning percentage, not everything about the 1924–25 season was a disaster. With all of those players coming and going, the Bruins managed to acquire perhaps the greatest player in NHL history who is *not* in the Hockey Hall of Fame. Yet when it was announced on the evening of January 8, 1925, that the Ottawa Senators had agreed to a loan, it seemed more like the player had picked the Bruins than Boston had picked the player.

Lionel Hitchman was born in Toronto on November 3, 1901, and began playing hockey there. His entire family later moved to Ottawa and Hitchman signed with the Senators late in the 1922–23 season. He spent most of his time on the bench with another young defenceman, King Clancy. Hitchman earned regular duty with the Senators in 1923–24, but in this era when starters — especially defencemen — still got nearly all of the playing time, he was mostly on the bench behind Clancy and veteran George Boucher during the 1924–25 season. In reporting on the deal with Boston, the *Ottawa Citizen* on January 9, 1925, said that Hitchman himself had "advanced the request that he be sent to the Bruins" in order to get more playing time. The Senators agreed, "on the understanding that any deal put through will be for this season only."

When Charles Adams heard about the loan, he was not impressed and his thoughts were quoted at length in the *Montreal Gazette*. "I cannot accept charity from the Ottawa club or any other club for that matter, and furthermore I do not intend to," said Adams. "I appreciate [Tommy] Gorman's offer but we would a great deal rather lose with our own men than win with players borrowed from other clubs. We will stand or fall upon merits of the team of our own that we can put on the ice…. I am ready," Adams continued, "to buy hockey players, or trade them but I haven't got to where I have any desire to borrow them."

The *Boston Globe* reported the next day that Adams hoped Ottawa would consider the outright sale of Hitchman's services, and the Senators obviously did. That morning, before the game against the Canadiens that snapped their 10-game losing streak, Hitchman was bought by Boston. It would take until midway through the 1925–26 season before the Bruins got things headed in the right direction, but Hitchman was instrumental in the turnaround. He would never score more than the seven goals he did that year, but he was a solid, steady, and physical presence in his own end. He was named captain of the team in 1927, and became the second player in NHL history to have his number retired after his playing career ended in 1934.

Hitchman was usually paired with Eddie Shore after Shore joined the team in 1926–27, and it was often said that it was Hitchman's defensive prowess that allowed Shore to become an offensive force. In his biography of Eddie Shore, author C. Michael Hiam quotes one sports columnist as saying: "Shore may be the dynamo of the Boston club, but Hitchman is the balancing wheel." Many of their contemporaries rated Hitchman as the better defensive player, and even Shore considered Hitchman a better checker. Hall of famer Frank Fredrickson, who played with them both, thought Shore was merely a country boy who made good. "He was a good skater and a good puck-carrier," Fredrickson told Stan Fischler in a 1968 interview, "but he wasn't an exceptional defenceman like his teammate Lionel Hitchman."

Hitchman apprenticed for his time with Eddie Shore by first playing with another teammate that nobody wanted to face, but who everyone wanted on their side: Sprague Cleghorn.

After the Wanderers folded in 1918, Cleghorn had joined the Senators and helped Ottawa win the Stanley Cup in 1920 and 1921. Unhappy when the Senators sent him to the Canadiens, Cleghorn saved his worst outbursts for members of his former team. During the playoffs in 1923, Cleghorn hit Lionel Hitchman in the head with a cross-check, and then jabbed at him again as he was falling down. Canadiens owner Leo Dandurand was so incensed by the dirty play of Cleghorn and teammate Billy Coutu (another future Bruin), that he immediately suspended both players. The Canadiens lost the series without them, but a year later Cleghorn was back to captain the team to the Stanley Cup.

Cleghorn finally wore out his welcome by the end of 1924–25 and there were rumours he'd be sold to the Maroons. Cleghorn knew his days were numbered. "They could have released me outright," he remembered, "or sold me for whatever they could get." Instead, the Canadiens held on to him, but in the late summer of 1925, Leo Dandurand summoned Cleghorn to his office.

"Sprague, I think Art Ross would like to have you in Boston. He needs an old-timer to steady that outfit. Make your own deal with him, and we'll let you go; but make your deal first."

Cleghorn and Ross worked out a deal for $5,500 for the 1925–26 season, as well as living expenses. Charles Adams okayed the contract, and Cleghorn was impressed by the way the Bruins paid him. "Each player was asked how much money he figured he would need as a weekly salary to keep him going comfortably. The sum he named was the amount he received. If he wanted it all, he could have it. If he was wise, he calculated the least he could get along on, and let the balance accumulate to his credit. When the season was finished he was paid in full — plus interest at a higher than savings-bank rate."

When the Bruins turned a profit in 1925–26, Cleghorn claimed that Adams split the amount with his players. In addition to the balance with interest due him on his salary, he was presented with 35 $20 gold pieces.

"That night, when I talked in my sleep, Mrs. Cleghorn tells me I was saying: 'God Bless Charles Francis Adams, and hurrah for Boston.'"

Boston's move to acquire Sprague Cleghorn was announced on October 13, 1925. When the Bruins opened practice a month later, Art Ross got Cleghorn and Hitchman together. Despite the bad blood between them, the young player offered his hand to the veteran. "If we can team up on defence with as much vigour and energy as we did against each other," Hitchman said in a story related by Kerry Keene in his book, *Tales from the Boston Bruins Locker Room*, "we should keep the league away from our net."

That must have been exactly what Ross hoped to hear.

# 21

# BUYING A
# BETTER TEAM

The team Art Ross assembled for 1925–26 appeared much improved over the year before. Carson Cooper had missed most of that first season with a knee injury, but was healthy and expected to lead the top line on the right wing of centre Sailor Herbert, who, it must be said, appeared anything but washed up. Boston-area amateur Hago Harrington later signed on to help Stan Jackson and Herb Mitchell at left wing. Still, the defence of Sprague Cleghorn and Lionel Hitchman, backed up by Red Stuart and Herb Mitchell, was the strength of the team. The Bruins would also have Charles Stewart in goal all season.

Stewart had taken over after the Hec Fowler fiasco in 1924–25, and he was clearly the goalie Ross had wanted from the beginning. Dr. Stewart, a practising dentist in the off-season, had played for Ross with the OHA Tigers in 1922–23 and was among the players he signed on his first scouting trip to Hamilton in October of 1924, but Ross agreed to let Stewart rip up the contract the following morning because, as Toronto's *Globe* reported, his father objected to him turning pro. It's unclear what had changed his mind by December.

As the 1925–26 season got under way, both Ross and Charles Adams expressed the belief that the Bruins would be very much in the hunt for the championship that winter. Two nights before the season got under way, Ross named Cleghorn the first captain in club history (records have long shown Lionel Hitchman was named Boston's first captain in 1927, but numerous contemporary newspaper clippings confirm it was Cleghorn), but he hurt his knee in the opener and was sidelined for eight games. Still, when a rival team enquired about purchasing the Bruins bruiser, Ross was said to have replied sarcastically, "Sure, I'll sell Cleghorn [for] $40,000, and if you wait five minutes, I'll make it $50,000."

Through the first half of the now 36-game schedule, the Bruins were only 4–11–3. But after losing their next game they went 12–1–1 in the 14 that followed. Two late losses to the NHL's newest teams — the New York Americans and Pittsburgh Pirates — hurt their playoff chances. The Bruins won their finale to finish the season 17–15–4, but wound up one point short of Pittsburgh for the third and final post-season berth in the seven-team league.

Finishing fourth behind the Pirates was a bitter blow, as the team was composed in large part of the former Pittsburgh Yellow Jackets, whose amateur teams had battled the Boston AA for years and won the last two USAHA championships. Making matters worse, the Pittsburgh team had openly expressed the opinion during the 1924–25 season that they were better than Boston's NHL team, and now it appeared they were. The Bruins also finished behind their expansion cousins, the deep-pocketed Montreal Maroons, who finished second overall in the NHL standings in 1925–26 and then eliminated Pittsburgh in the semifinals. The Maroons defeated first-place Ottawa in the NHL Final and went on to beat the Victoria Cougars of the Western League to win the Stanley Cup in just their second season. Ross knew his team still needed to get better, and shortly after Lester Patrick's Cougars lost the final game to the Maroons on April 6, 1926, Ross got in touch with Lester's brother Frank.

"Art Ross approached me in Montreal about securing individual stars for the Bruins," Frank Patrick remembered. "He found me in a very unreceptive mood with regards to selling odd players."

The two Patrick brothers had become convinced their western markets could no longer compete with the NHL now that it was becoming established in the United States, but Frank didn't want to peddle players a few at a time. As far as he was concerned, "it was going to be sell all or none." Knowing that the NHL was looking to add another team in New York as well as in Detroit and Chicago, Frank planned to merge the players of the western teams into three strong rosters and sell them intact for $100,000 a piece — although he knew he didn't actually have the rights to do this. "Our Western League contracts with the players did not carry reserve clauses. That is, we had no option on their services the following year any time. The one item that might have protected us if the East just started taking our players was the interleague agreement. But I was glad it was never put to the test."

Frank explained his plan to Ross, and after John Hammond of the Rangers refused to buy in, Ross got in touch with Charles Adams. Adams was in Bermuda at the time, but Ross told Frank that Adams agreed to underwrite the whole deal to the extent of $300,000.

As Frank remembered it, he received $50,000 from Adams before he left New York for an NHL meeting in Montreal at the beginning of May. By the time he walked out of the Windsor Hotel a few days later, he'd received another $100,000 on behalf of Chicago, and $100,000 more from Detroit. "Some other odd players brought in about $17,000 more on sales so that I actually distributed $267,000 throughout the Western League for my part of the coup de grace. As Saskatoon got $40,000 for its players, the Western League didn't do so badly."

Telling the story in the seventh installment of the series about his life in the *Boston Sunday Globe* nearly nine years later, in the spring of 1935 — shortly after his old friend had hired him to coach the Bruins — Frank Patrick was more than happy to give credit as he saw it due. "I want to say now that without the assistance of Art Ross, I doubt if I ever would have succeeded in my quest."

But the deal didn't go nearly as smoothly as Frank related it. After the issue finally came to a head at the NHL's fall meeting in Montreal on September 25, 1926, Charles Adams told his version of the events since May in the following day's Sunday edition of the *Boston Globe*.

"The original underwriting for the entire Western League involved $300,000: $50,000 for each club. When Saskatoon took the position that it preferred to negotiate for itself it reduced the amount to be guaranteed to the other five clubs, to $250,000." Adams said that he agreed to put up the amount. There was, however, some dissatisfaction, "particularly in Toronto," of the power Adams might have if he was able to control the distribution of the players. So, "I released my option and permitted [Frank] Patrick to deal directly with the management of the prospective owners of the Chicago, Detroit and New York franchises." The timing doesn't quite match Frank's telling, but Adams states that, "New York felt the price for a good hockey team was too high and did not complete negotiations with Patrick." Interests in Detroit and Chicago did, agreeing to pay $100,000 each. "This left $50,000 more to raise out of the leftovers."

"Toronto was given an opportunity to purchase a first class defenceman at a reasonable price, but said it was too high," related Adams. This likely turned out to be good news for the Bruins. That player may have been Eddie Shore, whom longtime sportswriter and future Hockey Hall of Fame referee Mike Rodden — working for the St. Pats at the time — later claimed wanted to sign with Toronto.

After the Canadiens picked up the three players they wanted, Adams offered John Hammond "an opportunity to buy the remaining lot of players together with myself, putting up $25,000 each, which he declined." At that point, "in order to complete the deal, I then alone paid Patrick $50,000 for the remaining players."

For Adams's money, the Bruins claimed seven men, although two of them were sold almost immediately. However, several teams were still squabbling over players they felt they had claimed and the only thing everyone seemed to agree on was that Adams's arrangement was self-serving. So, at the meeting on September 25, the NHL nullified the deal and formed a three-man committee of Frank Calder, James Strachan, and Leo Dandurand to re-distribute the western players.

Adams blamed Calder for quashing his deal, and burned quietly for a while until it was learned on October 14, 1926, that he was threatening legal action. In Montreal the following morning, Adams and Ross met with the Canadian lawyer Adams had hired to discuss the issue with

Calder, Strachan, and Dandurand — who could not even agree among themselves how best to proceed — ahead of an NHL meeting in Toronto the next day. After speaking with his lawyer, Adams decided it would look bad to try and influence Calder et al before the league meeting.

When the day-long session in Toronto finally ended, the NHL agreed to give Boston all seven players. That meant the sale of Frank Boucher to the Rangers and Ty Arbour to Pittsburgh went through immediately, while the Bruins landed Archie Briden, Duke Keats, Harry Oliver, Amby Moran, and Eddie Shore for themselves. Some newspapers missed out on reporting the acquisition of Shore — while others referred to him as Ernie — but in landing the big defenceman, the Bruins had the player who would become the heart of their franchise.

Acquiring Eddie Shore seemed to involve as much good luck as good management, but Art Ross also picked up Percy Galbraith, whom he'd been after since 1924, in an unrelated transaction. He then dealt Amby Moran to Montreal for Sprague Cleghorn's former roughhouse teammate Billy Coutu. Still, the Bruins hadn't gotten the Western League player Ross wanted most.

From the first time he contacted Frank Patrick after the 1926 Stanley Cup Final, Ross had, according to Eric Whitehead, expressed "a special admiration for Frank Fredrickson." Fredrickson had captained the Winnipeg Falcons to a league championship, the Manitoba provincial championship, and then to the Allan Cup as national amateur champions in 1920, before going on to win a gold medal at the first Olympic hockey tournament held that spring prior to the Summer Games in Antwerp, Belgium. Fredrickson, a high-scoring centre, then went on to great success playing under Lester Patrick in Victoria.

"Art Ross … arranged to have me play with the Bruins," Fredrickson told Stan Fischler during an interview in 1968. "But I wouldn't sign up with Boston and Ross sent me a wire threatening me with expulsion for the rest of my life." Still, when the rest of his Victoria teammates were sold, "I signed with Detroit and got $6,000, which was a lot of money then." When Fredrickson was awarded to Detroit at the September 25 meeting, Adams said he considered it to be a trade for Duke Keats. But

Ross remained interested in the Icelandic star. On January 6, 1927, he sent Keats and Archie Briden to Detroit for Fredrickson and Harry Meeking.

With the NHL expanded to 10 teams for the 1926–27 season, the league split into two five-team divisions and the schedule grew from 36 games to 44. Boston was placed in the American Division along with Pittsburgh and the new teams in Detroit, Chicago, and New York. The Bruins were originally slated to play in the Canadian Division (sometimes referred to as the International Division) along with Toronto, Ottawa, and the two Montreal teams, but Charles Adams said in the *Boston Globe* on September 28, 1926, that he suggested it would make more sense to place one of the New York teams there, "believing that it would forestall any talk of syndicate hockey or collusion by separating the two New York teams who otherwise would be in the same group." Adams suggested moving the Rangers, but it was the New York Americans who wound up playing in the Canadian Division.

The new season opened on three fronts, including Boston, on November 16, 1926. Seating capacity at the Boston Arena had been expanded with an upper balcony added, and a large crowd was expected to see the home team take on the Canadiens. The Bruins had lacked depth in 1925–26, but the busy offseason fixed that. "Ross has strength in every position," the *Boston Globe* reported on game day, "and he can be counted upon to juggle his players to the best interests of victory." Ross wouldn't reveal his starting lineup, but "the Boston manager does not conceal his plans to keep full strength on the ice always. He plans to run players in and out of the game frequently." Ross would alternate two forward lines, while rotating through Lionel Hitchman, Sprague Cleghorn, Eddie Shore, and Billy Coutu on defence. Red Stuart, a fan favourite from the first two seasons, would fill in as a forward or defenceman as needed.

The weather was wet and warm that evening and a crowd of 8,000 filed through the ornate lobby. The Bruins won the game 4–1, and the general consensus after just one game was that the team was much improved. It was the New York Rangers, however, that would be the best team in the American Division during their inaugural season. Ottawa was the league's best team overall atop the Canadian Division. Boston never seemed to get on track. They never lost more than three in a row, but never won more than three straight either, and always seemed to hover around .500. "Things go bad for a while," Ross used to remind the press when the Bruins were struggling, "and then they get worse." The low point during the 1926–27 season came shortly after Fredrickson was acquired, near the midway mark of the schedule, when the Bruins took on the 15–2–2 Senators in Ottawa on Saturday night, January 15, 1927. Boston's record fell to 9–11–1 that night, but the aftermath of the game may have saved the season.

Doc Stewart let in a couple soft goals in a 5–4 loss to Ottawa and, according to the *Montreal Gazette*, Art Ross "wired to his headquarters in the Hub-town that Goaltender [Moe] Roberts, who is at present playing with the New Haven team of the Canadian-American League, be recalled for duty with the Bruin clan." Ross was unsure if Roberts would take over in goal, but stated that he was not satisfied with Stewart's performance. Roberts never did get the call to Boston, but Stewart's NHL career was over. Charles Adams was quoted in the *Boston Globe* saying that Stewart was only being given a rest, that he'd been handicapped by poor health, and that "the dentist needs a layoff," but Michael Hiam, in his biography of Eddie Shore, writes that the goaltender had developed a drinking problem. Ross replaced Stewart with Hal Winkler, whom he purchased from the Rangers for $5,000.

In an era of low scoring, Stewart's goals-against average of 2.26 was among the worst in the NHL, whereas Winker's mark of 1.66 in Boston, and his overall average of 1.72 for the season, was more in line with the numbers put up by future hall of famers Clint Benedict, George Hainsworth, and Alec Connell. The Bruins improved to 12–9–2 under Winkler and finished the season with a record of 21–20–3 for 45 points. They were still a distant 11 points back of the first-place Rangers, but finished four up on third-place Chicago, whom they faced in their first playoff appearance. After defeating the Black Hawks 10–5 (6–1 and 4–4) in a total-goals series, the Bruins played the Rangers for the American Division championship. Winkler was the hero, blanking his former teammates in a 0–0 tie in the opener and surrendering only a single goal when Boston took the series with a 3–1 victory in game two.

The Bruins next faced the Canadian Division champion, the Ottawa Senators, who had posted a final record of 30–10–4 during the regular season and defeated the Canadiens in the playoffs. With the demise of the Western League, and all other top professional circuits considered either to be outlaws or of minor-league calibre, the NHL championship now carried with it not only the O'Brien Cup (a holdover from the National Hockey Association) and the Prince of Wales Trophy, but the Stanley Cup as well.

The Senators boasted several players who had won the Stanley Cup for Ottawa in 1920, 1921, and 1923, and had finished first in the NHL standings on three other occasions. As a team, the Bruins had no playoff experience, but as individuals, almost all of their personnel had played for the Stanley Cup before. Captain Sprague Cleghorn had won it three times, and Frank Fredrickson had won it just two years before and had reached the final again the previous season. And not that it could really have had any bearing on the outcome, but Boston teams had a reputation for winning it all when they got this far. The Red Sox had fallen on hard times in the nine years since their last title in 1918 (and the seven seasons since they'd sold Babe Ruth to the Yankees), but they did have a perfect record of 5–0 in the World Series. Boston fans were eager to add another title to their collection, and some 30,000 requests for tickets were received for the two opening home games even though the Boston Arena could barely accommodate 9,000 people. The Senators were certainly the favourites, but Art Ross promised the hometown fans his club was ready. "If Ottawa wins," John Hallahan quoted Ross in the *Boston Globe*, "it will know that it has been in a hockey game, for my players will give it everything they have."

Coming from Ross, this was no idle boast, and when the Bruins gave it everything they had, the rules didn't always get in their way. Writing about the team nearly 40 years later, Canadian media legend Peter Gzowski summed up the Bruins nicely when he said the team had always displayed a good deal of the "lusty, saloon-tough seaport" atmosphere that carried over from the turn of the century. "They seem," Gzowski wrote during the Original Six era, "to take as much pleasure out of knocking someone down as in scoring a goal." A *Time* magazine story in 1933 claimed: "[N]owhere is sheer roughness on the ice a greater drawing card than in bloodthirsty Boston."

This was the style of play Charles Adams wanted when he hired Ross, and now, with Eddie Shore, Sprague Cleghorn, and Billy Coutu, Boston had the team for it. "They play a game typical of Art Ross, who, in his day, was not afraid to 'hit' an opponent," wrote John Hallahan in the *Boston Globe* on the evening the Stanley Cup series opened.

As a coach, Ross wore elegant suits on game day, but his posture sitting on the bench — not standing behind it — gave a much better indication of his competitive drive. Hunched toward the ice, with his hat pulled down low to focus his vision forward, Ross sat with his hands draped over the boards, which he often pounded to attract the attention of the players he shouted instructions to ... and the referees he hurled insults at.

Complaining about referees was already a time-honoured hockey tradition, but the Bruins added a nationalistic wrinkle. Almost from the beginning of franchise history, Adams protested that his American-based team was not getting a fair break from Canadian-born officials. Ross was often fined by the referees for using abusive language towards them, such as on one occasion earlier in the 1926–27 season when Lou Marsh dinged him for $25 during a 3–2 loss in Detroit on January 13. "He threatened to 'puck' me," Marsh wrote under the "Remarks" section on the Official Report of Match ... and it doesn't take much imagination to believe it was a different four-letter word Ross uttered!

Boston fans reveled in the rowdiness, and would for decades. Ross and Adams were often accused of not just accepting the boorish behaviour, but encouraging it. During the 1927 Stanley Cup Final, Stanley Woodward wrote in the *Boston Herald* that the Ottawa crowd was different from Boston's in some fundamental ways. "It does not throw truck on the ice, except under greatest stress," he said. Between periods, "it sings cheering songs" rather than "cursing or blackguarding referees." Professor Stephen Hardy of the University of New Hampshire writes: "Woodward was probably too kind to Ottawa's fans, but he hit a central point about hockey's attraction in Boston. Throwing curses, eggs, or lemons at a referee both reflected and built a sense of ownership." But

Boston's disdain for referees would mar the end of the 1927 Final, which was already a strange one before it finished.

The 1927 Stanley Cup Final opened in Boston on April 7. It was the evening before the hometown Red Sox and Braves inaugurated the baseball season with a two-game exhibition series at Fenway Park, and the weather was more conducive to baseball than hockey. Warm temperatures softened the ice, which was so chewed up at the end of 20 minutes of overtime that the game was declared a 0–0 tie. (Both teams had goals called back; Ottawa in the first period and Boston late in OT.) NHL President Frank Calder — who made the decision along with representatives from both teams — quickly announced the series would not be extended. He didn't want anyone to infer that the game had been halted in order to add a potential extra gate. The series would still be a best of five, and if the teams split the remaining four games, they would split the players' pool of bonus money and the Stanley Cup would not be awarded.

Game two was played in Boston two nights later, and the Senators scored a 3–1 victory. The series then moved to Ottawa, where the teams played another tie game, this time 1–1, in game three on April 11. Calder declared this one a draw after a single overtime session because of his concern the players might be injured if they played longer. The tie was almost as good as win for the Senators, who now needed just one more victory in the final two games on home ice to take the series. The Bruins had to win both.

"Telegrams wishing the Bruins well — and the referees ill — were pouring in from Boston," writes Hiam in his Shore biography, pointing out that the Bruins were nursing a grudge against referee Jerry Laflamme from game three, when he apparently called a tripping penalty on a Boston player after Ottawa's King Clancy had fallen of his own accord. "All through the contest there were squawks from the Boston bench over the rulings of the officials," said the *Ottawa Citizen* of game four. What started out as "a spectacular and speedy struggle" soon took a turn for the worse.

Shortly after Frank Finnegan put Ottawa up 1–0 at 5:10 of the second period, Sailor Herbert led a rush into the Ottawa zone. Hec Kilrea hooked him from behind, and Herbert lost the puck. He retaliated by giving Kilrea a shove with his stick. The *Boston Globe* noted that this all took place directly in front of referee Billy Bell, but Bell either decided to "let them play," as a later era of TV broadcasters might say, or simply hadn't seen the foul. Laflamme was back in the Boston end, but he had a clear view of the play and whistled down Herbert for a two-minute cross-checking minor. Kilrea got nothing. According to the *Citizen*, Herbert then "directed some very uncomplimentary remarks to the official," while the *Montreal Gazette* reported that he "took a wild poke with the butt-end of his stick at Referee Laflamme." Whichever was correct, Herbert's penalty was upped to a five-minute major. The Bruins were not pleased.

Cy Denneny soon put Ottawa ahead 2–0, but the game didn't really get out of hand until Denneny scored again at 11:25 of the third. Boston forwards were pressing hard to get back in the game, with Shore often aiding in the rush, but the Senators had been masters of defensive hockey since that night back in 1915 when kitty barred the door. With time running out, the game got nasty — though Ottawa seems to have been just as guilty as Boston.

With 4:20 remaining, George Boucher and Lionel Hitchman got into a wild fight that required police intervention and saw both men kicked out of the game. At about 17:15 of the third, Harry Oliver finally got Boston on the board only to be rewarded a short time later with a butt-end in the face from Hooley Smith, who then tangled with Eddie Shore after he came to the defence of his fallen teammate. When time ran out, the final score was 3–1 Ottawa.

"We lost the game — and the Cup," Frank Fredrickson later recalled, "but after it was over, Ross got us together in the dressing room and said, 'Okay, the first man who gets the referee gets a $500 bonus.'" He then describes Billy Coutu letting the ref have it … and receiving the money too.

It may all have happened as Fredrickson described more than 40 years later, but contemporary accounts of the game make the trouble sound much more spontaneous. "Referee Jerry Laflamme was struck in the face and knocked down while on his way to the dressing room after the championship hockey battle tonight," read an Associated Press account from Ottawa. "He was accosted by Manager Art Ross and Charles F. Adams, owner of the Bruins, and a free-for-all followed, players joining in." The

*Ottawa Citizen* claimed that, "Manager Art Ross of the Boston team grabbed [Laflamme] by the sweater to prevent him entering the room and an officer of the Boston Club, Billy Coutu and several other Boston players assaulted him." According to the *Gazette*, "Just who of the Boston team clouted the official it is hard to say. Those who jumped in as peacemakers made free mention of Billy Coutu, but there were other Bostonians, players and supporters alike, who would have planted a fist if they could have got close enough." The story in the *Ottawa Journal* noted that the referee's report of the fracas named Coutu as "the main culprit," but the *Journal* also admitted to some confusion as to who else was involved.

All reports agreed that Laflamme had not been seriously injured and that he planned to take no action other than to report the incident to Frank Calder, who had been at the game but not witnessed the assault. Calder acted quickly, announcing fines and suspensions within less than 24 hours. Sailor Herbert was docked $50 for his outburst. Lionel Hitchman and George Boucher also received $50 fines, which were automatic for match penalties. Hooley Smith was fined $100 and suspended for the first month of the next season for his deliberate attack on Harry Oliver. For his attack on Laflamme, Billy Coutu was also fined $100 ... and expelled from the NHL for life. (He was permitted to play in the minors, and later had his NHL ban lifted, but he never played in the league again.) Calder also stated that: "The actions of all others alleged to have been implicated in the disturbance after the game at Ottawa are subject to further investigation and will be dealt with by the board of governors at its next meeting."

At the meeting, held in Montreal on May 14, the governors upheld the fines and suspensions, but apparently decided something needed be done about the quality of the refereeing. They created the position of referee-in-chief, to which Frank Calder would later appoint Cooper Smeaton. As to the further investigation into the actions of all others, there was apparently no proof whatsoever of Charles Adams having taken any part in the melee and he was exonerated from all blame. The *Toronto Star* reported that the evidence against Ross was that "he had probably started the trouble with the referee by holding Laflamme up at the dressing room … and starting an argument with him." The decision as to what action to take against him would be left up to Calder.

It seems that no punishment against Ross was ever announced. However, after the next governor's meeting, held in Chicago on September 24, reports all state that Charles Adams replaced Ross as Bruins governor. Before he gave up the position, Ross made a motion for an addition to the rules, asking that it be illegal "for managers to address abusive or offensive language to any official or to any player, nor shall any manager step on the ice during the progress of a match, nor shall he attempt in any way either by his own actions or by causing any action on the part of any person, to hamper the officials in their duties." Could this new rule have been Ross's penance?

The Ross family, circa 1891. Standing, left to right: Simon Peter, Sybil, Thomas Robert. Seated, left to right: Charles, Donald in the lap of Margaret, Thomas Barnston, Art, and George. Seated in front: Colin, Alexander, and Roderick. (Photo courtesy of the Ross Family.)

Art Ross's mother, Margaret McLeod Ross McKenzie, was said to be the prettiest woman in the Saguenay district. (Photo courtesy of the Ross Family.)

The Ross family, circa 1900. Standing, left to right: Alexander, Sybil, Thomas Robert, and Colin. Seated, left to right: Jennie Louis Ryan (wife of Thomas Robert), Peter McKenzie, Maggie Ross McKenzie, and Donald. Art is on the floor in front. (Photo courtesy of the Ross Family.)

This photograph was taken in Westmount around 1900. It is likely a school or church group. Art Ross is standing second from the left. The two boys standing at the right might be Lester Patrick and his younger brother Frank. (Photo courtesy of the Ross Family.)

The Crescent basketball team was the senior champion of the Westmount Amateur Athletic Association in 1902–03. Art Ross sits on the floor at the right. (Photo courtesy of the Ross Family.)

The 1903 Westmount rugby-football team won the Canadian intermediate championship. Art Ross stands second from the left. Frank Patrick is seated at the far right. The Westmount hockey club wore the same winged W sweaters Ross and some of the others are wearing. (Photo courtesy of the Ross Family.)

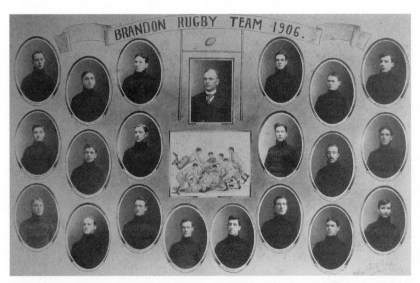

Art Ross is pictured in the circle to the right of the drawing in the centre of the photograph. He played centre-half and captained the Brandon rugby-football team in the fall of 1906. The Brandon hockey team likely wore the same "Wheat City" sweaters. (Photo courtesy of the Ross Family.)

The Kenora Thistles pose with the Stanley Cup in a Montreal studio after defeating the Wanderers in January of 1907. Standing at the back, left to right: Russell Phillips, John McGillivray, James Link, and Fred Hudson. Seated in the middle, left to right: Roxy Beaudro, Tom Hooper, Tom Phillips, Billy McGimsie, and Joe Hall. Seated in front, left to right: Si Griffis, Eddie Giroux, and Art Ross. (Photo courtesy of the Hockey Hall of Fame.)

Though it has long since disappeared, Art Ross was obviously allowed to keep the Kenora Thistles sweater he wore during the Stanley Cup series against the Wanderers in January of 1907. Here, he is wearing the sweater while on a fishing trip. (Photo courtesy of the Ross Family.)

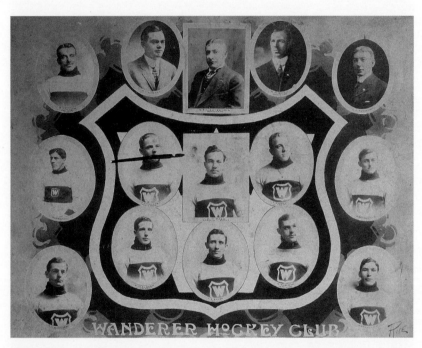

The Montreal Wanderers of 1911–12. Team owner and president Sam Lichtenhein is in the square at the top of the photo. Captain Art Ross is in the square in the centre. Odie Cleghorn (with the blemish on the photo) is to Ross's left. Sprague Cleghorn is immediately below his brother. (Photo courtesy of the Ross Family.)

Art Ross led the NHA Eastern All-Star Team west to face the Pacific Coast Hockey Association All-Stars in the spring of 1912 and 1913. This is the 1912 team. Standing, left to right: Sprague Cleghorn, Hamby Shore, Art Ross, Skene Ronan, Paddy Moran, and Odie Cleghorn. Seated, left to right: Jack McDonald, Cyclone Taylor, Jack Darragh, and Joe Malone. (Photo courtesy of the Ross Family.)

This portrait of Art Ross was used in a 1915 guide to businesses in Montreal. (Photo courtesy of the Ross Family.)

ARTICLES OF AGREEMENT Between the BOSTON PROFESSIONAL HOCKEY ASSOCIATION, INCORPORATED, of the City of Boston, State of Massachusetts, U.S.A., hereinafter called the "Association", PARTY OF THE FIRST PART - and ARTHUR H.ROSS, of the City of Montreal, Province of Quebec, Dominion of Canada, hereinafter called the "Manager", PARTY OF THE SECOND PART

**Witnesseth;**

That in consideration of the mutual obligations herein and hereby assumed, the parties to this contract severally agree as follows:

The Association agrees to pay the Manager for five years, beginning on or about October 1, 1924, a salary at the rate of not less than Forty-five hundred ($4,500.00) Dollars, and Fifty (50) Shares of the Common Stock of said Association for each year. Said stock being in consideration of an option by the Association on the services of said Manager for an additional five years of service, commencing October 1,1929, at an annual salary of not less than Sixty-seven Hundred and Fifty ($6,750.00) Dollars and Seventy-five (75) Shares of the Common Stock of the Association for each year.

The Manager agrees to perform for the Association, the duties of Coach and Manager efficiently and successfully, and for no other party during the period of this contract unless with the written consent of the Association it being understood that said Manager shall be permitted to conduct his regular business at such time as his services are not required in the conduct of his duties to the Association.

Should the Manager be unable to perform his duties at any time during the period of this contract, it is agreed that his compensation shall be reduced in proportion as the time of such inability may bear to the term herein described, it being understood that no such deduction shall be made by reason of any accident or injury received by the Manager while in the performance of his regular duties.

IN TESTIMONY WHEREOF, the parties hereunto have executed this contract in duplicate and each shall be considered an original, one copy being retained by the Association and one by the Manager.

DATED AT BOSTON this 29th day of November 1924.

Signed:   BOSTON PROFESSIONAL HOCKEY ASSOCIATION,INC.

Witness                                by   C.F.ADAMS
       L.M.Burk                                  President

                                        ARTHUR H. ROSS
                                             MANAGER

Received Fifty (50) Shares of the Common Stock of the Boston Professional Hockey Association, Inc., which is the number of shares due me as a bonus for signing the above contract.

                    Signed:        ARTHUR H.ROSS

A copy of the first contract Art Ross signed with Charles Adams and the Boston Professional Hockey Association, better known as the Boston Bruins. (Photo courtesy of the Ross Family.)

An old friend of Art Ross, and one of the roughest players in hockey history, Sprague Cleghorn was brought to Boston in 1925–26 to give the Bruins a veteran presence. Cleghorn's departure from the team after the 1927–28 season ended his friendship with Ross. (Photo courtesy of the Ross Family.)

The trade of Jim "Sailor" Herbert from Boston to Toronto during the 1927–28 season may have sparked the feud between Art Ross and Conn Smythe. (Photo courtesy of the Ross Family.)

The Boston Bruins circa 1930. Cooney Weiland is the first player to the right of Art Ross. Dit Clapper is seated second from the left. Eddie Shore and Tiny Thompson are seated directly in front of Ross, with Lionel Hitchman, George Owen, and Marty Barry to the right of Thompson. (Photo courtesy of the Ross Family.)

*Boston Globe* cartoonist Gene Mack captured Art Ross as fans in arenas around the NHL knew him best: staring intently at the action on the ice and banging on the boards to get the attention of a player or a referee. (Photo courtesy of the Ross Family.)

# 22

# NEW RULES, NEW INVENTION, AND A NEW JOB

The NHL introduced a lot of new rules for the 1927–28 season. After a serious drop in offensive production during the previous year, it was felt that something had to be done. Of the 220 games played by the 10 teams in 1926–27, an astounding 81 (nearly 37 percent) ended in shutouts. Four of those games were 0–0 ties, meaning there had actually been 85 shutouts during the season. Many of the new, or modified, rules introduced in 1927–28 were intended to speed up the game and create more scoring. Art Ross, who had been named to the committee to consider revisions to the rules as noted in the minutes of an NHL meeting on April 11, 1925, must have come up with many of the changes.

Among the new rules for 1927–28 was one reducing the width of goalie pads from 12 inches to 10 inches. The length of the blade of a goalie's sticks was capped at 14¾ inches. Rules about interfering with a player who was not in possession of the puck were strengthened, as was the NHL's anti-defence rule. This rule had been on the books for several years, and stated that not more than two players, in addition to the goalie, could remain in the defensive zone when the puck was being played in any other zone. However, only a warning had to be issued the first time any player violated this rule, so it was easy enough to work around. Now, each time any player violated the rule, he was to receive a two-minute penalty.

Forward passing, which the NHL had previously allowed only within the neutral zone, was expanded into the defensive zone in 1927–28. This was expected to make it easier for a team to get the puck out of its own end. Only the defensive team could make a forward pass in this zone, though. Forward passing in the offensive zone (which was, of course, the opposing team's defensive zone) was still not allowed and would result in a whistle for offside.

The NHL adopted another important innovation this season. This one was purely an Art Ross idea. In an effort to cut down on bad bounces and the resulting disputes when goals were disallowed, he had designed a brand new goalie net.

"Art Ross says that his Boston hockey team lost so many games in the NHL last winter over disputed goals," wrote *Toronto Star* sports editor W.A. Hewitt in his column on October 1, 1927, "that he decided to invent a more efficient goal net." Ross himself told a similar story to Fred Cusick 33 years later in their 1960 WEEI interview. "The old style was square nets and there were very stiff chords, and we used to have an argument — not one, but maybe three or four — every night. The puck would go in and out so fast the goal umpire couldn't see them."

Ross's new net featured a distinctive B-shape design with, essentially, two hoop-shaped frames. Unlike the old nets — which were actually rectangular, not square — this meant there would be no iron uprights at the back for pucks to bounce off. In addition, he angled the B-shaped bar resting on the ice in such a way as to deflect pucks up into the netting, unlike the flat bar straight across the base of the old nets that caused pucks to rebound out. As for the netting, it could be draped much more loosely over the rounded frame, allowing for a more noticeable bulge as it actually trapped the puck inside. The NHL, and virtually everyone else who played hockey, used Ross's net through the 1983–84 season. All the new nets used since then are still just a variation of his original design.

Still, there was one problem, according to Ross's son John. When he had his patent on the puck, Ross got 4¢ every time a new one was put into play to replace one that went into the seats. "That was nice," John remembered. "But then, when he made the net, he made one major mistake. He got the goal patented, but he never patented [the mesh], which is going to be replaceable after three years. That he didn't patent. The goal itself lasts for 25 years, or forever, but the netting lasts for two. That, he said, was one of the major mistakes in his life."

\*   \*   \*

In these early years when Art Ross was in Boston for the hockey season, John and Arthur and their mother Muriel stayed behind in Montreal. "We didn't see him a whole lot," John remembered. "He used to come in when Boston was coming to Montreal. I'd get all excited. He would let me take his American money to the Montreal bank and change it. You'd get 25¢ on each dollar and I'd bring it back to him and I'd keep the 25¢ and that was a great thing for me." The house got a lot busier whenever his father was home. "He'd show up and the phone would start ringing. The phone was ringing for free tickets all day long."

During the winter of 1927–28, John probably saw more of his father than usual, though not for a reason anyone would have liked. The trouble began shortly after January 14, 1928, when the Bruins reached the halfway point of the 44-game season with a 4–2 win in Ottawa. Boston's record was 10–6–6, good for 26 points, three ahead of both the Rangers and Detroit, with Pittsburgh and Chicago a long way back in the American Division standings. Over the next two weeks, the Rangers won four of their five games, while the Bruins suffered three losses and two ties. Suddenly, the Rangers were three points ahead of the Bruins in first place, and Art Ross wasn't feeling very well.

When the Bruins snapped their five-game winless streak with a 2–1 victory over the Americans on January 31, Sprague Cleghorn — whom Ross had given the added responsibility of coaching the defence as well as playing on it this season — was running the team while Ross was sick. Two weeks later, with Ross at home in Montreal undergoing treatment for a stomach ailment, a headline in the *Boston Globe* read:

"Ross' Retirement Forecast by Adams." The story had Charles Adams announcing after an NHL board of governors meeting in Toronto on February 13, that he did not expect his manager to be back in charge of the club the following season.

Whether or not the team's five wins and a tie in six games under Cleghorn had anything to do with it, by the time the Bruins travelled to Montreal for the first of a home-and-home set with the Maroons on February 25, Ross had shown great improvement. It was reported that he would rejoin the team in Boston for a game against the Rangers on March 10. He returned with the team following its 3–1 loss to the Maroons and was on hand when the Bruins beat them 2–1 at home on February 28. Cleghorn still ran the Bruins that night, as he also did when Ross chose not to make the trip to Toronto for what turned out to be a scoreless tie on March 3.

Ross made his return to the bench one game earlier than expected when the Bruins hosted the Ottawa Senators on March 6, 1928. Boston scored a 1–0 victory on a goal from promising rookie Dit Clapper, purchased that year from the Boston Tigers, a local minor league club in the Can-Am Hockey League that was not yet (but soon would be) officially affiliated with the Bruins. With the Rangers losing 3–1 to the Maroons in Montreal that night, the Bruins had finally regained sole possession of first place in the American Division, and their final record of 20–13–11 was good for a four-point advantage over the Rangers. Boston received the Prince of Wales Trophy, which had been newly designated as the champion's prize of the American Division, but with Eddie Shore suffering from a bout of neuralgia, and injuries to Dit Clapper, Dutch Gainor, and Harry Connor that all required post-season surgery, the Bruins' Stanley Cup dreams ended in a playoff upset against the Rangers, who went on to defeat the Maroons for the game's top prize in just their second season.

Normally, when the hockey season ended, Art Ross returned to Montreal, and then took an annual vacation to the wilds of northern Quebec for some hunting and fishing. During the 1928 offseason, however, he remained in Boston. One year earlier, Charles Adams had purchased an interest in the Boston Braves of the National League and become vice president. Majority owner and team president Judge Emil Fuchs was said to be a big fan of Ross and convinced Adams to loan Ross to the baseball team for the summer. Other stories maintain it was Adams himself who wanted Ross to "instill ginger" into the longtime, listless cellar dwellers.

Eight days after the Rangers eliminated the Bruins on April 3, 1928, Ross joined the Braves in New York for their season opener against the Giants, which they lost 5–2. He served as the team's travelling secretary, which in those days was not a secretary responsible for the team's travel, but an assistant general manager who travelled with the team. John Thorn, the official historian for Major League Baseball says, "Ross was the 'eyes and ears' for Judge Fuchs in a particularly fractious time for the Braves."

Boston finished with a record of 50–103, 44.5 games behind the pennant-winning St. Louis Cardinals, but were spared last place by the even-more-woeful Philadelphia Phillies, who finished 43–109. Adams retained his interest in the cash-strapped, non-contending baseball team until 1935, but Ross never worked for the club again. "You got out just in time," longtime Braves player Johnny Cooney told him in 1963.

There were almost 20 more years of lean times ahead for the Braves, who'd win the National League pennant in Boston in 1948 but move to Milwaukee in 1953, and then to Atlanta in 1966. As for the Bruins, they were about to become a powerhouse.

# 23

# A BIG YEAR
# IN BOSTON

During the summer of 1928, while Art Ross was travelling with the Boston Braves, a huge new arena was rising over the old North Station of the Boston & Maine Railway on Causeway Street near Boston's North End. Backed by Tex Rickard, impresario of Madison Square Garden in New York, the facility was originally called Boston Madison Square Garden, but would soon be known simply as the Boston Garden. By October, Ross was busily assembling the Bruins team that would call this new rink home.

One year earlier, before the 1927–28 season, the Bruins had carefully worked future hall of famer Dit Clapper into the lineup and introduced Dutch Gainor as well. Ross had also acquired Ralph "Cooney" Weiland during the 1927–28 season, but the former Memorial Cup champion with the Owen Sound Greys had been playing in Minneapolis since 1924–25 and finished out the 1927–28 season with the Millers before joining the Bruins in 1928–29. Another future hall of famer, Weiland was soon centring Clapper and Gainor on a combination the *Boston Globe* called "The Dynamite Trio" but is better known as "The Dynamite Line."

There doesn't seem to have been any formal relationship between the teams in Boston and Minneapolis, but an awful lot of Canadian-born players moved between the Bruins and the Millers in this era. Cecil "Tiny" Thompson — yet another future hall of famer — was one of them. Ross claimed to have bought Thompson sight unseen after he'd posted spectacular numbers in Minneapolis, and the new netminder was on hand when the Bruins began a pre-season conditioning stint in the gymnasium at Boston's University Club on October 25, 1928. Thompson would battle Hal Winkler for the Bruins goaltending job.

Seventeen players were expected for the team's opening workout. Eddie Shore was late. He'd rejected two contract offers from the Bruins before finally accepting a third. Terms of his new deal weren't announced, but Shore was entering his third season in the NHL and was already established as the league's best defenceman. If he was not yet the league's best-paid player, he soon would be, and was likely paid $10,000 or $11,000 in 1928–29. Getting a late start from his farm in Alberta, Shore didn't show up in Boston until October 29. Sprague Cleghorn wouldn't be there at all. He was now coaching the Newark Bulldogs of the Can-Am Hockey League, and he hadn't left Boston happily.

During the 1926–27 season, both Art Ross and Charles Adams had made promises to Cleghorn. When rumours spread in mid December of 1926 about a possible trade, Ross told reporters: "I want every club to know that Sprague will never be sold or traded by us. When he is forced to quit actual play, he can have a bench job with the Bruins if he wants it." Adams made a similar statement in January of 1927, saying Cleghorn "will remain with the Bruins until he is 50, unless he wants to better himself."

Cleghorn had a very specific recollection of a promise he received from Ross during the 1927–28 season. "He assured me," Cleghorn said in 1935, "that in the event of my sale to another club, he would do his best to see to it that I received the amount of the purchase price." Cleghorn admits there was no written agreement to that effect, or anything in his Boston contract. "It was a verbal understanding."

Whether he'd found a way to better himself, or whether the Bruins decided to part ways despite the kind words, Boston asked waivers on Cleghorn in June of 1928. They sold him that fall to Newark for $5,000. "I believed myself entitled to receive that amount from Boston," Cleghorn said, "and I so believe to this day." He never saw a cent of it. "That is why Art Ross and Sprague Cleghorn, close friends for twenty-five years, today just say 'hello' as they pass."

This would not be the only long-time friend whose relationship with Ross ended badly, but business was business and Ross already seemed to have another veteran player in mind for the Bruins. He'd selected Francis Xavier "Moose" Goheen in a draft of minor league talent at an NHL meeting on May 12, 1928, but Goheen, who is still considered one of the greatest American hockey players in history, wanted big money to leave his native Minnesota and his job with Northern States Power. Ross refused to meet his demands; instead, he replaced Cleghorn's veteran presence (though minus the violence, and at forward instead of defence) with long-time Ottawa Senators star Cy Denneny. Denneny signed up for part-time duty on the ice (it would be his final season as a player), and worked with Ross as his assistant (though he is sometimes incorrectly credited with being the coach).

With the Boston Garden not yet complete — and apparently no ice at the Arena — the Bruins had nowhere to practise when they opened training camp. After engaging in exercises at the University Club for a week, Ross completed arrangements to use the rink in Providence, Rhode Island, beginning on November 1. Eighteen players were bussed an hour or so each way between Boston and Providence for daily two-hour practices until Ross and the 15 players who made the cut (only 12 would be allowed to dress) left for Pittsburgh on November 14 and the first game of the season the following night. The situation wasn't great, but one week into the practices, Ross proclaimed that his squad was looking better every day. By the end of training camp he was convinced the team was stronger than the previous year's version and would be in the thick of the fight all the way.

Ross decided to open the season with both Tiny Thompson and Hal Winkler on his 15-man roster. Winkler was battling a cold, so Thompson got the opening start against Pittsburgh and earned a shutout in his first NHL game. Still, it took a goal from Dit Clapper at 7:30 of overtime for the Bruins to score a 1–0 victory. After a 2–2 tie in Ottawa two nights later, the Bruins returned to Boston for their first game at the Garden on November 20, 1928.

By the time the Boston Garden closed 67 years later, it was considered small and cramped, hot and smelly, and completely out of date. Its undersized rink dimensions of 191 by 83 feet had become a huge advantage to the home team over the years, but it had barely earned a comment when the building opened, except to note that the surface was slightly smaller than what the Bruins had played on in the Boston Arena. (The NHL regulation of 200 by 85 was not added to the rule book until 1929–30.) When it opened to much acclaim with lavish ceremonies and a boxing card on November 17, 1928, the Boston Garden was state of the art.

Tex Rickard had built the Garden with boxing in mind, say Stewart Richardson and Richard Leblanc, authors of *Dit: Dit Clapper and the Rise of the Boston Bruins*, and he "wanted the seats of the new venue to be close enough so that every spectator could see the sweat on the boxers' brows, and they nearly all could." Seats practically hung from the walls and for hockey, the front row of the upper balcony was almost directly over the ice. There were separate entrances taking those who could afford the more expensive seats directly to the main floor or the first balcony. "Less prosperous patrons," writes Michael Hiam, "the ones with cheap passes for open seats, had their own entryways, which led them via a labyrinth of ramps and stairwells to a pair of second balconies situated almost within touching distance of the rafters." These seats became home to the Garden's famous Gallery Gods, who thundered their approval of the home team for decades and heaped abuse — and sometimes garbage — upon the visitors.

For the first game, and for many years afterwards, Charles Adams continued a tradition he'd begun at the Boston Arena of holding back a block of inexpensive seats for sale on the night of the game. The last 1,500 tickets went on sale for just 50¢ apiece at 7:00 pm for the 8:15 start. Newspapers claimed the Garden could accommodate 14,500 for hockey, but that if every single ticket was sold, "500 standing room admissions in the first balcony will be sold for $1 each." John Hallahan, writing in the *Boston Globe* the next day, claimed that a crowd of almost 16,000 stormed their way in. His use of the word "storm" was no accident, as the hockey-mad crowd literally broke down the doors of the Garden when they were late in opening. "It was a riot, a mob scene, a re-enactment of the assault on the Bastille," wrote Stanley Woodward in the *Boston Herald*. To fans in Boston, hockey was already "bread and butter and beer to them, not caviar and champagne, and they reacted accordingly," said Neil D. Isaacs in his 1977 book *Checking Back: A History of the National Hockey League*.

To the large crowd's disappointment, the Bruins were beaten 1–0 by the Montreal Canadiens that night, dropping their record to 1–1–1 on the young season. By the end of November they were 2–2–2 and not looking nearly as strong as Ross had promised. Goaltending didn't seem to be the problem, as Thompson — who'd played every game — allowed just six goals while the team scored only five. Hal Winkler was soon loaned to Minneapolis, and Ross never had any reason to regret hanging on to Thompson. He gave the Bruins 10 great seasons and won the Vezina Trophy four times. But something more had to be done to shake up the team, and on December 20, 1928, Ross traded Frank Fredrickson to Pittsburgh.

Fredrickson, who loved Boston, and whose family was happy there, claimed that his relationship with Ross had never been the same after the Billy Coutu/Jerry Laflamme incident. He also claimed that Ross began using him less and less after a ridiculous story appeared in the *Boston Herald* saying that Fredrickson would take over the running of the Bruins. Fredrickson did become a player-coach with the Pirates in 1929–30, but at the time he was dealt for Mickey MacKay and cash (Fredrickson told Stan Fischler it was $10,000 while the *Boston Globe* at the time says only that it wasn't the $12,000 reported elsewhere) it appears to have been merely a trade of two aging stars whose offensive production was no longer near what it once was. The Bruins were only 5–7–2 through the end of December, but the biggest reason the team's fortunes finally began to turn around in January of 1929 had little to do with this deal; it was the improving play of the Dynamite Trio as the team's second line, and the powerful presence of Eddie Shore.

Two of the most famous incidents involving Art Ross and Eddie Shore occurred during the 1928–29 season. The first involves Myles Lane, a Boston-area sports star who made the then-rare jump from American college hockey to the NHL that year to play for the New York Rangers after three stellar seasons at Dartmouth.

With the Bruins struggling to start the season, Colonel Hammond thought the box-office appeal of a homegrown player might interest the Bruins and instructed Lester Patrick to send a telegram to Art Ross suggesting they trade Lane for Eddie Shore. Ross's reply has become a hockey legend: "You are so many Myles from Shore you need a life preserver."

Some versions of this story have the words a little bit different, and some say the exchange occurred between Hammond and Charles Adams, but Dick Patrick — grandson of Lester and a longtime part-owner and president of the Washington Capitals — grew up hearing the story in his family and always heard it with Ross and his grandfather. The Bruins would later acquire Lane from the Rangers on January 22, 1929, but for a straight purchase of $7,500.

The second story involves Shore missing the Bruins' train from Boston to Montreal the day after a 1–0 victory at home over Ottawa on January 1, 1929, and before their January 3 game against the Maroons. Shore was desperate to make it to Montreal for the game, but the next train wouldn't get him there on time and a call to the airport revealed that the runway in Montreal had been closed due to a storm. Shore hired a car for $100. "It was a lot of money," he said, "but I figured it would cost me twice as much if I didn't show," as Ross had imposed fines on any player who missed the team train.

Shore made a harrowing overnight journey through New Hampshire's White Mountains in a blizzard and arrived in Montreal a few hours before the game exhausted and frost-bitten. Once there, he ate a couple of steaks and then took a quick nap. When he awoke, he insisted on playing. Games between the Maroons and Bruins were always rough — games between the Maroons and anyone were always rough — and Ross thought Shore was in no condition to play. "I know how durable Shore is," Ross said to himself. "But after all, there's a limit to human endurance." Ross decided to let him start, but "at his first sign of weakness or sleepwalking on skates off he goes to the dressing-room, to stay!" He didn't want Shore hurting the team or getting himself badly injured, but he needn't have worried. Shore played brilliantly, and scored the only goal in a 1–0 Bruins win. Whether or not Ross upheld his standing fine is uncertain.

The Bruins posted 10 wins and two ties during the 12 games they played in January after Shore's overnight drive. The streak brought them neck and neck with the New York Rangers for top spot in the American Division standings.

Two other acquisitions made by the Bruins in January also helped the team's turnaround. The second one came on January 25, 1929, and proves that no matter how bad the personal relationship got between Art Ross and Conn Smythe, business was still business.

Bill Carson had been a star under Smythe at the University of Toronto and was a top scorer with the Maple Leafs. He was struggling and unhappy during the 1928–29 season, so Smythe sold him to the Bruins — making him the second hockey-playing dentist in franchise history. The other player Boston acquired in January was George Owen, whom they picked up a couple of weeks before the Carson sale. Owen's signing is yet another one of the possible explanations of the hatred between Smythe and Ross.

George Owen was born in Hamilton, Ontario, on December 2, 1901, but moved with his family to the Boston suburb of Newton, Massachusetts when he was five years old. Owen first gained attention as a hockey player at Newton High School from 1915 to 1919, and then starred at Harvard from 1919 to 1923. He was equally talented at baseball and football, winning nine varsity letters in all. Hockey was the sport Owen loved best, but he turned down repeated offers to turn pro after graduation. As a Harvard man, Owen had likely been conditioned to believe that professional sports were beneath him. He continued to play hockey on several of the top amateur teams in Boston while pursuing a career in banking, but Ross kept after him. "[He] was always on my neck saying, 'How about it, George,'" said Owen.

During the 1928–29 season *Boston Transcript* writer A. Linde Fowler was lobbying in his newspaper for the Bruins to sign Owen. Weston Adams, who'd recently graduated from Harvard himself and had played goalie on the university hockey team, was working behind the scenes on behalf of Ross and his father, Charles Adams, to land Owen for the Bruins. Despite all this, the local star may well have wound up in Toronto if not for a chance encounter between George Owen Sr. and Art Ross.

In a 1986 interview with Richard Johnson of the Sports Museum in Boston, Owen admitted it was Smythe who finally convinced him to turn pro. They were to meet on Tuesday, January 8, 1929, to iron out a contract while the Maple Leafs were in Boston to face the Bruins. When Owen Sr. ran into Ross that Monday and told him the news, Ross moved quickly, working out a deal with Owen that night. Smythe learned about it when he arrived in Boston the next day and read the story in a newspaper.

According to Michael Hiam, Charles Adams told the press he was willing to pay Owen $12,000 with an $8,000 bonus if the Bruins won the Stanley Cup — though Hiam believes these lofty figures were probably just a publicity stunt. When Owen wrote a column for the *Boston Globe* a few days later explaining his reasons for finally going pro, he said of the money: "I don't for a minute deny that the financial consideration played a part, because it certainly did. I have discovered in this present-day world of ours one can always find use for a few extra dollars." But he never said what he was being paid.

Owen suited up for Boston right away, facing Toronto in the January 8 game and playing defence alongside Eddie Shore. Lionel Hitchman was out with an injury, so Shore and Owen played almost the entire game. The only time Owen was off the ice was when he served a two-minute penalty for tripping during the first period. He scored the final goal late in the third as the Bruins downed the Maple Leafs 5–2 and was hailed in Boston as the star of the game.

Boston fans loved having a local star to cheer for, and Owen helped to attract a good deal more of the caviar-and-champagne crowd. He did his part in the team's turnaround too. In the 17 games before his signing, the Bruins were 8–7–2. With Owen playing in all 27 remaining games in 1928–29, the team was 18–6–3. They finished the season with a record of 26–13–5 for 57 points, trailing only the Montreal Canadiens in the overall standings and beating the Rangers by five points for their second straight American Division title. "Owen has been a wonderful acquisition," said Ross after the season, adding that his love of the game was a big help to the team and a value beyond just being a good hockey player.

The NHL featured a new playoff format in the spring of 1929. Charles Adams and Art Ross had created it. With a few tweaks over the years, it would essentially remain in place until the 1942–43 season — although it looks awfully strange from a modern perspective.

The format basically created a two-tier playoff. It seems to have been born from the fact that in 1927–28, both division champions were eliminated by second-place teams, who then played each other for the Stanley Cup. Now, the first-place team in the Canadian Division would face the first-place team in the American Division in a best-of-five series with the winner to advance directly to the Stanley Cup Final. "The change in the rules," reported the *Montreal Gazette* on September 24, 1928, "guarantees that at least one of the teams winning the top rung at the end of the scheduled series will be assured of a place in the [Final]." Of course, it also guaranteed that one team would be eliminated! Meanwhile, the two second-place clubs would face each other in a two-game, total-goals series, as would the two third-place clubs. The winners of those series would then play each other in a best-of-three to decide the other Stanley Cup finalist.

Under this new format, the Bruins opened the playoffs at home for two games against the Canadiens, with however many of the next three games were necessary to be played in Montreal. Game one was a tame affair with Boston getting out front on a first-period goal from Cooney Weiland. A Canadiens goal in the second period was called back on an offside, and with the three-man rotation of Shore, Hitchman, and Owen playing strong defence and the Boston forwards backchecking brilliantly, Tiny Thompson let nothing else get past him in a 1–0 Bruins victory. With more than 16,000 fans jamming the Boston Garden once again, game two was much rougher, but the results were the same. Thompson was unbeatable and Boston won 1–0. The Dynamite Trio struck again, with Weiland scoring another first-period goal when he picked up the rebound of a Dutch Gainor shot and put it past George Hainsworth with the Canadiens a man short.

Eddie Shore was the hero in game three, ignoring the boos of the Forum faithful as the Bruins completed a series sweep. After the Canadiens took a 2–0 lead in the first period, Shore set up the first Boston goal and later scored the winner to cap a three-goal second that gave the Bruins a 3–2 victory. When the final bell sounded, Canadiens star Howie Morenz skated over to the Bruins bench to praise their coach and manager. "Art, I want to congratulate you. You have a wonderful team." To this, Ross replied, "You are a great hockey team."

The Bruins spent that Saturday night in Montreal, returning to Boston the following evening. A crowd of 3,000 fans turned out at the North Station to greet them. Bells rang and the crowd cheered each player as they made their way from the train to waiting taxicabs on the street. The biggest cheers were for Eddie Shore. "[I]t was the first time that a hockey team representing Boston has been given such a reception," wrote John Hallahan in the *Boston Globe*. "Heretofore only the Olympic athletes of 1896 and World Series baseball champions have been accorded such a tribute."

Something else that Hallahan wrote in his March 25 story will be of interest to hockey historians who like to debate how quickly the challenge era of the Stanley Cup ended after the agreement between the NHA and the PCHA was signed in the fall of 1913. "It is not generally understood," the *Globe* writer told his readers, "that the Bruins [have already] won the historic Canadian trophy but, as winners of the interdivisional series, they have that honor, under a ruling by Pres Frank Calder of the National Hockey League." However, "according to the rules that govern playoffs this season, [the Bruins] are forced to meet the winner of the other playoffs in a series of two out of three games in a challenge round."

When the Rangers beat the Maple Leafs in overtime the following night to sweep their best-of-three semifinal, it set up the first all-American Stanley Cup Final in hockey history — and added a little more confusion to who would actually be defending the Stanley Cup. "Pres Calder of the National Hockey League says the Bruins won the Stanley Cup by beating Les Canadiens," reconfirmed the *Globe* on March 26 in the "Live Tips and Topics" column compiled by a writer known only as Sportsman. But, "over in New York they proclaim the Rangers as holders of the trophy until they are eliminated from the 1929 series." So, where is the Cup right now?"

The Bruins quickly eliminated any confusion as to the rightful champion, or whether or not there might have to be two different names engraved if the Rangers — who'd lost five of six games to Ross's team during the regular season — pulled off an upset. A crowd of 15,000 filled the Boston Garden on Thursday night, March 28 for game one. They saw Dit Clapper and Dutch Gainor score goals, while Tiny Thompson made 22 saves for this third shutout in four games. The Bruins won the Stanley Cup opener 2–0. With the circus due to move into Madison Square Garden on Saturday and a women's indoor track and field meet set for the Boston Garden that same night, the hockey schedule was compressed, with game two played in New York on Friday. Both teams left Boston on late-night trains after Thursday's game, but while the Rangers arrived home bleary-eyed and tired in the early-morning hours, Art Ross had the Bruins' Pullman car disconnected in New Haven so the team could get a full night's sleep.

Whether or not the travel plans helped, the Bruins swept the series with a 2–1 victory. Harry Oliver was the star of the game, scoring the first goal and setting up Doc Carson for the game winner with just under two minutes remaining.

"The Bruins are on top of the hockey world and there are no more worlds to conquer," said Sportsman. "Great credit is due the boys piloted by Art Ross. They filled every demand made on them, came from behind to win their division title, then cleaned up both the Canadiens and the Rangers.... Now the National League season is over so farewell to a real championship team and good luck to the Bruins next season."

# PRACTICE DOESN'T
# QUITE MAKE PERFECT

The Bruins ended the 1928–29 season in style. Three days after winning the Stanley Cup, owner Charles Adams held a banquet for the team at Boston's Copley Plaza Hotel. In addition to the bonus money promised to players in their contracts, and the pool of playoff money from the NHL to which they were entitled, Adams gave each player an additional $500 in gold. The players, in return, presented Adams with a bronze statue of a bear, and gave Art Ross a new set of golf clubs. "Manager Ross spoke of each and every player, praising them for the manner in which they went about their work," reported the *Boston Globe* on April 3. Two in particular were singled out, with Ross announcing, "that he considered Tiny Thompson, expert goalie, the most valuable man on the team, and next to him, Eddie Shore."

Both Shore and Thompson had enjoyed brilliant seasons. Shore finished third in voting for the Hart Trophy as NHL MVP for the second season in a row, but the fact that Ross considered Thompson (who didn't even finish among the top five in the league vote) as his team's MVP was indicative of a problem the NHL's newest rule change hoped to fix. The problem was that goal scoring had continued to decline, hitting an all-time low in 1928–29 when teams combined to average just 2.8 goals per game. That meant the average score each night was less than 2–1! Thompson led the league with 26 wins during the 44-game regular season (he'd seen action in every one of his team's games, as had eight of ten NHL netminders this year), and added five more wins, three shutouts, and a 0.60 average in five playoff games. But Thompson's 12 shutouts and 1.15 goals-against average during the regular season were nowhere near the numbers put up by George Hainsworth. The Canadiens goaltender set records during the 1928–29 season that will never be matched, with 22 shutouts and a goals-against average of 0.92! None of the 10 NHL team's starters had an average higher than 1.85 during the season, and Toronto's Ace Bailey was the league's top scorer with just 22 goals and 10 assists in 44 games. Clearly, something had to be done.

Complaints about the lack of scoring had been common since the 1926–27 season. On February 21, 1927, sports editor Frederick Wilson of the *Globe* in Toronto noted a suggestion made in New York to widen the nets to seven feet, as well as reports from Montreal and Chicago advocating plans to do away with goaltenders. "Hockey is a great game," Wilson quotes Albion Holden, the Chicago-based editor of *Big Ten Weekly*, "but the importance of the goaltender is out of proportion to that of any other player in any other sport." Holden further opines that, "two or three goals a game out of a hundred shots or so is not the proper proportion" and that, "basketball wouldn't be a popular game if each team had a goaltender sitting on the basket to sweep aside all but two or thee shots in each game."

Presumably those championing the removal of goalies also planned on shrinking the nets to basketball-like sizes, but fortunately, cooler heads prevailed. When Art Ross and the rules committee presented their recommendations after the 1928–29 season, their plan to increase scoring called for forward passing by either team everywhere on the ice. The rule change — which had been adopted by the PCHA back in 1922–23 — was passed at the NHL's semi-annual meeting in New York on September 28, 1929. The league was not yet ready for long passes from deep inside the defensive zone, through the neutral zone, and all the way to the far blue line, although what modern commentators usually refer to as "stretch passes" today were discussed quite often over the next few years. Forward passing, as it had been out west, was therefore restricted to within each zone and not allowed across the blue lines. Among other new rules, players would be allowed to kick the puck in every zone, although then, as now, a goal would be waved off if an offensive player kicked the puck in. The anti-defence rule allowing no more than a goalie and two players to hang back when the puck was up ice was also to be more strictly enforced. Still, forward passing was the key innovation, though it would take one more tweak in midseason to truly modernize it. In the meantime, Ross planned to ensure that his Bruins were ready to play the more wide-open style, even if that meant changing his usual approach to coaching.

* * *

Harry Sinden held many of the same jobs in Boston that Art Ross did. When Sinden joined the Bruins in the early 1960s, he loved to talk about the old days with local legend Milt Schmidt. "When I'd ask him, he didn't always have good things to say about the old-time players, even those considered to be all-time greats." Sinden wouldn't say which players Schmidt bad-mouthed, but did say that, "he thought Art Ross was a really great coach. Milt thought Ross was a really tough individual to deal with, but he liked that, because he was tough himself."

Ross had a few pet peeves as a coach. "He would not allow us to slap the puck," Schmidt himself remembers. "He'd say, 'If you slap your shots you'll slap your passes and they'll be difficult to handle.'" He also believed that defencemen should leave the shooting to the forwards. When Eddie Shore was asked to compare himself to Bobby Orr in 1970, he told reporters it would have cost him too much money to win the scoring title, as Orr was about to do. "You see, when I carried the puck in, if I shot instead of passing, Art Ross had a standing fine of $500." Ross, on the other hand, had claimed in a story in 1958 that he could give Shore a signal allowing him to score at will.

As to his coaching style, Sinden's impression from Schmidt was that Ross "could really 'game manage.'" Schmidt says, "I think Ross was one of the smartest guys behind the bench. He was excellent at playing one line against the other." But when it came to fundamentals, Ross was "only so-so." Then again, "fundamentals weren't impressed in those days as they are today," says Schmidt.

Milt Schmidt didn't encounter Ross's coaching style first hand until later in the 1930s, but stories about Bruins practices from earlier in the decade make it clear that little had changed. "Ross does not have much teaching to do," wrote Art Siegel around 1930, when he was the hockey editor at the *Boston Herald*. "Fundamentals are taught through competition. Fundamentals are taught through experience. Every practice is a test of speed, of skill, of wits." Veterans were expected to help the newcomers, and in his biography of Eddie Shore, Michael Hiam writes that Shore would sometimes take it upon himself to coach his teammates — even after Ross thought he was going too far and threatened to fine him for doing so.

When he'd been a player, Ross had kept himself in great shape. As a coach and general manager, he expected the same from his players, but it appears he was not a stickler for hard work in practice. When Ed Sandford joined the Bruins in 1947 as part of a post-Second World War youth movement, he thought Ross was still trying to run his young team the way he'd run his great old clubs. "We didn't practise a lot," Sandford remembers. "He'd say, 'Don't waste yourself in practice,' but ... I thought we should practise [more]."

Ross told a similar story about those times in a 1962 interview with the *Boston Globe*'s Harold Kaese. Ross recalled the players' complaining about lack of practices, so he told Dit Clapper, who was coaching the team, to, "get 'em out on the ice twice a day and work 'em hard for an hour." Ross remembered the players gloating when they won the next game, but "then we lost the next five, showing them that as long as they were in shape, it was better not to leave their game on the practice ice."

The approach of the 1929–30 season marked at least one time when Ross felt differently about practice. He'd kept his Stanley Cup team virtually intact, with only Cy Denneny and a few other veterans gone. Ross wanted his team working extra hard in their pre-season practices, not just because they were defending champions but because of the new passing rules.

Even before the September 28 meeting that introduced the new rules, Ross planned to bring the Bruins together early. He hoped to have the whole team in Boston by October 14 — a full month before the start of the season — for a week of workouts in the gym before getting on the ice on October 22. As it turned out, the team didn't gather until October 28, working out with medicine balls and doing some general conditioning for about 30 minutes before hitting the ice at the Boston Arena to begin passing drills and to take shots at Tiny Thompson.

The Bruins practised for two hours a day for the next two-and-a-half weeks as they prepared for the upcoming season. On the evening of November 6, 1929, the team held an open practice at the Boston Arena to demonstrate the new forward passing rules for local fans. About 3,000 turned up. Goalie Herb Rheaume was borrowed from the Boston Tigers so the Bruins could play a true scrimmage game. It lasted 40 minutes, and nine goals were scored! Obviously, things were going to be different this season.

For several years, Ross had maintained a policy of playing no exhibition games during training camp. However, with the new rules, Ross wanted to give the Bruins a chance to play under actual game conditions, so on Saturday, November 9, he took the team to Philadelphia to face the Arrows of the Can-Am league. Boston lost 4–3, but Ross was said to be satisfied with his team.

On November 13, the Bruins left for Detroit, where they opened the season the following night. The game was tied at 2–2 through the first 20 minutes before Boston pulled away for a 5–2 victory. The general consensus was that Boston was in better shape, but as to who was better with the new rules, the jury seems split. One news service reported that, "the Bruins apparently knew the trick system frontward and backward," but the *Montreal Gazette* claimed, "the Cougars made much better use of the three-zone forward pass system than the champions."

When the Bruins won their next three in a row, it became clear they'd learned the new rules well. "It was Ross, aided by Les Patrick of the Rangers, who devised this new game," reported the *Daily Sun* of Lewiston, Maine, on November 21, "… so it is only natural to expect a Ross coached team would be the first to master the new game." By

December 15, 1929, the Bruins were 10–2–0 and four points clear of the next best teams in the overall standings. But everything wasn't perfect.

Two days earlier, newspapers in Toronto (where nobody seemed to like the new rules) reported on dispatches out of Boston claiming that Ross and the Bruins were now in favour of reverting to the old rules. That seems unlikely, although Ross had probably come to the conclusion — as many others had — that the new passing rule was in need of an important adjustment. At this point in the 1929–30 season, scoring was up a whopping four goals-per-game (to 6.91) from 1928–29. Forward passing seemed to be working a little too well!

The way the rule had been written, the puck could not be passed across the blue line into the offensive zone, but there was nothing to stop a player from crossing the blue line ahead of the puck. He could take up a position in front of the net and wait for a teammate to bring the puck into the zone and pass it to him. The *Ottawa Citizen* referred to the situation as being "similar to a 'basket hanger' in basketball." In the words of a different generation, the current rule encouraged goal sucking … and Boston's Cooney Weiland was among the best at it.

To remedy the situation, the NHL made a slight alteration at a governors' meeting in Chicago on December 16. Coming into effect on December 21, 1929, a new rule stated that no attacking player could precede the puck across the blue line into the other team's zone. With that, the modern offside rule was born.

The Bruins beat Ottawa 6–2 in their final game under the old rules on December 17, and then defeated Chicago 4–1 in their first game under the new one on December 21. Ross continued to drill the players on passing in practice, making sure they developed effective techniques for scoring under the new system. The team responded by running its winning streak to 14 straight. After two losses in their next three games, the Bruins rattled off 17 in a row without a defeat, winning 16 and tying one. Clearly, the team had adapted!

Exploiting another new rule that let teams use 15 players in a game instead of just 12, Ross often used three forward lines over the course of the season. Even in his days as a player with 9- and 10-man rosters,

Ross had been a proponent of unlimited substitutions at any time, and as many times, as necessary. Now Charles Querrie, writing in the *Toronto Star* on November 13, 1929, made it seem that Ross had invented a new, three-line tactic and planned to use his lines evenly. Neither claim is true. Odie Cleghorn is generally credited with introducing two set forward lines to the NHL as coach in Pittsburgh in 1925–26 and hockey historian Iain Fyffe notes that Cleghorn occasionally used nine forwards that season — not that he ever rolled three lines evenly. Chicago, however — with no true stars beyond goalie Charlie Gardiner, but a lot of depth — also began using three lines in 1929–30, and probably rotated them more evenly than the Bruins did that year.

In terms of who usually started the games in Boston, the combination of Harry Oliver at right wing, Percy Galbraith on the left, and originally Doc Carson, and then newcomer Marty Barry, at centre was considered the team's first line. They saw most of the action against other team's best forwards. The third line used a variety of players, including Barry, Carson, Mickey MacKay, and George Owen, who split his time between forward and defence during the season as Ross relied heavily on Shore and Hitchman. The second line was the Dynamite Trio, and they did most of the scoring. By season's end, Cooney Weiland had 43 goals in 44 games. His 30 assists gave him 73 points, which shattered the previous record of 51 set by Howie Morenz two years earlier. Right winger Dit Clapper scored 41 times, while left winger Dutch Gainor had 18 goals and finished second in the NHL with 31 assists. (The Rangers' Frank Boucher led with 36.) Tiny Thompson's goals-against average jumped from 1.15 to 2.19, but that number was the best by far in the NHL.

In a year in which no other team won more than 23 games, the Bruins went 38–5–1 for 77 points out of a possible 88. Their winning percentage of .875 remains the best in NHL history. To put Boston's 1929–30 season into perspective, consider that the record 132 points posted by the Montreal Canadiens when they went 60–8–12 in 1976–77 equals only an .825 winning percentage, while Detroit's record-setting 62 wins (62–13–7, 131 points) in 1995–96 produced only a mark of .799. To better Boston's record in a modern 82-game season, a team would have to get 144 points!

As the playoffs neared, Michael Hiam writes that Ross began sneaking movie cameras in to other NHL arenas to spy on potential opponents. He also filmed his own players to better study their various flaws, but "picking out the weak spots of the Boston Bruins is just about as difficult as forecasting the probable evolution of mankind," said former fan favourite Frank Fredrickson, who was now the player-coach of the Pittsburgh Pirates.

"Art Ross," continued Fredrickson, "backed by the owner of the Boston Bruins, Mr. C.F. Adams, has gathered under his wing an aggregation of hockey stars who have displayed this season, beyond question of doubt, a brand of hockey that will place them on a pedestal for many years to come." Bruins captain Lionel Hitchman also gave tribute to his bosses: "Due credit must be given to Mr. Adams for his liberality and determination to build up a world's championship team for Boston," said Hitchman. "A big share must [also] be allotted to Art Ross.... Art is the boss. He commands and directs the club through the playing season and brooks no interference.... Art Ross demands and secures co-operation. Strict discipline rules this club, its value recognized and respected by all the players.... [His] sense to recognize hockey ability and how to place it in position and develop it is responsible for the results obtained by this really great club."

Hitchman, who played the latter part of the season with a broken jaw, said that the team was "an optimistic crew" and that "over the rough, turbulent, and uncertain hockey season," the Bruins were convinced they were good enough to win the Stanley Cup again. Fredrickson thought so too, but added: "it is always unwise to make predictions for fear that the unexpected may occur."

The truth was, that for weeks prior to the end of the NHL season, there were those who believed that if the Maroons won the Canadian Division and met Boston to open the playoffs (which they did), the team that survived this best-of five series would be too beaten up to defeat anyone in the best-of-three Stanley Cup Final. The bad blood between the two teams had only gotten worse over the course of the season, and when Boston defeated the Maroons three games to one, the physical series did indeed take its toll. The wounded Bruins could only get in a couple of light workouts in their four days off before taking on the Canadiens for the Cup. Dutch Gainor would be unable to play at all, breaking up the powerful Dynamite combination.

When the Final opened at the Boston Garden on April 1, 1930, it marked the Canadiens' fifth game in 10 nights. With a triple overtime game and a quadruple one among those, it was as if they'd actually played six full games, not just four. But instead of appearing tired, the Canadiens seemed to be in peak condition, while the Bruins had gone stale. Boston lost the first game 3–0.

Facing elimination in the short series two nights later at the Forum, Ross assured everyone that his team would make a fight for it, but the Bruins still seemed dazed. They trailed 3–0 midway through the game and were down 4–1 entering the third period before Ross's shouts from the bench finally aroused the signs of life he'd promised. Goals by Percy Galbraith and Dit Clapper got Boston close, but then a goal to tie the game in the dying seconds was called back. The red light flashed, but referee George Mallinson wiped out the goal. The Bruins maintained that it was good and that Marty Barry had scored it, only to have the puck immediately bounce out of the Art Ross net, strike Weiland's skate, and bounce back in again. Barry and the Canadiens' Howie Morenz were sent to the penalty box for fighting about it, but unlike 1927 there would be no attack on the referee. The Bruins accepted their stunning defeat gracefully. Ross and Hitchman even visited the Canadiens dressing room after the game to congratulate them. It was the first time all season that Boston had lost two games in a row, and the huge upset is usually cited as the reason why the NHL went back to a best-of-five Final the following season.

Lester Patrick attributed Boston's shocking loss to stress. "Art Ross's great team had something to shoot at in the finals," he explained. "First, they were defenders of the Stanley Cup. Next, they created such a remarkable record during the regular season.... The players just had to win, and consequently were under too great a strain to beat the Canadiens." The sports reporter for *Time* magazine chose to credit the Canadiens' defensive tactics, and the brilliant play of Howie Morenz, who "seemed to be in a thousand places at once, shooting oftener than anyone else, checking back like a lightning bolt."

Art Ross himself offered little in the way of a post-mortem, as the Bruins left Montreal immediately for the West Coast. They relaxed briefly in Banff, Alberta, before playing a series of exhibition games against minor-pro teams in Vancouver, San Francisco, Oakland, and Los Angeles, as well as against the Chicago Black Hawks, who were also touring California. It was a good way to forget the disappointing end that ruined a spectacular season.

# BATTLING THE
# GREAT DEPRESSION

According to a column by Harold Kaese in the *Boston Evening Transcript* on January 31, 1941, the Stanley Cup champion Bruins net a record profit of $200,660 in their first year at the Boston Garden in 1928–29. Then they netted $202,317 in 1929–30. The Bruins were the best team in the NHL again in 1930–31, but they weren't nearly as dominant on the ice or at the box office. Boston finished 28–10–6 for 62 points, which was 11 points up on Chicago for top spot in the American Division but just two ahead of the Montreal Canadiens who were easy winners in the Canadian division.

Goal scoring dropped dramatically in the 1930–31 season. It was nowhere near as low as in 1928–29, but not nearly has high as it had been in 1929–30. The worry over goal scoring was such that an experiment was tried in Toronto. From late January until the season's end in early March, the Toronto Mercantile League was given permission from the Ontario Hockey Association and the Canadian Amateur Hockey Association to use nets that measured seven-and-a-half feet wide. The results were mixed, with many games still ending in 2–0 or 3–1 scores but some that were 10–5 or more.

Though the NHL kept apprised of the experiment, it's unlikely that Art Ross saw any of the wide-net games in Toronto. Still, he did give his thoughts on the experiment to *Boston Traveler* hockey editor Ralph Clifford. "Adhere to the rules," Ross said. "Have them strictly enforced, especially the anti-defence rule, and you will have a game that is wide open enough to satisfy the most exacting fan."

The Bruins won the American Division title for the fourth year in a row in 1930–31 and faced the Montreal Canadiens in the opening round of the playoffs. It was a tight series, with four of the five games decided by a single goal, including the last one, which the Canadiens won 3–2 in overtime to eliminate Boston once again. Montreal then went on to win the Stanley Cup for the second year in a row.

Game two in the Bruins-Canadiens series featured an interesting moment. With under a minute to go in a game Boston trailed 1–0, there was a faceoff deep in the Montreal end. Even though Boston was a man short with George Owen in the penalty box, Art Ross took a gamble. The *Boston Globe* is rather nonchalant about it (and says the player involved was Red Beattie), but the *Montreal Gazette* provides the details: "As the referee was about to face the puck, the crowd first gasped and then applauded as Tiny Thompson skated to the bench and [Art] Chapman came on." There were now five forwards — or Eddie Shore and four forwards, depending on the report — in the Montreal zone with an empty net in the Boston end. "It was a daring move and the Bruins kept the Frenchmen hemmed in, but the gong sounded before there was any score." The huge crowd of 16,500 moved dejectedly out of the Boston Garden, "having witnessed a move that made history in an NHL series, but failed to gain the victory."

Ross pulling Thompson in the game does seem to be an NHL first. It's often attributed to Ross as an all-time hockey first, but it isn't. Minnesota hockey historian Roger Godin notes a March 26, 1929, story in the *St. Paul Pioneer Press* describing coach Lloyd Turner of the Minneapolis Millers having removed Hal Winkler from the net during a playoff loss to the St. Paul Saints the night before. Frank Patrick may have preceded even that move by a few years in pulling Hugh Lehman during Vancouver games in the Pacific Coast Hockey Association.

After a disappointing end to another season, the Bruins suffered through a horrible year in 1931–32. The Dynamite Line had been broken up with the trade of Dutch Gainor to the Rangers prior to the season — though Marty Barry had already begun seeing action in his place. Cooney Weiland followed Gainor out of town after the season, although he would return a few years later. There were also injuries to a few key players, but nothing that kept anyone out long enough to really account for the collapse. Boston fell to 15–21–12, last in the American Division, and out of the playoffs for the first time since 1925–26. Still, the season provided some moments that would change the way the game was played. Eventually.

On December 8, 1931, the New York Americans beat the Bruins 3–2, ending Boston's streak of 24 games in a row at home without a loss, dating back to the previous season. Though the *Boston Globe* only described the Americans' play as a great example of old-time defensive tactics, Charles Adams accused them of icing the puck (which was not yet against the rules) 61 times under direct instructions from their coach, Eddie Gerard. He promised similar tactics from Boston when the two teams next met in New York on January 3, 1932. The Bruins did indeed give the Americans "a taste of their own medicine … in the first period [when] they 'golfed' the puck down the ice no less than 40 times while making no pretense of a serious attack." In all, it was said that Boston iced the puck 87 times in a 0–0 tie.

Boston had probably been the most offense-oriented team over the preceding seasons. In fact, Art Ross sometimes used all five of his skaters on the attack at a time when most teams left their defencemen to lag behind in the neutral zone. (This led to the first use of the term power-play, which had nothing to do with a man advantage when it was initially coined.) Still, other league governors jumped all over the Bruins after their display in New York. John Hammond of the Rangers felt the Bruins should be fined a least $1,000. James Strachan of the Maroons felt a $10,000 fine was in order. No fines were issued. President Frank Calder had been at the game, and told the press he'd seen worse. Besides that, Boston had done nothing to break the rules.

If Ross had his way, the rules would change. "We want to stop purely defensive hockey," he said a few weeks later, "and to forestall any attempt of one team to stall when it has a lead.… We want to give the public the most for its money but we can't tax players beyond their physical limits, nor make the game too strenuous for comparatively small squads." His proposal to eliminate "golfing the puck" was: "Any team may be permitted to shoot the puck up the ice into opponents' territory once, but if it does the same thing again without having carried the puck into neutral territory, a penalty face-off will be called in front of the offending team's net." With a bit of tinkering, Ross's rule would eventually be adopted ... but not until September 24, 1937!

The Bruins bounced back strong in the standings with another first-place season in 1932–33, though they suffered yet another first-round playoff defeat, this time to Conn Smythe's Maple Leafs. But the Bruins, and the entire NHL, faced bigger problems over the course of the season. The entire world was now fully immersed in the Great Depression, and hockey was not immune. There would be no more huge profits in Boston for many years to come.

The league had dropped to eight teams in 1931–32, and although the Ottawa Senators returned after one year off, they wouldn't last. The economic collapse from 10 teams to the so-called Original Six was under way. With so many people out of work, total attendance across the NHL dropped by over 100,000 fans in 1931–32, falling from 1,733,317 to 1,627,703. Among the eight teams, only the Bruins, Leafs, and Canadiens made money. Despite its poor year, Boston led the way with attendance of 295,549 (12,315 per game) while Detroit drew less than half that at 130,207 (5,425 per game).

The Depression was not letting up as the 1932–33 season began. "You could see the effects ... in the arenas that fall," Conn Smythe would write in his autobiography. "Only two thousand for the opener in Detroit; four thousand for our first game in Chicago." With nine teams in action in 1932–33 instead of eight, total attendance still dropped by 4 percent to 1,556,180 (7,205 per game). Due to steep reductions in ticket prices, total receipts were down by 20 percent. After the 1931–32 season, the NHL had voted to impose a salary cap of $70,000 per team, with no individual player to be paid more than $7,500. After 1932–33, the cap was lowered to $65,000 for 1933–34, though the maximum remained at $7,500. Another year later, the cap fell to $62,500 and the maximum to

$7,000. Very few players were paid to the upper limit, which remained at $7,000 well into the years of the Second World War.

*  *  *

In his younger days, Art Ross had always advocated on behalf of players' rights to higher salaries. Even when he'd been involved in the management of the Montreal Wanderers, he'd spoken out against salary cuts and cap limits. But the money in his playing days was nowhere near the money of the 1930s, and the monetary worries of the years around the First World War were nothing like those of the Great Depression. So, as he neared his fifties, and was approaching 10 years as an NHL coach, manager, and a part-owner, was he still supporting the players' financial interests?

"He sure as hell wasn't!" says Milt Schmidt. "I read something about before he came to Boston, he was one of those players that used to hold out all the time. It was amazing to find him just completely the opposite."

Schmidt went to his first Bruins training camp in 1935 when he was only 17 years old. "After a week, I was called up to Mr. Ross's suite and he says, 'I think you've got some ability to have a good career in this game of ours.'"

Schmidt worried that he was too young to compete with players like Dit Clapper and Eddie Shore, but wasn't happy when Ross told him he planned to send him to the minors. "I said, 'No thank you, Mr. Ross. I think I'm too young to sign a contract. I think I'll go home.' I got as far as the door, and I said, 'by the way, what are you offering?'

"He said '$2,000.'

"I said, 'Mr. Ross, you can arrange for me to go home tomorrow!' I could make more money than that playing junior hockey in Kitchener. They got me a good job, and I got a few dollars more just for playing."

A year later, Schmidt did sign with the Bruins, and began the 1936–37 season in Providence. "They signed me to a bigger contract," he says, but Schmidt told Ross he wanted $500 more. "He said, 'I'll speak to Mr. Adams.' He went out and when he came back, he said. 'Mr. Adams can't see his way clear to give you $500 more.' I said I'd go home then, and he said, 'Think about it for a day.'"

On his way out of Ross's office, Schmidt saw Charles Adams's name on another door. "I decided to stop and ask him why he wouldn't go $500 more," Schmidt says, "and his secretary told me he wasn't in yet!"

Schmidt says he challenged Ross on that. "I told him I wanted X and I got it. Otherwise I'd have gone home."

Harry Sinden, who heard similar stories from Schmidt, believed the only way a player could get what he wanted from Ross, or any general manager in that era, was to truly be willing to walk away. "These days," says Sinden, "in most cases, there's very little problem getting a deal. A player says, 'take it or leave it,' and they get it. The GM says, 'OK, we don't want to fight.' In those days they'd say 'go home!'"

"What's good for the goose is good for the gander," says Schmidt, who wound up signing a three-year contract. He would only say that it was "very satisfactory for the time." (A 1999 *Boston Globe* story says he received a salary of $3,500.) Still, when his first check arrived, it was made out for $1,500 less than he expected. "I said, 'Mr. Ross. What's this all about?' He said. 'I sent it home to your mother and dad.'"

Ed Sandford had a similar experience when he signed his first contract in 1947. Sandford and his father met Art Ross at the Royal York Hotel in Toronto to work out a deal. Sandford, who was only 18, signed a contract for $6,000. "My dad said, 'you can't give a boy that young that much money.' Ross agreed to pay $3,000 [to my father] up front, and the rest was paid over the season as my salary."

So, in a sense, Art Ross still had his player's backs financially, though he was never one to throw money around, even in the headier postwar days. "I remember one time," says Paul Ronty, who joined the Bruins the same year as Sandford and played in Boston until 1951. "Weston Adams came in and called us aside. 'Come to my apartment' he said, 'and we'll have a drink and talk about contacts.' There was me, Kenny Smith, Johnny Peirson.... We cut a contract that Ross wasn't happy with, so he wouldn't let Adams sign us anymore! 'You can't give away money like that,' he said. It wasn't a lot of money either, only about $9,000."

"Everyone was trying to get an extra thousand," Sandford remembers, "but [Ross] was a tough negotiator. He had all the cards. Where else are you going to go? They'd ship you down to the minors."

NHL coaching legend Scotty Bowman recalls another story from that era. Bowman heard it from Lynn Patrick when they worked together in St. Louis in 1967–68. Patrick was the Bruins' coach under Art Ross at the time of the incident. The facts of this story don't quite line up, perhaps because Patrick told it to Bowman some 17 years later, or maybe because Bowman was relating it another 47 years after that. Still, it illustrates that Ross had become tight with a dollar and that he was just as quick-witted and sarcastic as his critics often claimed:

> Boston had made a trade one year with Chicago. Ross ran a pretty strict ship in Boston and Chicago was a little different. Bill Tobin in Chicago traded Pete Horeck to Boston. He had a pretty good ending to the season, but Boston got knocked out in the playoffs. Horeck came in to get his train fare home from Boston. It wasn't in his contract, but he had a letter from Chicago saying that he was entitled to transportation home.
>
> Mr. Ross said, "Well, we don't pay transportation. I'm sorry."
>
> Horeck pulled out the letter, but Ross said, "That's Chicago."
>
> Horeck got upset and banged his fist on the table. "Mr. Ross, if I don't get my transportation paid home, then don't count on me for next year."
>
> Ross pushed down his glasses and stared at Horeck over them. "Don't worry," he said. "We're not."

But during the depths of the Great Depression, Ross's hard line on money may well have played a part in one of the darkest moments in hockey history.

# 26

## THE ACE BAILEY
## INCIDENT

There were several Boston stars that weren't very happy with Art Ross and the Bruins when they received their contracts prior to training camp at Quebec City in the fall of 1933. "One of the things which you can't keep secret very long is a pay cut," wrote Victor O. Jones in the *Boston Globe* on October 19, 1933, "and news leaked out yesterday that [the] Boston Bruins ... had been sliced in the vicinity of 10 percent." Jones noted that Dit Clapper and Marty Barry had refused to sign, but after three days of holing up in Montreal, Clapper and Barry took a morning train to Quebec City on October 23. They agreed to the terms Boston was offering and signed their contracts. Only Eddie Shore remained a problem.

From his farm in Alberta, Shore gave an exclusive to the *Edmonton Journal* on November 3, 1933, which was picked up in papers all across North America the next day. "Sure I'm a holdout," said Shore, who'd won the Hart Trophy as MVP in 1932–33 (his first of four, which is still an all-time record for defencemen). "I am not going to take a $2,500 cut this year, and it is up to Manager Art Ross and Owner Charles Adams to make the next move."

According to Shore biographer Michael Hiam, the star defenceman (who held out as regularly as Art Ross once did) had demanded a salary of $17,500 before the start of the 1929–30 season. If he truly received that much, he certainly didn't get it again in the years that followed. Shore never gave a starting figure for his 1933 negotiations, but he did elaborate on the pay cut in the *Edmonton Journal* story. "A couple of weeks ago I received a contract that was satisfactory to me. Then, apparently, because I did not pack up at once and leave for the east, they turn around a chop $2,500 off that contract." Shore must have known there was a cap at this time of $7,500 for any one player, but he felt he was worth something extra. "I figure that if I am to play 60 minutes a game and if I can save the Boston Club some money, due to the fact that they do not have to employ another defenceman, then at least I should receive something extra for my time."

Because the Bruins had suspended Shore for his failure to report, the next move wasn't actually up to Ross and Adams. Signing him now was a two-step process. First, Shore had to make his peace with NHL president Frank Calder, and then agree to a contract. He was still holding out when Boston opened the season with a 6–1 loss in Toronto on November 9, but there were reports he'd arrive in Montreal in time for Boston's next game.

Stories claimed Shore would catch an airplane in Edmonton on Saturday morning, November 11, and arrive in Montreal in time to sign his contract and play that night. Art Ross put an end to such talk. "Eddie Shore left Edmonton last night by train," he said, "not a special train and not an airplane but just an ordinary, everyday train. He will arrive in Montreal about 8 a.m. Monday and then discuss the situation with the NHL authorities."

Ross wasn't there when Shore arrived, having taken a train back to Boston with the team on Sunday night. According to a story in the *Boston Globe* on November 13, he clearly felt there was nothing to negotiate. "Shore and Pres Calder will meet Monday morning and the matter of the signing of the contract should not take long," Ross said. "We never have offered Shore a new contract which was really acceptable to him. Finally, however, we agreed to pay him the highest salary allowed by the league. We could not do more than that."

Shore met Calder early Monday morning and a telegram soon reached Ross stating that the holdout star had signed his contract. Terms were not made public. Michael Hiam claims Shore "certainly got far more than the supposed maximum" and there are stories saying he received as much as $13,000 — although it's hard to imagine the NHL president giving such a number his approval. Whatever he signed for, Shore quickly caught a train for Boston, and, though the Bruins had already concluded their two-hour afternoon practice before he got there, he had a brief workout by himself and was in the starting lineup for the home opener against Detroit on November 14. Boston lost 4–2. Only about 10,000 fans were on hand, but Sportsman in the *Boston Globe* the next day called the attendance "encouraging" and added: "No doubt exists as to who is the darling of the Boston ice crowds. Eddie Shore." Shore played nearly the entire 60 minutes, taking just one short rest on the bench and sitting for a two-minute break in the penalty box for slashing in the second period.

The Bruins won their next three in a row, but were spinning their wheels at 6–6–0 when the Maple Leafs came to town on December 12. Shore always kept himself in excellent condition with his farm work in the offseason, and had practised with the minor-league Edmonton Eskimos during his holdout. Still, he was not playing up to his usual high standard. Conn Smythe blamed Art Ross, saying that Shore "had not yet recovered from the load he was made to carry last year," and was now struggling to carry a weak team on his shoulders. Smythe's Leafs were 9–2–1 on the young season and Boston fans hoped Toronto's visit — which usually brought out the best in the Bruins — would give Shore and his teammates the extra motivation they needed.

A crowd of 13,000 watched a game that referees Odie Cleghorn and Eusebe Daigneault were accused of letting get out of hand. The worst incident on the night — and one of the worst in hockey history — occurred with about six minutes to go in the second period.

The Leafs had been playing two men short, but had just killed the penalties to Red Horner and Hap Day, when Eddie Shore led a rush on the Toronto end. Horner himself recalled delivering a clean hip check, though Michael Hiam writes that Horner tripped Shore. Frank Selke, then an executive with the Maple Leafs who was watching the game from the press box, recalled for *Canadian Weekly* in 1962, that King Clancy had tripped Shore with an "innocuous" tap on the front of his skates.

Whoever did what, most accounts have Shore sliding into the boards and getting up slowly and angrily. Clancy sped up ice with the puck, while Ace Bailey — who'd done great work to kill the Toronto penalties — dropped back to cover Clancy's defensive position. Even at the time, eyewitness accounts differed, but as he raced out of the Leafs end, Shore seemed to go out of his way to hit Bailey from behind. Bailey somersaulted backwards and hit his head on the ice.

The Boston crowd first roared its approval, but then fell silent. Bailey lay with his head at an unnatural angle, his knees raised, and his legs twitching. Horner was Toronto's roughest player and he went after Shore. There are different accounts of what was said before Horner threw a punch. Shore went down, his own head striking the ice and spilling a pool of blood. All the players were on the ice now, as were Art Ross, Conn Smythe, and several Boston policemen. Tempers quickly calmed and the two injured players were carried off the ice unconscious.

Shore was not hurt as badly as it appeared — though it took seven stitches to close the three-inch gash in the back of his head. Bailey slipped in and out of consciousness, and even asked to be put back in the game at one point. When Shore and Ross arrived at his side so that Shore could apologize, Bailey was lucid enough to reply: "It's all in the game, Eddie." But he was badly hurt. His skull was fractured, and in the next few days there was a blood clot discovered and extensive hemorrhaging of his brain. It seemed Bailey was going to die, but a series of operations performed by Boston specialist Dr. Donald Munro saved his life.

The hockey world was horrified, and even the Boston fans turned against Shore. (Once it was determined that Bailey would live, Shore — who truly seemed to be under a great mental strain — left Boston to recuperate in Bermuda.) Frank Patrick, who'd taken a job as managing director of the NHL that season, issued indefinite suspensions to both Shore and Horner the day after the game, which the Leafs won 4–1. Patrick then launched a thorough investigation. One week later, he announced that Horner's suspension would end on December 31, meaning he'd sit out six games. On January 4, 1934, one day after receiving assurances from Boston surgeons that Bailey was out of danger, Patrick addressed Shore's suspension.

In making his decision, Frank Patrick had contacted lawyers in both Toronto and Boston. Fifty-one depositions were taken, involving every player in the game, as well as Boston sportswriters, prominent Boston citizens, and other spectators. It turned out that only five Toronto players and four Boston players actually saw the collision, and they had sharp differences of opinion as to whether Shore hit Bailey in an illegal manner. Rough as he was, Shore had played some 400 games in his career and had never before received a match penalty. Patrick chose to believe there was no true malice behind what he deemed a spontaneous act. He announced that Shore's suspension would end on January 26. He could return to action when the Bruins faced the Rangers in New York two nights later. Shore would miss 16 games in all, or one-third of the 48-game season.

Art Ross had little to say about Patrick's decision. "We think the sentence is a pretty severe one," but he added that the Bruins would not appeal. Whether or not he was covering for his star player, Ross was certainly among those who believed Shore's hit was a tragic accident. In the first interview Ace Bailey gave from his hospital bed on January 4, he admitted that he couldn't remember what happened, but that Ross had given him his version of events the day before and Bailey took him at his word.

"Art Ross said Shore was offside in our defence zone and he was skating back fast to avoid a penalty and I was skating fast to protect Horner and Clancy's territory. I didn't see Eddie and he didn't see me and we crashed and that's all." Bailey's version of events changed somewhat over the years, but he always maintained there was nothing malicious about the hit.

In the immediate aftermath of the Ace Bailey incident, Art Ross was busy. He acquired Babe Siebert from the Montreal Maroons, whom the Bruins later converted from left wing to defence. Siebert became an all-star, and often partnered with Eddie Shore, although the two rarely spoke, such was the animosity between them from the rough battles they'd fought over the years. In addition to tinkering with the lineup, Ross was busy in his workshop too.

Bruins players had worn helmets before. Lionel Hitchman (who was protecting a broken jaw), Eddie Shore, and George Owen had all worn helmets during the 1930 playoff series with the Maroons. "Owen had a brand new one on that made him look something like a halfback," John Hallahan had written in the *Boston Globe*. Ross set about designing something better. On December 21, 1933, he brought a sample to the Bruins dressing room. "The headgear is essentially like a football helmet," reported the *Globe* the next day. "Instead of a solid top there are strips of leather projecting from the rim to the top. The entire headgear is equipped with a sponge-like substance which will have plenty of 'give' to protect a player when he falls and strikes his head and also from high sticks which would ordinarily land on the unprotected skull."

The Bruins all appeared in helmets for the first time in a game in Ottawa on January 4, 1934. Even Tiny Thompson wore one in goal, and, according to the *Montreal Gazette* a few days later, "[W]henever Thompson went down in a scramble his helmet time and again would come down over his eyes. By the time he pushed it up again, he would generally find the puck safely lodged in the net behind him." Boston lost 9–2. The Maroons beat the Bruins 4–2 on January 6, but the Montreal players gave the headgear a passing grade. "Maroons' attitude to Ross's helmet is that it is the best of its kind they have seen. But they are not partial to helmets of any description." No one was. The chief complaint among the players was that the helmets were too bulky and too warm and the sweat that dripped down into their eyes was a greater hazard than going bareheaded. The Bruins wore their headgear for the rest of the season, and then most of them abandoned them the following year. But Boston had bigger problems than helmets.

The Bruins had gone into a tailspin without Shore, and attendance — both at home and on the road — was plummeting. Ross continually spoke of the mental anguish Shore was suffering, which annoyed Conn Smythe no end, and got on the nerves of other NHL governors too. "Many people must wish that Art Ross would stop talking about Shore's mental agony," said Ottawa Senators owner Frank Ahearn. "All this talk will not make people forget poor Bailey lying in hospital with two holes sawed in both sides of his skull. Nor will they forget the real mental agony of Mrs. Bailey and Bailey's family."

Ahearn backed Smythe's request that Frank Calder call the NHL governors together to reassess the Shore suspension and discuss the financial ramifications of Bailey's injury. The Maple Leafs had already spent $2,500 on Bailey's medical expenses. The Bruins donated the proceeds from their home game after the Bailey incident (reported first as $6,642.22 and later as $6,741.21) directly to Mrs. Bailey, but Smythe called on Boston to pay $8,000 more.

A meeting took place at the Lincoln hotel in New York on January 24, 1934. Charles Adams and club attorney R.R. Duncan represented Boston. Art Ross was there, but didn't sit in on the meeting. He told reporters the suspension of Shore had hurt the Bruins badly. "We can't win without him," Ross admitted. "Since he's been out ... we have dropped in the league standings until now we're at the bottom. More than that, the team doesn't have the appeal that it has when Shore is playing. I for one am willing to admit that he is half our team. He has been out for seven home games and the receipts have fallen off more than you would believe." Ross estimated that the suspension had already cost the team $50,000 in lost revenue.

Ross spoke even more bluntly to Alexandrine Gibb in the *Toronto Star* on January 25. "Professional sport hasn't any sportsmanship in it," Ross said. "It is a business. A racket if you like. Sportsmanship went out the door long ago in pro hockey. So why should we have to do without the services of one of our major attractions? It shouldn't happen in any business.... As a business move it was a bad thing. And hockey is business, pure and simple, when you get into the professional ranks. The same thing should go that goes for theatricals. 'The show must go on.' And our show can't go on as it should without Shore. And it hasn't."

The question of whether to extend Shore's suspension never seems to have been discussed at the nearly three-hour-long meeting. Compensation was the only issue. The governors clearly believed Bailey was entitled to something, but seemed worried about setting a precedent that would make teams financially liable for injuries to an opponent. In the end, it was James Strachan of the Maroons who suggested a benefit all-star game, although *Ottawa Journal* sports editor Walter Gilhooly had already written the league with a similar proposal. A game pitting Toronto against a team made up of two stars from each of the other eight clubs was soon set for Maple Leaf Gardens on February 14, 1934. After much deliberation, Eddie Shore was included among the all-stars.

Shore's suspension ended as scheduled on January 26. A full house — including 400 fans from Boston — greeted him at Madison Square Garden two nights later. Rangers fans cheered him. A crowd of 12,500 was on hand for Shore's Boston return on January 30 and saw the Bruins score just their second win in 12 games. By February 14, Shore had played seven games (Boston was 2–4–1) and was warmly welcomed in Chicago, Detroit, and Montreal. The big test came in Toronto at the Ace Bailey benefit.

Bailey was there and took part in the pregame ceremonies, handing out commemorative medals and windbreakers to all the players. The second player to step up for his mementos was Eddie Shore. "It was a tense moment, and instinctively that vast crowd hushed its hubbub," wrote W.T. Munns, assistant sports editor of Toronto's *Globe* newspaper. "Shore advanced, Bailey extended his hand, and a cordial handshake gave mute evidence of Shore's regret and Bailey's willingness to forgive." As Lou Marsh then described it in the *Toronto Star*, "the crowd blew the roof off with the mightiest cheer of the evening." The Leafs beat the all-stars 7–3, but most importantly the capacity crowd of 14,074 paid a total of $20,909.40 for their tickets, which was turned over to Bailey. "I bought a house with that money and had plenty left over," he later remembered.

Bailey received a similar ovation from 12,000 fans in Boston a few weeks later when he returned for a medical checkup and shook Shore's hand and dropped the puck before the Leafs played the Bruins on March 6. Clearly, they key players and the fans in both cities had put the ugly incident behind them. It was hoped that Art Ross and Conn Smythe would do the same, but their feud still had a few more years to run.

# BIG
# CHANGES

The Bruins had a record of 18–25–5 in 1933–34, and it took six wins in the last seven games to do that well. Boston finished last in the American Division and seventh overall in the nine-team NHL. Art Ross was sidelined late in the season with stomach troubles for the second year in a row, though neither time was for as long as he'd been out in 1927–28. Still, after 10 years running the Bruins hockey operations it was time to cut back.

Ross announced in mid March of 1934 that he was retiring as Bruins coach. By the end of April, there was strong speculation that Frank Patrick would replace him. Frank Calder hadn't formally accepted his resignation as managing director of the NHL yet when Charles Adams (who'd recently cut back his own involvement with the Bruins) announced the hiring on May 8, 1934. Stan Fischler wrote in *Total Hockey* that Frank's salary of $10,500 was thought to be high for a coach, but that he quickly proved it to be worthwhile with his decision to move Babe Siebert to defence.

"I have no doubt that the Bruins will give a fine account of themselves under Mr. Patrick's able direction," said Adams. "His entire time will be devoted to maintaining a club worthy of the name of Boston Bruins." Adams was very happy "that Art Ross may now devote his entire time to the general business interests of the club in his position as general manager." Adams wanted the Bruins to do a better job of finding and developing promising young players for their farm system. Freed from his coaching concerns, Ross would certainly do that.

During the 1934–35 season, Ross scouted Bobby Bauer and Woody Dumart, who advised him to take a serious look at their 16-year-old teammate Milt Schmidt. Schmidt says that Frank Selke was also keen on him, but Conn Smythe — who wasn't aware how young Schmidt was — thought he was too small. The three Kitchener kids who would soon be known as the Kraut Line were invited to Bruins training camp at Saint John, New Brunswick, in October of 1935. So was Roy Conacher, a younger brother of NHL stars Lionel and Charlie Conacher. Bill Cowley was also there after Ross had recently picked him in the dispersal draft of Ottawa Senators/St. Louis Eagles players when the NHL shrank to eight teams. Only Cowley made the Bruins in 1935–36 (Dumart played one game), but all five players would be key components of the Boston Stanley Cup winners to come.

In addition to his duties in Boston, Ross also spent 1935–36 as president of the Can-Am Hockey League. By season's end, every one of the five league teams was said to have made money under Ross, who "leaves the Can-Am league healthier than it has ever been under any previous administration." In 1936–37, four of those five teams joined with four teams from the International Hockey League to form the forerunner of today's American Hockey League. For Ross, however, the most satisfying aspect of his presidency may have been his freedom to tinker with the rules. Not all worked out, but Ross was very happy with his experiment that allowed teams to clear their own zone more effectively by passing the puck across their blue line and right through the neutral zone. The NHL was still not ready for this innovation, and would not permit passing across the blue line until 1943–44 when the centre-ice red line was added to restrict the length of those passes. The NHL wouldn't allow "stretch passes" through the neutral zone until 2005–06.

Under Frank Patrick, Boston jumped back into first place in the American Division in 1934–35 in a close race with the defending Stanley Cup champions, the Chicago Black Hawks. The playoffs proved disappointing, with a three-games-to-one loss to the Canadian Division champions from Toronto. Art Ross then made several trades heading into the 1935–36 season. Lionel Hitchman had left the Bruins to become coach of the minor league Boston Cubs midway through the 1933–34 season, and now Ross acquired Flash Hollett from the Maple Leafs to back up Eddie Shore and Babe Siebert on defence. He also re-acquired Cooney Weiland after four years away.

The Weiland deal cost Ross Marty Barry, who would help the Red Wings win back-to-back Stanley Cup titles. The trade paid off for Boston in the long term, but the immediate result of Ross's many deals was a drop to second place in the American Division standings. This was followed by another early playoff loss to the Maple Leafs, who'd fallen to second place in the Canadian Division. Boston took a 3–0 lead in game one against Toronto, but an Eddie Shore penalty, plus his additional 10-minute misconduct, resulted in five quick Toronto goals in game two. The Leafs romped to an 8–3 win and took the total-goals series 8–6. Even Conn Smythe admitted to reporters that referee Odie Cleghorn made some questionable calls.

The Bruins had done fairly well on the ice under the Ross-Patrick combination, but actions off the ice put an end to their life-long friendship. By the midway point of the 1935–36 season the two men were barely on speaking terms. Charles Adams called stories about their feud nothing more "than a tempest in a teapot," but Gerry Moore of the *Boston Globe* had reported colourfully on February 4 that, "the players themselves have known for some time that all has not been beer and skittles between Patrick and Ross."

"I think Frank is too goddamn soft," Ross told Lester Patrick in a conversation retold by Eric Whitehead. "He's too chummy with the players, and he thinks every referee is his best friend. He protects everybody. He's just too goddamn nice." Ross paused before adding, "And he's drinking."

Victor Jones, writing after Boston's playoff loss in Toronto, noted: "The Ross-Patrick feud was at its worst during this series. The club's general manager and manager established separate headquarters in Toronto, were in different drawing rooms on the train, and didn't see or speak to each other." Frank's son Joe Patrick told Whitehead: "A Boston paper alleged that my father had been drinking the day of the [second] game and wasn't fit to handle the team from the bench that night. It was a terrible thing to happen, if, in fact it was true," Frank's youngest daughter Francis Donnellan believes her father suffered from bipolar disorder that was undiagnosed (and perhaps impossible to diagnose) at the time but adversely affected much of his behaviour as he aged.

One further issue must have complicated the relationship between Ross and Patrick and could account for the animosity between them. Charles Adams was looking to sell the Bruins, and Ross was said to be putting together a syndicate to meet the $250,000 asking price. Others interested in buying the club included Leo Dandurand, who, along with his partner, Joe Cattarinch, had recently sold the Montreal Canadiens, whom they'd owned since 1921. If Dandurand did buy the Bruins, newspapers reported that Frank Patrick would be put in charge.

When the end came for Frank in Boston, it would seem that neither Ross nor Adams ever actually fired him. It was likely just a case of not renewing his contract. Rumours began immediately after the loss to Toronto that he would not return as coach, and while Frank may have been told privately before returning home to Vancouver, there was never any word for public consumption. During the summer of 1936, it was rumoured that Lionel Hitchman would take over as Bruins coach. Finally, on September 14, 1936, Charles Adams announced that Ross would return to coaching duties. Hitchman took on the new position of Ross's assistant manager.

The news that Ross would again be coach indicated there would be no sale to Dandurand, and a few days later Adams sold the Bruins to a group headed up by his son, Weston Adams. According to stories in the *Boston Globe* during the fall, Weston bought a 51-percent interest in the team and replaced his father as president. Ralph Burkard, the team's long-time treasurer and a minority shareholder, bought in at 10 percent. A group of 30 or 40 small shareholders split another 6 percent. Art Ross reportedly increased his hold in the team to about 33 percent, although future transactions involving the Bruins indicate his share was smaller than that.

With the sale transacted and Frank Patrick gone, Art Ross was fully in charge once again in 1936–37, but not much changed. Tiny Thompson was back for his ninth season in the Boston net and Eddie Shore was back for his eleventh year, though he would miss most of the season after breaking a vertebra and displacing his spine. Ross traded Babe Siebert to the Canadiens for three players and $10,000, so Flash Hollett and Jack Portland saw the bulk of duty on defence. Dit Clapper, in his tenth season, played with Cooney Weiland and Charlie Sands on the first line, while Bill Cowley played between a revolving door of wingers on the second. Milt Schmidt, Bobby Bauer, and Woody Dumart all saw action as well this year, but spent most of the season in the minors with Providence. Boston finished in second place again and suffered yet another first-round playoff exit, this time to the Montreal Maroons.

The severity of Eddie Shore's back injury had many speculating that his career was over. Fortunately for the Bruins, Shore returned to action in 1937–38. Amazingly, he seemed to be as good as ever and the team improved dramatically. Shore was given a new partner in Dit Clapper, who'd often filled in over the years, and now, with the rapid improvement of Cowley and the Kraut Line, was moved permanently to defence. Cowley teamed with Charlie Sands and Ray Getliffe this year, while Weiland centred the third line with various wingers, including rookie Mel Hill, who spent most of the year with Providence but would soon make his mark.

Ross had his eye on some other young offensive talent this year too. According to a column in the *Montreal Gazette* on March 29, 1938, he and Cecil Hart with the Montreal Canadiens were both looking to add Max Bentley, a rising star from Saskatchewan, to their negotiation lists. It was also reported that Ross had damaged his long friendship with Hart by making disparaging comments about the Canadiens unrelated to the Bentley chase. Bentley was playing in Alberta with two of his brothers, Reg and Wyatt (known as "Scoop") on the Drumheller Miners, a team that would soon feature five Bentleys after the addition of Doug and Roy in 1938–39. Drumheller just happened to have a club executive named Thomas Ross who doubled as the team's doctor and was Art's older brother. Still, the Canadiens wound up with Max Bentley on their list, although the Bruins were able to put Doug's name on theirs. Both players were later dropped and picked up by Chicago where they would soon launch their Hall of Fame careers.

Meanwhile, Bauer and Cowley appeared among the NHL leaders in goals and points in 1937–38 (Cowley for the second straight season) as Boston featured a balanced offense. Cowley was a First Team All-Star at centre, but it was the Bruins' league-leading defence that made the difference. Shore won the Hart Trophy for the fourth and final time in his career, while Thompson posted an NHL-best 1.80 goals-against average and won the Vezina Trophy for his fourth and final time. Both were also First Team All-Stars. The Bruins led the league by a comfortable margin with 67 points on a record of 30–11–7, but the playoffs proved a disappointment once again. Toronto swept Boston in three straight in the opening round, although all three were one-goal games and two of them required overtime.

\* \* \*

Long before Boston's bitter defeat, a banquet had been planned for the end of April in Art Ross's honour. While it had been hoped that the Stanley Cup might decorate the head table, the dinner went ahead as scheduled at the Copley Plaza Hotel on April 21, 1938. Some 500 guests were in attendance, and speakers included Charles Adams, Weston Adams, Cooney Weiland, Lionel Hitchman, and NHL president Frank Calder, as well as golf legend Francis Ouimet, and former Bruins season-ticket office manager and current PGA tournament director Fred Corcoran. The biggest news to come out of the evening was Ross's announcement that he'd taken out his first United States citizenship papers. "You call it your country," he told the large gathering. "I hope to call it mine in the very near future."

The news seemed to come as a surprise to everyone, although by this time, the Ross family had called the Boston area home for several years. It's unclear exactly how long this had been the case, as the family seemed to relocate from Monteal in a slow shift between 1933 and 1935, eventually spending winters in the suburb of Brookline and summers halfway down the coast to Cape Cod in Marshfield, where Ross was involved with the local golf club.

Whether or not he ever followed through with his citizenship application — which granddaughter Victoria Ross believes he did not — one thing is certain: The first big move Art Ross made with the Bruins after announcing his intention to become a U.S. citizen had fans ready to run him out of Boston.

# 28

## BACK ON TOP ...
## TWICE!

Art Ross understood that he couldn't let sentiment get in the way of doing his job. In later years, he'd warn his children not to become too close to the players, as he didn't want any hurt feelings if he had to trade a friend or a favourite player. Still, Ross's choice to replace the popular and talented Tiny Thompson with Frank Brimsek at the start of the 1938–39 season was one of the biggest gambles he ever made. The decision to go with the 23-year-old native of Eveleth, Minnesota, is often said to have come like a bolt out of the blue. To those paying attention, it shouldn't have been such a shock.

As reported in the *Boston Globe* on April 6, 1938, Tiny Thompson told Ross at the end of the 1936–37 season that he was thinking about retirement. He advised the Bruins to start looking for his successor and even offered to give up part of his salary to help pay for the new goalie's development. The Bruins didn't take Thompson up on it, but when Thompson suggested Brimsek as his own replacement, Ross signed the Pittsburgh Yellow Jackets' star in October of 1937 and invited him to training camp at Hershey, Pennsylvania. Brimsek was then farmed out to Providence, where he helped the Reds win the AHL championship and was a nearly unanimous selection to the league All-Star Team.

Thompson again made statements about ending his career in the spring of 1938. "I am seriously thinking of retiring," an Associated Press reporter quoted him from his home in Calgary. "I have been in the National Hockey League with the Bruins for 10 seasons and I'm beginning to think that is about long enough." Thompson added that even if he did return to Boston for 1938–39, it would only be as a part-time player.

In June of 1938, there were reports that Thompson would be traded to Toronto. Ross denied this. The story persisted into August, with the rumours insisting that Thompson would be dealt for either Red Horner, Busher Jackson, or Charlie Conacher. By late September, several other hockey rumours had become fact: the Montreal Maroons were the latest team to lose the economic battle to the Great Depression, reducing the NHL to seven clubs for 1938–39; the league would revert to one division for the first time since 1925–26; and Lionel Hitchman left the Bruins to become head coach of the Springfield Indians.

Cooney Weiland replaced Hitchman as assistant manager in Boston in 1938–39, though he would continue to play for the team and serve as its captain as well. The Bruins returned to train in Hershey, Pennsylvania, and Frank Brimsek was there again. This time it was announced that Brimsek would alternate with Tiny Thompson in the Boston nets for several games during the upcoming season.

The Bruins opened the 1938–39 campaign in Toronto on November 3. Brimsek was scheduled to leave Boston for Baltimore the day before to play an exhibition game with Providence before its season opener on Saturday, but Thompson took a puck above his right eye during a Bruins intrasquad scrimmage on October 30. The five stitches needed to close the cut and the swelling, plus a huge wad of adhesive tape, left his eye practically closed. "Tiny may be ready to play by Thursday night," declared Ross, "but we won't take the slightest chance of his hurting it again." Brimsek skipped the Baltimore trip and went with the Bruins to Toronto, where he was solid in a 3–2 win over the Maple Leafs.

Ross was especially pleased with Boston's defence in Toronto, noting that veteran Dit Clapper and rookie Johnny Crawford were "particularly outstanding," in filling in for Eddie Shore, who was once again holding out (he would come to terms with the Bruins two weeks into the season). Ross was also impressed with Brimsek, saying he looked "like a real star" and that his play warranted giving Thompson a little more time to heal. Ross was positively ecstatic about the goalie's play in a 4–1 win in Detroit on November 6. "Brimsek's a peach," he said. Still, with Thompson fully recovered, the young goalie was off to Providence for the next few weeks.

Boston went 3–1–1 in five games under Thompson, who allowed just 8 goals in 310 minutes of play for an average of 1.56. Nonetheless, Ross couldn't get Brimsek out of his mind. Branch Rickey's long-held belief in baseball that it's better to trade a player a year too early than a year too late was not yet a famous quotation, but Ross certainly had the same idea. On November 28, 1938, he announced Thompson's sale to Detroit for $15,000. It was the richest deal for a goalie in NHL history and Thompson was given $1,000 of it to soothe any hard feelings. "We regret that we were forced to dispose of Tiny," said Ross, "but we realize it was to his advantage. He's good for at least five more seasons with Detroit, where I am sure he will be very happy. But if he remained with us, it would be a matter of only two seasons at the most before we would be forced to replace him with the younger Brimsek, a big league goalie if I ever saw one."

Thompson agreed he'd last longer in Detroit (though he'd be out of the NHL after the 1939–40 season), but admitted it was hard to go. The deal shocked many of his Boston teammates. Victor Jones wrote in the *Boston Globe* that Dit Clapper, the goalie's long-time roommate, was so upset he asked Ross to trade him too. Ross refused, and Jones wrote that Clapper and the others had shrugged off the trade by the end of the day, saying: "Well, that's hockey." The team's public was slower to come around. Michael Hiam writes that some Boston fans considered the loss of Thompson to be the worst thing to happen to a local team since the Red Sox sold Babe Ruth to the Yankees in 1920.

Boston fans had yet to see Brimsek play on home ice, and wouldn't for a few more days. The Bruins played their first game after the Thompson trade in Montreal on December 1 and lost 2–0. They played in Chicago three nights later and beat the Black Hawks 5–0. Returning home to face Chicago again on December 6, Brimsek admitted to feeling "a ton of pressure."

"I couldn't eat," he reminisced to the *Boston Globe* on May 29, 1977. "I knew people would be sitting back and waiting for me to boot one. And they were. Boston fans used to roar when the Bruins skated onto the ice; they probably still do. And I'll never forget the reception that first night — total silence! Not a sound. Wow! Then I knew I was on trial and that I'd be on the next train out of town if I had a bad night." Brimsek turned in another shutout and Boston scored a 2–0 victory. Next came a 3–0 win over the Rangers in New York. After defeating Montreal 3–2 at home, Brimsek rattled off another three straight shutout victories.

After the Thompson trade, Brimsek posted seven wins and six shutouts in eight games. His performance won over the Bruins fans and the triple shutout streaks earned him the nickname Mr. Zero, but Brimsek remained modest. "To reporters, taciturn Frankie Brimsek announced that the triples he liked most were triple features at the movies." As for the shutouts, "If the customers are giving me credit for that they're way off base. A team's defencemen turn in the shutouts, not the goalie, and the Bruins defencemen are the best in the National Hockey League.... We're out to win games and the greatest goalie that ever put on pads couldn't win one victory by himself."

By the end of the first week in February, the Bruins were 24–7–2, with only the New York Rangers anywhere close in the seven-team standings. "The Boston Bruins of this year are the greatest team I have ever seen," said Ross to the *Montreal Gazette*. He also called Brimsek the greatest goalie he'd ever seen. "Of all the goals scored on him this season, which isn't very many, I have only seen one that possibly could have been stopped."

At season's end, the Bruins were 36–10–2 and their 74 points were 16 better than the runner-up Rangers. Brimsek led the league in wins with a record of 33–9–1. He also had a league-best 10 shutouts and 1.56 goals-against average and became the first goalie in history to win both the Vezina Trophy and the Calder Trophy as rookie of the year. Brimsek, Clapper, and Shore were all named to the First All-Star Team as Boston allowed just 76 goals on the season compared to a range of 105 to 157 for everyone else. There were no Boston all-stars on offense, but left winger Roy Conacher led the NHL with 26 goals in his first season and finished as the runner-up to Brimsek for the Calder Trophy. Bill Cowley, centring Conacher and Mel Hill, played only 34 games due to an injury, but still led the league with 34 assists.

Under the NHL's new playoff format for 1938–39, only one team — the defending champion Black Hawks, who finished last — was eliminated during the regular season. Boston opened the post-season against the second-place Rangers for a berth directly into the Stanley Cup Final, while teams three through six battled for the other spot. The Bruins-Rangers matchup marked the first best-of-seven series in the NHL since 1919. Given that the Rangers had only managed three wins in eight games against the Bruins during the regular season (no one else had beaten Boston more than twice) it seemed unlikely they would now beat them four times in seven tries. Still, given the Bruins' poor playoff history in the 10 seasons since they'd last won the Stanley Cup, nothing was impossible. Regardless of what Ross had said in February, no one would consider the Bruins the greatest team ever if they faltered in the playoffs once again. So, en route to New York by train for game one, the coach and GM gathered the players together in the smoking room of their Pullman coach. Victor Jones quoted his tactical discussion at length in his column for the *Boston Globe* on March 21:

> The only thing that can beat us is a lot of dumb penalties or a lot of dumb plays.... [So] you're to take whatever is handed out without any talking back.... As to your general style, with both sides even we're going to play 'em close to the chest, typical Stanley Cup hockey. The lines will rush with a trailer and the defencemen are to stay back. The forwards won't do any body checking because we don't want to take the chance of any penalties, but you defencemen, Eddie, Dit, Jack [Portland] and Johnny, I want you to hit those birds hard.
>
> Playing that kind of a game, the percentages ought to be with us. We've got two great scoring lines. The third line ... I'm counting on you for defensive purposes. Your first duty is not to get caught up the ice. If you fellows can give our other two lines some rest, you'll have done all you're supposed to do.
>
> If we go a goal up and they start to gang us, the only player I want to be looking for a break is the center — Cowley,

[Gord] Pettinger, or Schmidt. The rest of you are to cover your men. During the season we sometimes lost games because too many men were looking for breaks.

When we're a man up and are ganging, I want the wings to go into the corners and the defencemen to move up, but let me caution the defencemen against ever trying to check in the enemy zone. The Rangers are pretty fast and when your side loses the puck, you're to get back in a hurry. Any passes you get, shoot right back in. Don't fool around with the puck or you'll wind up hitting some Rangers in the leg and giving 'em a clean break.

In the series opener, the Rangers scored the first goal late in the second period, but Bill Cowley evened things early in the third. The game then went almost three full overtime periods. All night long when the Cowley line was on, the Rangers paid close attention to Roy Conacher. Mel Hill had scored just 10 times all season, but Ross advised Cowley to look to him when he could. Finally, with just 35 seconds remaining in triple overtime, Hill cut sharply for the Rangers' net, shouted for a pass, and Cowley fed him the puck. Hill was already half past the goal, but twisted his body just enough to flick a backhander past Dave Kerr for a 2–1 Bruins victory. Back in Boston two nights later, Cowley set up Hill again at 8:24 of the first overtime session for a 3–2 victory and a 2–0 series lead. A record crowd of 16,981 jammed the Boston Garden for game three and saw the Bruins score a 4–1 victory.

The series seemed over, but the Boston playoff bugaboo almost struck. The Rangers bounced back for three straight wins and then pushed game seven deep into overtime. Once again it was Cowley and Hill to the rescue, with Cowley picking up the puck in the corner after a wild Conacher shot and feeding it to Hill out front. Hill took two strides towards goalie Bert Gardiner and fired. The puck sailed into the net at the eight-minute mark of the third overtime period, giving the Bruins a 2–1 victory in front of another huge crowd of nearly 17,000. Hill remains the first and only player in NHL history to score three overtime goals in a single series, and has been known by the nickname "Sudden Death" ever since.

For the rest of his life, Art Ross considered the 1939 playoff victory over the Rangers to be the greatest thrill of his Bruins career. Still, there was the matter of the Stanley Cup Final and Boston's playoff jinx against Toronto. The Bruins ended that with a five-game victory. Fireworks exploded in the Boston Garden after game five and the organ played "Paree," the Bruins' theme song since the late 1920s. Frank Calder presented the Stanley Cup to Ross, who immediately passed the trophy to captain Cooney Weiland. Meanwhile, the fans shouted for Eddie Shore, who was given a thunderous send off in his last great moment in a Bruins uniform.

The only disappointing aspect of the entire season was at the box office, where the Bruins lost $37,000. Saturday night crowds had been good during the season, but other nights were poor, and Ross blamed the situation on Walter Brown of the Boston Garden and the Boston Olympics independent hockey team Brown operated in direct competition with the Bruins. "There is too much hockey for the town," said Ross of his team's failure to turn a profit despite its tremendous season. For his success that year, Art Ross earned his only selection to the First All-Star Team as a coach after the Cup win. Even so, there'd been rumours throughout the season that he'd had enough of coaching.

During the Final against Toronto, Ross stated that regardless of the outcome, he would confine his future duties to those of general manager. Victor Jones thought the job that really interested him was Frank Calder's, but Ross proved lukewarm toward accepting the position of NHL president at the league meetings held in Boston in May. Newspapers suggested that Weston Adams had talked him out of it.

By the end of June, there were reports that Ross wanted Cooney Weiland to take over as coach. Ross was behind the bench when the NHL All-Stars scored a 5–2 victory over the Montreal Canadiens in a pre-season benefit game for the family of Babe Siebert, who'd drowned in August of 1939 after retiring as a player to become a coach. But after that game, Weiland became coach in Boston for the 1939–40 season.

Eddie Shore and the Bruins parted ways this year and with Brimsek's rookie numbers almost impossible to match (he was only a Second-Team All-Star this season), the Bruins were not the same great defensive squad under Weiland. Instead, the offense exploded. Milt Schmidt, Woody Dumart, and Bobby Bauer finished first, second, and third in the NHL scoring race, with Bill Cowley placing fifth. Schmidt was a First Team All-Star, with Dumart and Bauer on the Second Team and Bauer claiming the first of two straight Lady Byng Trophy wins. Newly acquired Herb Cain scored 21 goals to join Dumart and Schmidt (with 22 apiece) among only five NHL players to top 20 that season. The Bruins led the league with 170 goals and finished with a record of 31–12–5, but were only three points ahead of the Rangers in the standings. Boston fell to the New York team in an opening-round playoff rematch and the Rangers went on to win the Cup, but the Bruins bounced back with another first-place finish in 1940–41.

After a slow start, Boston was practically unbeatable in the last two-thirds of the 1940–41 season, going 23 games without a loss at one point, and 21–1–10 in the final 32 games. The Bruins finished 27–8–13 and had a five-point margin over the second-place Maple Leafs. Again the offense was best in the league, with Cowley leading all scorers with 62 points and setting a new league record with 45 assists. No one else in the NHL had more than 44 points, meaning Cowley could have led the league on assists alone. Wayne Gretzky is the only other player in league history who can make that claim. Cowley won the Hart Trophy over runner-up Dit Clapper, and both were named to the First All-Star Team, with Bauer, Dumart, and Brimsek on the Second.

A knee injury sidelined Cowley for the first three games of the playoffs, and the Bruins' post-season followed a similar slow starting pattern to the regular season. Boston fell behind Toronto two games to one and three games to two, but then rattled off two straight wins to take that series. They won four in a row to beat Detroit for the Stanley Cup, the first sweep of a seven-game series in NHL history.

The Bruins seemed to be a dynasty in the making, but they wouldn't be able to follow through. Milt Schmidt is certain the team would have won the Stanley Cup two or three more times during the 1940s if not for the fact that he and so many other Boston stars left for the military during the Second World War. "Nobody was close to us," Scotty Bowman remembers Schmidt telling him, "if we could have held all those players."

# WORLD
# WAR TOO

Germany invaded Poland on September 1, 1939. Two days later, Britain and France declared war on Germany. Canada declared war on September 10. Five out of seven NHL teams were based in the United States, which didn't enter the Second World War until after Japan bombed Pearl Harbor on December 7, 1941, but almost all of the players in the league were Canadian citizens. At the NHL's semi-annual meeting in Detroit on September 20, 1939, President Calder announced that the league would carry on in a manner as close to normal as possible.

The NHL remained fairly unaffected by the War until the 1941–42 season, after which more and more players began to enlist in the armed forces. The 1940–41 season even saw attendance increase as the growing wartime economy finally put an end to the Great Depression. The NHL box office thrived throughout the war years, even as the star players were replaced by those too old or too young for enlistment, or those with medical or other deferments. During these early War years and beyond, Art Ross continued to fight his own personal battles.

"Art Ross was a man whom you either liked or disliked," said Boston writer Henry McKenna in a story for a Bruins program on November 19,

1961. "His friends were legion, old-timers swore by him, [and] young hockey personalities who respected his judgement … were quick to take his advice." McKenna also wrote that there was "another Ross that few people ever met or saw." This Art Ross was the genial host who "used to throw play-off parties that lasted until dawn, memorable nights of fun and horseplay, spiced with his French-Canadian stories of Joe LaPorte, his practical jokes and his amazing card tricks." McKenna admitted that there were plenty of people who disliked Ross too, but in Boston, he was generally beloved by the fans, and respected by the sportswriters, who'd dubbed him Uncle Arthur some time before 1935.

Ross was definitely more of a crusty uncle than a kindly old soul. In a Bruins publication from 1946–47, he is described as a man of raw courage and fierce spirit, but also as being "not the most tactful and sympathetic man, even in the NHL." The words "dour" and "sarcastic" were often used to describe him during his years in Boston. He told sportswriter Harold Kaese, for his *Boston Globe* column on January 6, 1959, "I never believed in praising players too highly. They're getting paid to do well."

"Art Ross was the kind of guy, when he made up his mind he wouldn't budge from it," says Paul Ronty. "It didn't make any difference who it was."

"He was a gruff kind of guy," says Ed Sandford, "but so was Connie Smythe and Jack Adams. They were all from the same mould."

Dick Patrick shares a family story passed down from his grandfather Lester, or perhaps through his uncle Lynn. "Art Ross, when he was stuck talking to someone he didn't want to, in a social situation, he had this signal. I'm not sure if it was to warn other people, or look for help, but he'd hold the lapel of his suit coat with one hand, and that was the signal." From this emerged a particular type of insult. "If you were really a guy that no one wanted to hang out with," says Patrick, "you'd be a 'two-lapel guy' according to Art Ross."

Clearly Ross was a person who didn't suffer fools gladly, which is not to say that Conn Smythe or Jack Adams (whom he also disliked) were fools. Nonetheless, Ross seems to have been the type of man who assumed he was the smartest person in the room. Smythe described him as "the most devious man I ever met." Frank Selke once said: "Art Ross writes the rules, and then lies awake at night thinking of ways to circumvent them."

Ross didn't just fight with the coaches and managers of opposing teams, but also with many of the Bruins' biggest stars. Vitriolic Boston sportswriter Dave Egan, who wrote as the Colonel, had a long-time feud with Ross, in addition to other Boston sports personalities, most notably Ted Williams. Still, Egan had a point when, as Michael Hiam relates, he wrote that Eddie Shore had been traded "because there can only be one great man of Boston hockey and his name is Art Ross."

The falling out between Ross and Eddie Shore in 1939–40 appears to have been sparked by the fact that Shore had bought the Springfield Indians and wanted to devote his time to running his own team. Hiam writes that Ross and Weston Adams seemed shocked by the fact that a mere player could afford to buy even a minor-league franchise. They made things difficult for Shore before trading him to the New York Americans. Shore had likely accumulated other resentments along the way, and he and Ross rarely had a kind word for each other in the years to come.

Those years also saw a feud between Ross and Bill Cowley. It's not clear how this one started, but it ended in a public blowup at the conclusion of the 1946–47 season which was well covered in the Boston papers.

The Bruins were planning a post-season barnstorming tour of the West Coast and some of the players were on edge because they'd begun hearing rumours about young call-ups from the farm system taking some of the spots on the roster. Cowley called Ross to ask him about it.

"Art, the boys are wondering who isn't making the trip."

"Well, what are you worrying about," Ross told him. "You're not going."

Cowley was crushed. That night, at an annual dinner for the team, he was called on to say a few words and decided to make his thoughts public. "This is the most disappointing night of my entire hockey career," he told the audience. "I was told I wasn't making the western trip with the Bruins. I had looked forward to it — to taking my wife who lives in Vancouver, and to using it as a honeymoon. After 12 years with the Bruins I was certainly disappointed to find my name left off the list. I am through with the National Hockey League." The greatest playmaker of his era and the NHL's all-time scoring leader at the time never played again.

Cowley, who'd been hurt the previous season and knew this year that he was nearing the end of the line, explained a couple of days later that he was angry because Ross had accused him of quitting during the playoffs. "I never quit in my life," said Cowley, who'd nearly come to blows with Ross after the dinner. "It was a rough, tough series [and] I just didn't have it. I know I'm washed up, but I didn't quit."

For his part, Ross claimed the decision to leave Cowley off the West Coast roster was simply business. "It is my job to hire and fire and it is not a pleasant one," he told the gathering in his own speech later in the evening. "My job is to rebuild the team. The men who were not picked to go ... don't figure too largely in the Bruins' plans for next year. I meant no affront to Cowley. There is a job waiting for him with the Bruins if he cares to see me about it."

Cowley never did.

Ross's feud with Herb Cain might also be considered simply business, but it certainly seems vindictive. Cain set a new NHL scoring record with 82 points in 1943–44. He had 32 goals the following season (although adding only 13 assists) and then fell off dramatically during the first postwar season of 1945–46. Still, he ended that season as just the thirteenth player in NHL history to top 200 career goals. The generally accepted story is that Cain held out prior to the 1946–47 season, and that an angry Ross sent him to Boston's minor league team and buried him there with instructions that he was not to be sold to another NHL team. Cain languished in the farm league for four seasons, falling just short of the number of games necessary to qualify for an NHL pension, and being blackballed from the Hockey Hall of Fame, where for years he was the only eligible former winner of the league scoring title not to be inducted.

Years later, Cain himself seemed to indicate that his holdout was in an earlier season, and that Ross turned on him because he felt that he was too old to play at 33. Cain clearly believed that several other teams were interested in him, but that Ross refused to sell him. "The NHL was like a little house league then," said Cain as quoted in Brian McFarlane's *The Bruins*. "The six owners simply made up their own rules, called each other up and made deals, and settled things among themselves. The players had no clout, no say in anything." That was certainly true, and it's possible the owners had enough clout to control the newspapers too, because nobody seems to have reported on Cain's case as anything out of the ordinary.

On July 2, 1946, the *Boston Globe* stated that both Cowley and Cain no longer fit into the Bruins' plans. Cowley returned for his last, bitter season, but rumours had Cain on the move to the Rangers or Maple Leafs. "Nobody, however, wants Cain, so, in all probability, he'll wind up in the minors if he chooses to play next Fall."

Similar stories appeared in many newspapers in September, saying the Bruins had offered waivers on Cain, but no one claimed him. Cain was on the Boston training camp roster when it was announced in newspapers on September 27, "but it is almost certain the veteran left wingman won't be with the club when the season gets under way." Cain was most definitely at training camp with the Bruins at Hershey, but was not with the team when they opened in Montreal on October 19. He reported to the Hershey team a few days later, and whether or not Ross truly intended to bury him there, Cain never played in the NHL again.

There are even fewer hard facts pointing to any issues between Ross and Cooney Weiland, but there was something personal between them too. Harold Kaese, writing in the *Boston Globe* on November 18, 1962, mentions only "a clash of personalities." Weiland certainly bolted the Bruins as soon as he could after guiding them to the Stanley Cup and being named a First Team All-Star coach in 1940–41. He didn't go far, taking a job coaching Boston's Hershey farm club, but he left the Bruins willingly, and had, in fact, been angling for this new job for quite some time. Richard Johnson, curator of the Sports Museum in Boston, heard stories that Ross never left Weiland alone as coach and treated him as little more than an errand boy.

There's not much need for guesswork when it comes to the relationship between Ross and Conn Smythe. Ross had little to say for public consumption about their feud, but Smythe said plenty. Many of the stories are told in detail in his autobiography, which was written with Scott Young and published shortly after Smythe died in November of 1980. Others appear in Kelly McParland's biography, *The Lives of Conn Smythe*, first published in 2011.

In addition to constantly attacking each other in the newspapers, one story has Ross planting a couple of longshoremen behind Smythe at a game in Boston and trying to goad him into a fight. Another has Smythe giving King Clancy a bouquet of roses to deliver to Ross (who was suffering from hemorrhoids) with a note written in Latin telling him where he could stick them. Smythe writes that this incident occurred on the same night that he wore a top hat and tails to the Boston Garden as a joking reply to Ross saying he had no class. Not that it really matters, but the *Lowell Sun* in nearby Lowell, Massachusetts, wrote on January 15, 1937, that Smythe would wear formal attire to the upcoming game on January 19 because Ross had mocked Chicago Black Hawks owner Fred McLaughlin as being too refined for professional hockey, and Smythe shot back that the NHL needed all the dignity, poise, and culture it could collect to make up for Ross's lack of the same.

There are also conflicting reports about whether Smythe or Ross wanted to employ a coin flip to decide game five of their 1933 playoff series that eventually went to six overtime periods, though Smythe writes that it was Ross who was in favour of it. He also writes with glee about Ross insulting Red Dutton so mercilessly throughout at NHL governors meeting in the late 1930s that the two finally came to blows. "I have never seen a man so completely cleaned in his life as Ross was.... His nose was broken, his cheek bone was broken, he'd lost some teeth.... Couldn't have happened to a more deserving recipient."

Smythe does not write about a different NHL governors meeting, held on September 26, 1936, a few weeks after a horse he owned named Shoeless Joe was caught up in a doping scandal at Saratoga. Smythe and his trainer were later exonerated, but the NHL governors didn't know that yet and were all very quiet as they awaited his late arrival at their meeting. "Smythe finally came in and sat down," remembered Leo Dandurand for a story in *The Hockey Book* by Bill Roche. "Ross, with a perfectly straight face, spoke up: 'Mr. President, I insist that a saliva test of all those present be taken before proceeding any further with the business at hand!'" Dandurand said that the laughter almost blew down the walls, "and the man who got the biggest bang out of the episode was Smythe." One has to wonder.

The last great blowup in the Ross-Smythe feud came in mid-December of 1939. Smythe was angry at what he perceived to be the Bruins' defence-first strategy in a 1–1 tie in Toronto on December 14. When he arrived in Boston a few days later ahead of a Leafs game there on December 19, he descended on the *Boston Globe* office "spouting fire and brimstone." Smythe blasted the Bruins in general: "They're still the champions aren't they? Everybody calls them champions? Why can't they play like champions?" He also went after Ross in particular: "I guess [he] is so busy inventing things that he doesn't find time to make his players play hockey." He then took out an ad that appeared above his signature in the *Globe* that evening:

> ATTENTION, HOCKEY FANS!
> If you're tired of seeing the kind of hockey
> the Boston Bruins are playing
> COME TO THE GARDEN TONIGHT
> and see a real hockey club,
> The TORONTO MAPLE LEAFS

The Bruins won the game that night 3–2 in overtime in front of a crowd of 14,107 that was the largest of the season. Even so, Ross demanded that Smythe be fined $1,000 for his unbecoming conduct. Smythe was still worked up about it eleven years later, telling a reporter from *Life* magazine, "Can you imagine that? I put money in their pockets and they want to fine me." The issue was raised at the next NHL meeting but was dismissed, although a motion was passed censuring both Ross and Smythe for their unseemly bickering over the years.

Several months later, on September 11, 1940, Ross's son, Art Jr., married Loretta Jane "Bunnie" Rabbitt in a quiet morning ceremony at the Rabbitt home in Hanover, Massachusetts. A story in the society page in the *Boston Globe* the following day noted that the groom had served as a ground instructor (essentially, a pilot-in-training) under the Civilian Air Authority in Rockland, Massachusetts. He now held a commercial pilot's license and the *Globe* reported that the newlyweds "planned to visit Montreal, where Mr. Ross is going to enlist in the Royal Canadian

Air Force." John Ross soon followed his brother into the RCAF. Conn Smythe, a First World War veteran who re-enlisted for the Second World War, was impressed. "I was a little sorry about having been on [Ross] all the time when his sons came up and joined the RCAF," he'd write. "We weren't so hard on one another after that."

# 30

## THE WAR YEARS

While Art Ross feuded off the ice during the War years, the Bruins struggled on it. With Cooney Weiland gone in 1941–42, many speculated that
Dit Clapper would become the team's playing coach. Instead, Ross made
another return behind the bench. He believed that the 1940–41 Bruins
might have been even greater than the 1938–39 team, but he wasn't prepared to make the same boast about the 1941–42 squad. "I'm not going to
say they're the best I ever saw," Ross told reporters prior to Boston's season
opener on the road in Toronto. "Too many things to take into consideration. Suppose Cowley doesn't have as a good a year? Suppose Clapper gets
hurt or something like that happens." Both Cowley and Clapper were hurt
during the 1941–42 season, but the bigger losses were War-related, as the
conflict in Europe finally began to take its toll on the NHL.

In June of 1940, the Canadian parliament passed the National Resources
and Mobilization Act. The act meant the government could take actions that
would require citizens to place themselves, their services, and their property
at the country's disposal for national defence. By September of 1941, there
were rules in place preventing unmarried men or those with no depend-
ents between the ages of 21 and 25 from receiving passports to work outside

the country. All five NHL teams based in the United States (the New York Americans folded in 1942, leaving the league with its so-called "Original Six" franchises) would be hurt by this rule, but Boston and Detroit faced the biggest losses. The Bruins could potentially lose Milt Schmidt, Woody Dumart, Pat McCreavy, Red Hamill, and Terry Reardon. It turned out that in 1941–42 they were only denied Terry Reardon, whom Ross sent to the Canadiens so that he could at least earn his living playing home games in Montreal and road games in Toronto. Reardon would be in the army by 1943.

Although unrelated to Japan's bombing of Pearl Harbor, word came shortly after the December 7 attack that Schmidt, Dumart, and Bobby Bauer would be called up by the Canadian military. On February 10, 1942, they received a lavish sendoff before they played their last game for the Bruins — an 8–1 thumping of Montreal — and headed to Ottawa to join the RCAF. Art Ross Jr., wearing his RCAF uniform as a pilot officer, and his brother John presented gifts on behalf of their father, while Ross and United States Naval Reserve Lieutenant Weston Adams had farewell messages read on their behalf. At this point, Adams was the Bruins' only active serviceman. He would serve in the U.S. Navy, in both the Atlantic and the Pacific, until May of 1946, rising to a full commander.

Schmidt, Bauer, and Dumart played the rest of the 1941–42 season with the Ottawa RCAF hockey team and led them to the Allan Cup. Shortly after their departure from Boston, Ross had suggested that, if the RCAF team won the Allan Cup, a series should be arranged with the Stanley Cup champions. Red Dutton of the New York Americans was reportedly amenable to the proposition, but nothing came of it. Perhaps it might have happened if the Bruins had won the Stanley Cup. Despite a stellar season from Frank Brimsek and a respectable record of 25–17–6, Boston lost a second-round playoff series to Detroit.

With six teams for the 1942–43 season, the NHL expanded the schedule to 50 games. The Bruins lost Roy Conacher to the RCAF, and among the players Ross used to fill the gaps in the Boston lineup was 16-year-old Bep Guidolin, the youngest player in NHL history. Ross played Guidolin with fellow teenagers Bill Shill (who soon left for the Canadian Navy) and Don Gallinger on a unit dubbed the Sprout Line. A return to First All-Star status by Bill Cowley and another strong season from Brimsek saw Boston remain contenders. The Bruins even reached the Stanley Cup Final, but the Red Wings swept them. After the loss of Brimsek to the U.S. Coast Guard in 1943–44, the Bruins' dropped to fifth place, which put them out of the playoffs. With other players gone (including Guidolin and Gallinger) the Bruins fell to 16–30–4 in 1944–45 but they returned to the playoffs because the Black Hawks and Rangers were even worse. "Hey, Ross! Where's your power play now?" an old Boston story has a disgruntled fan shouting at a Bruins game during the war. "In England, in France, in Germany!" Ross shot back, silencing his detractor. Nevertheless, the team was so weak that Ross admitted during the 1944–45 season: "I am now piloting the worst hockey team at which it was ever my misfortune to look."

\* \* \*

Throughout the War years, the NHL managed to keep quiet most of the squabbling between the league owners and governors, but it wasn't always possible.

With Conn Smythe serving in the Canadian army, Frank Selke was made acting manager of Maple Leaf Gardens. In January of 1943, he wrote an article in a Leafs game program that stirred up the old rivalry with Art Ross. Selke was critical of Boston hockey in general and the Bruins in particular. He also attacked Boston sportswriters and referred to Ross as a sourpuss. Ross was incensed, and fired off an angry four-page letter. It's unclear if he ever sent it, but a copy of the letter was found by historian James Andrew Ross (no relation to Art) in the papers of Boston writer Harold Kaese at the Boston Public Library. Ross recited a long history of grievances over his past treatment in Toronto and with his fellow NHL governors, including president Frank Calder. He also mocked the Toronto press as "the Froth Estate," ridiculed Selke as "Frank Sulky," and laid into the Maple Leafs' famed radio announcer, referring to "Foster — and how he can Hueit."

Ross seemed most angry that Selke had refused to provide discounted tickets to a former NHL player currently in the military — although Ross was likely unaware that Conn Smythe had left explicit instructions against any discounts. "Old Sourpuss has arranged that over

25,000 men in uniform here in Boston will see our games this season free of any charge whatsoever," wrote Ross. "Think that over, Stupid."

The Bruins also played several exhibition games to raise money for the War effort over the years and Ross was disappointed that the Canadian teams didn't do more. He got himself in trouble in February of 1944 for a speech he gave at a service club luncheon in which he blasted the Canadiens for backing out of a charity exhibition with the Bruins in Quebec City. He also sarcastically referred to the Montreal team, whose players were mostly employed in local war industries, as "The Essential War Workers." The owners of the Canadiens considered suing him, but didn't after Ross maintained he'd been misquoted. However, at the NHL board of governors meeting in May, Ross moved a resolution that the league passed saying that (with noted exceptions for students and farmers) "for the duration of the war, no person will be eligible to play in the National Hockey League whose induction into the Armed Forces of the Dominion of Canada or of the United States of America has been deferred or may hereafter be deferred for other than physical reasons."

\* \* \*

Like Conn Smythe, John Kilpatrick of the New York Rangers was a veteran of the First World War who re-enlisted for the new fight. Many other NHL executives had family members serving in the armed forces. Red Dutton had served in the First World War and lost two sons in the RCAF in the Second. Art Ross also had his boys in the RCAF. John Ross ended up flying a Spitfire in Burma fighting the Japanese. "I didn't shoot anybody down," said John. "Matter of fact, I didn't even see [any]one in the air."

The war experience of John's brother, Art Ross Jr., was significantly different.

"Our darkest and brightest moments were tied up with Art," Ross would say of his eldest son's exploits in a 1960 interview with Arthur Siegel. "First came the darkest moment when we were informed he was presumed dead.... The brightest moment was when we heard from the newspapers about his being alive."

Art Jr. had indeed enlisted shortly after his marriage. On August 24, 1941, he was posted in Brandon, Manitoba, when his wife, Bunnie, gave birth to their first child back in Boston. He was named Arthur Stuart Ross after his father. Art Jr. was given a few days leave to return home and see his son before returning to duty. He was such an adept pilot that he spent his early war years teaching others to fly, but by the summer of 1943, he was in the thick of the action flying over Europe in a Typhoon he named *Spirit of Lou Gehrig*. That November, Elmer Ferguson reported in the *Montreal Herald* that, "unofficial but very reliable sources of information say that the younger Ross ... bagged a Messerschmitt, two locomotives and a couple of barges on the same day with accurately placed bombs." When Ross was informed by telephone during a Bruins loss, he replied: "I'm glad somebody in the family is doing well, because we're taking a pasting here right now."

More news of Art Jr.'s exploits appeared in a supplement to the *London Gazette* on July 25, 1944. The story notes: "This officer has participated in a very large number of sorties, including attacks on enemy airfields, shipping, railways and mechanical transport. He is a skilful and courageous pilot whose determination to press home his attacks, often in the face of intense anti-aircraft fire, has been most praiseworthy. In air fighting, Flight Lieutenant Ross has destroyed 2 enemy aircraft." Unfortunately, by the time this story appeared in the *London Gazette*, the courageous pilot was thought to be dead.

Art Jr. was among the many flyers providing aerial support for the ground troops on D-Day, June 6, 1944. He then flew three and sometimes four missions a day over the next few days, shooting up tanks, trucks, and road convoys on the ground that were moving up to reinforce the German defence. On June 11, Art Jr. was flying inland from the Normandy coast at dawn. Some 80 kilometres in, he spotted a German truck and dived on it from two kilometres. "Then I saw it was only the last truck of a long road convoy," he said, and so he radioed to the other seven Typhoons in his group. "Come on down, quick! There's a whole slew of them."

Art Jr. then proceeded to drop his bombs. "I knew it was dumb as hell to go right down the line of vehicles. Everybody gets a shot at you when you do that. But I was committed now. I was going like the clappers, making about 500 mph and about fifty feet off the ground when I opened up on the last truck in the convoy." This last truck was filled with shells and explosives and it went off like a fireball. The inferno was so intense that Art Jr.'s plane was immediately engulfed in flames. "I jerked the plane over on its back and shoved the stick forward as hard as I could to shoot it upward so I could get enough height to bail out." He was still doing at least 600 kilometres per hour and was no more than 60 metres off the ground when he jumped. The parachute was almost horizontal to him, but slowed his fall somewhat. When he hit the ground, he bounced and skidded across a marshy field, but at least the flames on his uniform were extinguished as he rolled through the mud.

When he finally came to a stop, Art Jr. had a few broken ribs and a badly burned face. He managed to hide from the Germans beneath a pile of leaves and branches and for the next few days he travelled only at night, hoping to make his way through enemy lines while memorizing as much information as he could about the German military installations he passed. During this time, Bunnie (who, along with her son, was living with Ross and his wife Muriel while Art Jr. was overseas) received a telegram at home in Brookline, Massachusetts on June 15:

REGRET TO ADVISE THAT YOUR HUSBAND FLIGHT LIEUTENANT ARTHUR STUART ROSS C EIGHT THREE TWO THREE IS REPORTED MISSING AFTER AIR OPERATIONS OVERSEAS JUNE ELEVENTH STOP

Meanwhile, after several days where he'd received only bits of food from French villagers who were terrified of being found helping a downed Allied airman, Art Jr. eventually fell in with a group of French townsfolk who fed him and nursed his wounds. He was provided with a cover story and billeted in the home of the local mayor … hidden in plain sight in a room next to a German major who was already in residence there! Eventually, Art Jr. was put in touch with the French resistance. He was provided with forged papers claiming he was a local woodcutter and though he had only barely passable high-school French, he did his best to learn a few key phrases and mimic the accents of those he travelled with as they walked over 300 kilometres to Paris. He also roughened his hands by twisting them around a broom handle for days on end until they appeared appropriately calloused.

Eluding and escaping from German patrols along the way, Art Jr. finally reached Paris in late July. Without a way to get a message home to his family, who'd had nothing more than hope to go on for weeks, he planned to lay low until the inevitable arrival of the Allies. But as he became aware of the Nazi atrocities in the French capital, Art Jr. took up arms with the local citizens. When the city was finally liberated on August 25, he was able to relay a message home through a chance meeting with a *Chicago Tribune* reporter. The reporter slipped in a short note for his editor at the end of one of his stories, and so it was that on August 29, 1944, another telegram arrived in Brookline: "JOHN THOMPSON CABLES FROM PARIS HE DINED WITH YOUR HUSBAND LAST FRIDAY." This was how the Ross family learned that Art Jr. was still alive.

Art Ross called the *Chicago Tribune* office to confirm the story and sent his thanks to the editor by letter the next day. "Words fail me to adequately express our appreciation of Mr. Thompson's marvelous action and your thoughtfulness in conveying his message to us," he wrote. "A great cloud has been lifted from the minds of a wife, mother, and father. I would appreciate greatly that my thanks be conveyed to Mr. Thompson and when this terrible war is over, I do hope that I will have the pleasure of thanking him personally when he returns."

A few days later, another telegram arrived. This one was from Art Jr. Typically understated, it read: "SORRY IT TOOK SO LONG TO GET AWAY FROM THE RATS."

On October 20, 1944, Art Jr. arrived home, greeted by his mother, his wife, and his now three-year-old son. A few days later, husband and wife travelled to Quebec City, where the Bruins were training.

"People who saw Art Ross, rugged manager of the Boston Bruins … saw something a little new in him today," noted the *Boston Globe* on October 25. "The usually grim countenance, which has been presiding over the practice sessions of the 'Beantown' boys, was wreathed in smiles because Art was accompanied by a tall flight lieutenant of the RCAF."

When asked to express his feelings, the elder Ross could only manage: "I'm very happy and very proud."

# 31

## POSTWAR CHALLENGES

The Second World War ended during the summer of 1945. Many of the NHL players who'd enlisted were expected back in time for training camp that fall. Others returned as the 1945–46 season progressed. Throughout the War years, Art Ross had occasionally turned over the coaching of the team to Dit Clapper. Sometimes, Clapper ran the team for weeks on end as Ross and Bruins scouts, headed by former NHL player Harold "Baldy" Cotton, busied themselves with the business of securing players to fill out Boston's depleted roster. Now, the 60-year-old Ross was stepping away from coaching once again. This time, it was for good.

The news about Ross's coaching decision was made official on October 3, 1945, at a pre-season luncheon at Boston's Parker House hotel. Clapper was confirmed as the Bruins' playing coach, and it was reiterated that the word from Kitchener was that Milt Schmidt, Bobby Bauer, and Woody Dumart would all be back in time to open the season. Frank Brimsek hadn't been released from the U.S. Coast Guard, but "we're praying for his return," said Ross, who would have a new assistant general manager this year: Art Ross Jr.

Muriel Ross with her sons Arthur (Art Jr.) and John. (Photo courtesy of the Ross Family.)

This picture is a puzzle. Art Ross is seated next to an unknown person who may have been hired to play the part of one of the French-Canadian characters Ross created for the stories he told to help drum up publicity for the Bruins. (Photo courtesy of the Ross Family.)

Goalie Art Ross Jr. receives instruction from Bruins legends Eddie Shore and Tiny Thompson. (Photo courtesy of the Ross Family.)

A cartoon strip depicting the many talents of Art Ross. (Photo courtesy of the Ross Family.)

A Christmas present to Art Ross from cartoonist Gene Mack and the sportswriters of the *Boston Globe*. (Photo courtesy of the Ross Family.)

Art Ross beats Father Time. This gift for his 53rd birthday was probably presented to him in January of 1939 ... though Ross likely turned 54 that year. (Photo courtesy of the Ross Family.)

Ten long years after Boston's first championship, Art Ross drinks champagne from the Stanley Cup once again while inside the Bruins dressing room after defeating the Toronto Maple Leafs on April 19, 1939. (Photo courtesy of the Ross Family.)

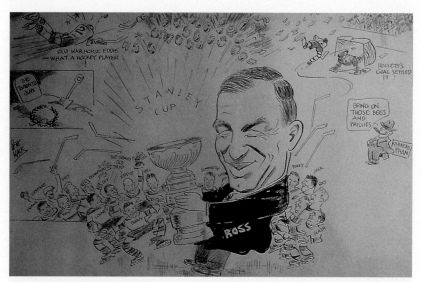

A Gene Mack cartoon depicting Boston's 1939 Stanley Cup victory. There had been a lot of playoff losses between the first Bruins Cup in 1929 and this one, including several to the Maple Leafs. (Photo courtesy of the Ross Family.)

A formal portrait of Art Ross, circa 1939. (Photo courtesy of the Ross Family.)

Art Ross with sons John and Art Jr., who both served in the Royal Canadian Air Force during the Second World War. (Photo courtesy of the Ross Family.)

Conn Smythe poses with Art Ross and Art Ross Jr. The patriotic Smythe was impressed that Ross's sons came north to Canada (where both had been born) to serve with the RCAF during the Second World War. This helped to ease the feud between the two hockey men. (Photo courtesy of the Ross Family.)

Art III and his mother Bunny welcome home Art Ross Jr. in October of 1944. Art Jr. was thought to have died behind enemy lines after being reported missing five days after D-Day. (Photo courtesy of the Ross Family.)

THE 1945 BOSTON BRUINS — Back Row, L. to R. — PAUL BIBEAULT, BEP GUIDOLIN, JACK CHURCH, JACK McGILL, DON GALLINGER, MURRAY HENDERSON, BILL SHILL, TERRY REARDON, PAT EGAN, HARVEY BENNETT. Front Row, L. to R. — BOBBY BAUER, WOODY DUMART, MILT SCHMIDT, COACH DIT CLAPPER, CAPT. JACK CRAWFORD, BILL COWLEY, HERB CAIN. Inserts, Upper — TRAINER WIN GREEN, GEN. MGR. ART ROSS, ASST GEN. MGR. ART ROSS, JR. Lower Insert — FRANKIE BRIMSEK.

The 1945–46 Bruins welcomed back many players who had served in the Second World War, including Bobby Bauer (17), Woody Dumart (14), Milt Schmidt (15), and Frank Brimsek (lower insert). Dit Clapper (5), Johnny Crawford (6), Bill Cowley (10), and Herb Cain (4) had not been overseas. Art Ross Jr. (upper right insert) served as the team's assistant general manager this season. (Photo courtesy of the Ross Family.)

Art Ross shakes hands with Elmer Lach of the Montreal Canadiens (who was sidelined with a broken jaw) during the first presentation of the Art Ross Trophy at the Montreal Forum prior to a game between Boston and Montreal on December 23, 1948. Lach had led the NHL in scoring in 1947–48. Ross's lifelong friend Lester Patrick (far left) and NHL president Clarence Campbell were on hand as well. (Photo courtesy of Imperial Oil-Turofsky Collection/ Hockey Hall of Fame.)

The scroll presented to Art Ross upon entering the Hockey Hall of Fame shows the correct spelling of his middle name (Howey) and the correct date of his induction: December 3, 1949. (Photo courtesy of the Ross Family.)

In perhaps the last photograph ever taken of him, Art Ross is wearing one dark lens in his glasses to help him combat a problem with his eyes. (Photo courtesy of the Ross Family.)

Clapper proved a capable leader, and Schmidt, Bauer, and Dumart slowly rounded into shape. Brimsek returned to the team in December and, after a few rough outings, was soon in pre-war form. He was named a Second Team All-Star, while defenceman Johnny Crawford (who'd been with the Bruins throughout the War) was selected to the First Team. Boston finished second to Montreal in the regular-season standings with a record of 24–18–8. However, the Maurice Richard–led Canadiens were too powerful for the Bruins when the teams met up in the Stanley Cup Final. Montreal took the series in five games.

Among the few things that hadn't gone well for the Bruins in 1945–46 was Ross's decision to hire his son. "It was a quintessential case of nepotism," observes Art Ross III, "but given his War record [he'd received Britain's Distinguished Flying Cross and would later receive the Croix de Guerre from France] nobody seemed to mind."

Many have spoken of Art Ross's great ability to size up talent. "Whether you like or dislike Art Ross," Frank Selke said in an undated story written by Henry McKenna of the *Boston Herald*, likely for a Bruins program, "there's one thing that must be said about him. He's the best judge of a hockey player I've ever seen. He can take one look at a player, and tell you whether he's got it or not. He's almost infallible in his judgment." His son did not share this ability. "Dad didn't have the skill set for the task," says Art III, and, given that he was already Art Ross Jr., "he said he didn't want to be a 'Junior Art Ross.'" On July 3, 1946, a small story appeared in the *Boston Globe* saying that Art Jr. wouldn't be back with the hockey club for the next season. He'd left for a job in the aviation industry.

Art Jr. likely had no input in a decision made after the 1945–46 season that his father came to regret. Roy Conacher was not discharged from the RCAF in England until February of 1946 and didn't rejoin the Bruins until March. A slow starter under of the best of circumstances, he got into only four games, but did manage two goals and an assist before being held pointless in three playoff contests. Always considered something of a reluctant athlete who'd been pushed into hockey by the success of his older brothers, Ross convinced himself that nearly four full seasons away from the NHL had ruined his former star. In June, he traded

Conacher for Joe Carveth, who'd played well for Detroit during the war. Carveth managed only one decent season with the Bruins in 1946–47 before Ross dealt him too. Meanwhile, Conacher bounced back as a top scorer in Detroit and then Chicago and was elected to the Hockey Hall of Fame in 1998. Writing at the time of Conacher's induction, Jim Proudfoot noted in the *Toronto Star* on November 16, 1998, that Ross always considered trading him to be his biggest mistake. In a column for the *Boston Globe* on December 12, 1956, Harold Kaese wrote that Ross had asked Detroit boss Jack Adams to throw in a young kid named Gordie Howe to even up the deal. If that's true, and if it had happened, Ross's memory of the deal — and the history of hockey — would have been considerably different.

*  *  *

Given his inventive mind, it's likely that the modern statistics known as analytics would have intrigued Art Ross. Then again, he was the type that liked to see something with his own eyes and form his own opinions. Craig Patrick, long-time general manager of the Pittsburgh Penguins and currently a special assistant to the hockey operations department of the Buffalo Sabres, shares a story from when Ross hired his father, Lynn Patrick, to coach the Bruins in 1950.

"They were sitting in Ross's office in the Boston Garden and Art was asking my dad about a particular player. My dad pulled out some stats and started looking at them, and said, 'well, he did this, and he did that ...' Art said to my dad, 'Lynn, if you have to look at stats to tell me about a player, I hired the wrong guy.'"

On the other hand, Ross wasn't against using statistics when it was to his advantage. "Every year," Ed Sandford remembers about his contract negotiations, "[Ross would] pull out the stats and tell you how you'd done and how you hadn't done." There was little more than goals, assists, and penalty minutes for Ross to go on during the late 1940s and early 1950s, but there is, at least, some indication that he understood the concepts that modern analytics hope to quantify.

In a column by Harold Kaese, then of the *Boston Evening Transcript*, on January 31, 1941, he wrote: "Ross likes to see the puck in the other team's zone. When people say the Bruins are futile trying to clear the puck, he replies, 'look at it from the other side. Don't other teams look even worse trying to get the puck out against us?'"

Puck possession, it seems, was just as important to Art Ross as to the analytics advocates today — although Ross probably believed this was something a smart observer could see for himself. Of course, it was much easier to see things first-hand in a league with only a handful of teams playing half the games of the modern NHL season. Even so, during the 1946–47 season, Ross tried to create a new statistical system. Today's analytics crowd will likely find his idea simplistic, but it shows that Ross was trying to look at the game differently. He wanted to generate a more reliable measure of a players' overall worth, particularly for players who were strong defensively.

"I am coming out of New York the other night after we have beaten the Rangers," Ross explained to reporters in his room at the Royal York Hotel in Toronto. "I have just read in one of the New York papers where [Milt] Schmidt had accidentally fallen and his fall saved [Bryan] Hextall from scoring a Rangers goal. But what actually happened was one of the best defensive plays I have ever seen. Hextall has broken away and is in the clear. Schmidt sails after him from the side. He takes one dive, lands in front of Hextall, takes the puck with him and ends on the boards. It was daring, effective and clever."

It was because of moves like this one, a defensive gem from a player still capable of challenging for a scoring title, that Ross considered Schmidt to be the greatest centre in hockey history. "Schmidt [is] a better player than [Howie] Morenz," he would claim while explaining his new defensive scoring system. As late as 1960, Ross still maintained that Schmidt was the best centre he ever saw.

Continuing his story, Ross said he was in his room on the train en route to Toronto, thinking about how important Schmidt's play had been to Boston's 3–1 victory, but realizing it would never show up in a statistical summary. "I figured something should be done to get the defensive player into the records."

His idea wasn't completely worked out yet, but Ross explained: "We could give, say, five points for defensive play. Two for the defence men and three for the forwards. One defence man might win both points for a sound game. Or they might be divided equally between two defence men. The same for forwards. One man might earn all three, or two, or one. After all, my argument is that it is just as important to save a goal as it is to score one. Hence some credit should be given and put into the records."

When asked who'd give out these points, Ross said: "I would appoint a defence scorer for each game — preferably some old time hockey player capable of judging good defensive play."

Ross later revised his system somewhat, suggesting that the old time hockey players be appointed (and paid) to award up to three points to each player in a game to rate his overall performance. A player might earn one point for his defensive play, and two for his offense, or perhaps no points at all. By the end of the season, Ross reasoned, a coach or manager would have a much better indication of the strength and weakness of all his players. "If you're making a deal," said Ross, "you have a real line on a player. In addition, fans get to know their real value and you have something of a guide to go on." Realizing his plan still wasn't perfect, he added: "I do not say the three point idea should be adopted, but some system should be devised along those lines."

Ross's system was never adopted, but NHL statistics did slowly evolve. By 1955, all six teams employed statisticians who tracked not just goals, assists, points, and penalty minutes, but shots taken by each player, saves made by each goalie, and which players were on the ice when goals were scored. The plus-minus information generated was used by general managers in contract negotiations, but was considered confidential. It was not until the 1963–64 season that the figures were made public. This was certainly a big step forward in recognizing defensive play, although many devotees of analytics can list dozens of ways in which plus-minus is flawed.

\* \* \*

The NHL season expanded from 50 to 60 games in 1946–47, and the Bruins took a slight step backwards that year, posting a third-place finish with a record of 26–23–11. In the playoffs, they lost their semifinal series four games to one to first-place Montreal, who was then beaten by Toronto in a six-game Stanley Cup Final. The Maple Leafs, who'd won the Stanley Cup in 1944–45 but missed the playoffs entirely in 1945–46, surprised the experts by bouncing back in 1946–47 on the strength a youth movement engineered by Conn Smythe. With the symbolism of the death of Charles Adams marking the end of an era in Boston on October 2, 1947, Ross took a page from his old rival's playbook and began to rebuild the Bruins around younger players.

Dit Clapper retired after having seen only limited action during his twentieth NHL season in 1946–47. He'd be back as coach only in 1947–48. Bill Cowley was gone, and Bobby Bauer also retired despite scoring a career-high 30 goals in 1946–47. All of them needed to be replaced. Among the newcomers to the lineup in 1947–48 was future hall of famer Fern Flaman, who played his first full season on the Boston defence. Promising forward Paul Ronty was promoted from the Bruins' farm team in Hershey, and Ed Sandford was signed to his first pro contract after leading St. Michael's College of Toronto to the Memorial Cup. The Bruins had been after Sandford since 1944 when he was only 16 and the *Boston Globe* called him the hottest amateur product in eastern Canada. Johnny Peirson appeared in a handful of games for the second straight winter in 1947–48 and became a regular the following year.

Clapper was the coach, but Art Ross certainly kept his hand in the on-ice decisions. In his *Globe* column on January 6, 1959, Harold Kaese quoted Ross as saying that he, "never bawled out a player in front of the team. If I had something to say, I made him come to the office the next morning and said it there." Ed Sandford recalls things differently. "Maybe that's how he did it in the 1930s when he was coaching," he says. Sandford remembers Ross the general manager occasionally calling his own meetings with the players, and that, "he was pretty rough. [Ross] would tell you if you, or your line, were playing poorly and how you could improve. He was actively involved; knew all the players; knew how they were playing. One time he criticized me for slashing and getting penalties, but he said 'you pass the puck well.'"

Even with the veteran presence of Milt Schmidt and Woody Dumart to lead the young team (Schmidt won the Hart Trophy as NHL MVP in 1950–51), Boston's youth movement was only moderately successful. The Bruins of the late 1940s and early 1950s generally finished third or fourth in the six-team league and usually exited the playoffs in the first round. Still, "it was a fun time," says Paul Ronty. "We were young guys. You'd go out for beers together, [but] you couldn't have a drink within three miles of the Garden. It was a Boston Bruins rule. They didn't want the guys to get involved with the guys in the North End!"

But it wasn't a problem with anyone in the North End that produced an incident in 1948 that Art Ross III remembers could still make his grandfather brim with anger many years later. It was the involvement of Don Gallinger with Detroit gambler and career criminal James Tamer.

Don Gallinger was only 17 when he joined the Bruins in 1942. He later spent time with the RCAF before returning to the Bruins in the fall of 1945, and was still just 22 during the 1947–48 season. He was a decent scorer and a solid second-line centre who was also an excellent baseball player.

In a series of stories about Gallinger in Toronto's *Globe and Mail* in January of 1963, Scott Young wrote that Gallinger had begun betting heavily on horse racing at Bruins training camp in 1947. Soon, with teammate Billy Taylor (whom Ross had recently acquired from the Red Wings), Gallinger was feeding information about the Bruins to Jim Tamer and gambling on his team — not always to win. Young notes that, in the minds of the players, they weren't throwing games intentionally, but simply taking advantage of what they knew of injuries, attitudes, and other performance factors. Gallinger told Young his bets varied from $250 to $1,000 and that he likely wagered on eight or nine games between December of 1947 and February of 1948.

Detroit police had a wiretap on Tamer's phone and on February 18, 1948, they picked up a call from Gallinger in Chicago. He relayed some key information about Bruins injuries and the death of Johnny Crawford's newborn daughter. Gallinger was sure the Bruins would lose and told Young he bet $1,000 on the Black Hawks. Boston beat Chicago 4–2 that night, but Tamer was arrested in a downtown Detroit bar a few days later. Police informed NHL president Clarence Campbell of their wiretaps and he began his own investigation. Soon word hit the newspapers that a couple of unnamed players had been gambling on games, though Campbell was quick to point out that none had been fixed.

Gallinger was visiting his family at home in Port Colborne, Ontario, prior to a game with the Maple Leafs, when he was summoned to Toronto. He had not been foolish enough to reveal his name during his phone calls to Tamer, and while on the train from Welland to Toronto, he made up his mind to deny his involvement, chiefly, he told Young, because of the disgrace it would bring to his family.

In Toronto, all the players were being called into Art Ross's hotel room one by one. From the questions he was asked, Gallinger sensed there was no hard proof against him, so he went ahead with his denials. Then, in the early morning hours after the game against the Maple Leafs, he was called back to Ross's room.

"[He] went at me for, oh, about an hour and before it was over he was cursing and swearing at me and saying, 'Don, I know it's you! Why in the hell don't you tell me?' And this went on and on and on, till it got to the point where I really thought he was going to punch me."

Gallinger told Young that, "When it boils right down to it during all these interrogations, Art Ross, I know, yet I didn't want to believe it, was trying to help me and yet I wouldn't give him the opportunity to help me."

On March 9, 1948, Clarence Campbell suspended Billy Taylor from organized hockey for life. Gallinger was suspended indefinitely before receiving the same lifetime ban on September 27, 1948. More than a year later, on October 9, 1949, Gallinger finally admitted his guilt in a private meeting with Campbell. He never admitted it publicly until his interviews with Scott Young. Gallinger said that Campbell had urged him not to tell anyone, and that he would keep it quiet also to spare Gallinger's ailing father. (Young found it odd that Campbell never altered his policy after Gallinger's father died in 1951.)

Around 1950, Gallinger approached Conn Smythe about reinstatement. Smythe told him he'd support a petition to allow him to play or coach in the amateur ranks if he could get Art Ross onside. Gallinger met with Ross, but Ross was still bitter. There was sympathy for Gallinger from many quarters, including Dave Egan of the *Boston Daily Record* who wrote in support of the banned player from time to time and blamed Ross for the continuing ban. Ross wasn't moved. To him, Gallinger was a cheat who'd gambled on his own team to lose. "This Gallinger comes back, I go," John Ross remembers his father saying. "He put his job right on the line."

After the Bruins fought to deny another appeal in 1955, Gallinger realized that Ross didn't know about his confession. In the fall of 1961, he decided to see him again.

"I went to Boston, and when we were talking, I mentioned about my first confession to Mr. Campbell. He interrupted. He said, 'Are you meaning to tell me that you confessed to the National Hockey League that soon after the incident?' And I said, 'Yes.' He was flabbergasted … and I told him about Mr. Campbell telling me not to tell anyone else and promising that he wouldn't tell, either."

Clearly Campbell hadn't told anyone and when Gallinger told Ross, the atmosphere between them changed completely.

"He said, 'Don, I don't have any active participation with the Boston hockey club or the National Hockey League now, but if I'm ever asked I will support you.' And we shook hands I think on the friendliest note that we'd had since the incident started."

Apparently, Ross was never asked. He never forgave Gallinger in public, nor did his family ever realize he'd had a change of heart. The NHL finally lifted the suspensions on Gallinger and Billy Taylor, but not until 1970.

# 32

## HOCKEY
## IMMORTALITY

The NHL had trophies for its most valuable player, its best goalie, its top rookie, and its most gentlemanly player, but until 1948, the league had no award for its leading scorer. Charlie Conacher had talked about this oddity in a column in Toronto's *Globe and Mail* back on February 12, 1937.

"It is the ambition of every forward to make his goals and assists reach a larger total than that of any of his rivals," wrote Conacher. "I know I was always under the impression that there was a trophy for realizing this ambition until I finally was successful. Then, the year I led the league I found that with the honor went no prize that I could keep for later years.

"Probably the scoring leadership is the most important thing any individual in the league can win," he added, "and, with prizes for the best goaltender, the most gentlemanly player and other distinctions that might be gained, I certainly think the best scorer of the season at least should be given equal recognition."

Ten years later, at the NHL meetings in Montreal in June of 1947, the league's governors voted to establish a $1,000 cash award to the player who led the league in scoring, with $500 to the runner-up. One year after, the governors announced that there would finally be a trophy presented to the scoring leader. The award was not named in honour of Art Ross, as is often written, but was named for him because he was the man who donated the trophy to the NHL. It was inscribed as follows:

THE "ART" ROSS TROPHY
PRESENTED TO
THE NATIONAL HOCKEY LEAGUE
BY
ARTHUR H. ROSS
F/LT ARTHUR S. ROSS, D.F.C.
F/LT JOHN K. ROSS

TO BE AWARDED EACH YEAR TO THE LEADING SCORER

The trophy was awarded for the first time retroactively to 1947–48 scoring champion Elmer Lach of the Canadiens and presented to him in a ceremony before a Boston game in Montreal on December 23, 1948.

The Art Ross Trophy has kept Art Ross's name alive and is probably the one thing he is best known for today. However, recognition for the NHL's top scorer was not originally what Ross had in mind. In May of 1941, the NHL had accepted a trophy from him that was supposed to go to the league's most valuable player. There was already the Hart Trophy for the NHL MVP, but sportswriters voted for that. Ross wanted the NHL players to vote for his MVP award.

"It will be up for competition for the first time next winter," reported the *Boston Globe* of Ross's trophy on May 17, 1941, but it was never put to use. "Wartime restrictions" is the reason given in the *National Hockey League Official Guide & Record Book*.

One year after the 1948 presentation of the Art Ross Trophy, Ross's hockey immortality was further ensured when he was elected to the Hockey Hall of Fame. Most sources list Ross's induction date as 1945, but like the donation of his trophy, his enshrinement was somewhat slow in coming.

Baseball first elected members to a hall of fame in 1936. Three years later, on June 12, 1939, the National Baseball Hall of Fame and Museum was dedicated in Cooperstown, New York. Soon, the hockey community was calling for its own such shrine.

During the early 1940s, Captain James T. Sutherland of Kingston, Ontario, led the charge for a Hockey Hall of Fame and lobbied to have it established in his hometown. Over the weekend of September 10–12, 1943, the NHL endorsed a proposal put forward by the Canadian Amateur Hockey Association, and already approved by Kingston city council, to establish the Hockey Hall of Fame in Kingston. However, construction delays meant no building was erected in Kingston until 1965 — seven years after the decision to relocate to Toronto, where the original Hockey Hall of Fame building finally opened in 1961.

A few weeks after the 1943 endorsement, seven prominent hockey executives were appointed to a board of governors to have jurisdiction over the election of those to be inducted into the Hockey Hall of Fame. Shortly after the initial seven were announced, two more men became Hall of Fame governors. One was Art Ross.

By January of 1944, newspaper writers and old-time players were speculating on possible honourees. That February, Ross refused to commit himself to any names, but offered the opinion that any player who was still active should not qualify. When the first inductees to the International Hockey Hall of Fame (as it was originally called) were officially announced in newspapers on May 1, 1945, not only were no active players named, no living players were elected either. It's not clear if a decision was made only to vote for deceased greats, but that may well have been the case.

"Each member of the board of governors cast a ballot for 12 players," reported the *Toronto Star*, "with eight to be chosen according to the voting." When two players tied for the final spot, the decision was made to induct nine men. The actual tallies weren't noted, but the first inductees to the Hockey Hall of Fame, in order of the votes they received, were: Howie Morenz, Tommy Phillips, Georges Vezina, Hod Stuart, Frank McGee, Eddie Gerard, Charlie Gardiner, Hobey Baker, and Harvey Pulford.

News of the Hockey Hall of Fame's first honoured members didn't create much of a stir, but the announcement of a second set of inductees in 1947 certainly did. Seven players were elected this time, and all seven of them were still alive. Six of those elections were announced together on February 21, 1947, but one name had already been announced alone, 15 days earlier, on February 6. The solo announcement was that of Dit Clapper.

Though he had been expected to retire from playing after the 1945–46 season, Clapper was filling in as an injury replacement in 1946–47. He was to be honoured before a game at the Boston Garden on February 12, 1947. The game would mark the final one of Clapper's career, and he would be presented with his Hall of Fame scroll that night. Surely Ross must have orchestrated this.

Bruins fans loved the classy Clapper, and were happy to celebrate him. (Conn Smythe was at the Clapper Night festivities and noted that, "Even if Dit couldn't play hockey, he'd deserve all this for having stood Art Ross for 20 years.") But the decision to elect Clapper to the Hockey Hall of Fame before the player everyone in Boston believed was the greatest in Bruins history proved unpopular.

"Why isn't Eddie Shore in the Hockey Hall of Fame?" asked writer Roger Birtwell in the *Boston Globe* on February 7. "In hotel lobbies, in corner drug stores, even in the corridors of Greater Boston high schools, it was the chief subject of conversation yesterday."

Birtwell wrote that Shore seemed "genuinely delighted" that Clapper had been honoured, but admitted that he had no idea who'd been elected previously, or by whom. When informed that Ross was one of those on the selection committee, Shore laughed, and added: "I guess there are some things that are best not mentioned."

Two weeks later, when the six other Hall of Fame players were announced, Shore's name was among them. Whether or not Ross had intentionally slighted him with the early announcement of Clapper's induction, Shore seemed bitter. "I would like to have the presentation at the Garden because of the Boston fans," he said, "but I wouldn't be fussy for the sake of anybody else connected with the Bruins." Shore and Ross shook hands publicly before a Boston playoff game in Montreal on March 25, and Shore received his Hall of Fame scroll at the Garden one week later.

Shore's election to the Hockey Hall of Fame had been announced along with those of former players Cyclone Taylor, Russell Bowie, Frank

Nighbor, Aurel Joliat, and Lester Patrick. Now, the fact that Patrick was being honoured and Ross was not caused more consternation in Boston. Dave Egan had never been a Ross fan, but even he wondered in his *Boston Record* column why the Bruins boss was overlooked. It turned out that even if his friend Lester had no such concern about conflicts of interest, Ross had refused to allow his own name on the ballot. "Perhaps when some other governors come in," he said, "but not now."

In January of 1948, the International Hockey Hall of Fame announced the names of seven more governors creating a 16-man selection committee. Ross must have found it less of a conflict to put himself up for induction among a larger field of selectors. Either that, or he liked the idea of going into the Hall of Fame in conjunction with the Bruins' upcoming 25th anniversary season. Both reasons were probably true.

Ross was at home in Brookline when his election to the Hockey Hall of Fame was announced on October 21, 1949. "I am very happy about the selection," he said, but he preferred to talk about his fellow inductee Donald (Dan) Bain, who'd starred with the Winnipeg Victorias in the 1890s and early 1900s. "It would take an old-timer like myself to remember Donald Bain," said Ross. "I remember the thrill I got watching him when I was in my teens. He was one of the best skaters and stick handlers I have ever seen."

Three weeks after the Hall of Fame announcement, Weston Adams declared that the Bruins would honour Ross for his 25 years of service to the team with a pre-game ceremony and post-game dinner when Boston hosted Chicago at the Garden on December 3, 1949. Before the game, Kingston mayor and Hall of Fame president James B. Garvin delivered Ross his Hall of Fame scroll. NHL president Clarence Campbell presented Ross with a silver tray decorated with the insignias of all six teams and the signatures of the club's governors. Representatives from the Garden's famed Gallery Gods received the loudest ovation of the pre-game ceremony when they presented a silver tea service. Ross addressed the crowd briefly, expressing his thanks and appreciation to the Boston fans.

The gift giving continued after the game at the Hotel Statler. Weston Adams presented Ross with a beautiful watch; Milt Schmidt gave him a Paul Revere service bowl on behalf of the players; and the local hockey writers and radio commentators gave him a solid gold cigarette case. Still, the gift that he appreciated most was that his struggling team, the youngest in the NHL that season, beat the Black Hawks 5–3. "Thanks, boys, for winning the game for me," he said quietly.

In the days before and after the ceremony, Boston writers filled the local sports sections with stories about Ross. Gordon Campbell in the *Boston Traveler* on December 3 wrote: "Much has been said about Art as a player and executive. Much more can be said of him as an inventor. He designed the net universally used today, and an intimate sidelight to that invention is the secret that Art's charming wife, Muriel, crocheted the webbing used on the original model Art submitted to the league for approval.... Ross designed the puck used today, although it took a war to disclose that synthetic rubber was better than pure rubber, since it didn't bounce readily." Campbell also noted, "Art had the guard for his players' Achilles tendon long before it was adopted by the league." As for rules, he said: "Art practically wrote the rule book."

Victor Jones wrote similarly in the *Boston Globe*, saying, "It would be almost impossible to play [hockey], as now played, without Mr. Ross' gimmicks.... He has also been one of the leading factors in rule revisions and the introduction of new tactics."

When it came to tactics, Herb Ralby, writing in the *Globe* on December 4, thought there was no better story than how Ross had outwitted Jack Adams during a 1945 playoff series between Boston and Detroit: "Adams was talking to himself because Jack had been trying to maneuver certain Wings lines against particular Bruins lines [but] Ross shifted every other minute and Adams never could get his club settled because he was too busy shifting and watching for Ross' next move. Finally, the shrewd Ross dug into his bag of tricks and came up with an unorthodox line of a right wing from one line, a centre from another, and a left wing from a third. Adams, on the Detroit bench, was stymied. He didn't know which of his forward lines to use, and he almost had apoplexy. 'It's illegal,' he screamed at the referee. 'He can't do such a thing.' But there was nothing the referee could do except [drop the puck]."

There were 350 guests invited to the Art Ross tribute, but one big name was absent. Conn Smythe stayed home in Toronto, where he was involved in a very public (and almost purely promotional) battle in which he insisted that Maple Leafs goalie Turk Broda lose weight. Smythe telegrammed his regrets, and stole the show:

> Owing to Leafs entry into Lard league and Battle of the Bulge that is now in progress, I find it impossible to be in Boston....
>
> Although I have been personally against anybody living being put in the Hall of Fame, on second thought, perhaps that does not disqualify Art. With all the talk of fat in our team at present, some people might have been unkind enough to say that is what is the matter with Arturo's head.
>
> However, never have I met anybody who even suggested there was any fat around Art's heart. I believe this is one of the very best choices made to date for the Hall of Fame. It adds great and real distinction to the project.
>
> I send him my heartiest congratulations and also congratulate those who had enough sense to enroll in the Hall of Fame one of the all-time greats in hockey.

# A GREAT LOSS
# TO THE GAME

By the summer of 1950, Art Ross was 65 years old. He wasn't ready for retirement yet, but he was planning for the Bruins' future without him.

Dit Clapper had seemed the type that might take over Ross's front office job one day, but Clapper resigned as Bruins coach after the 1948–49 season. His wife was ill and his off-season business concerns in Peterborough, Ontario, were taking up more of his time. Still, the news came as a shock. There was no player Ross was ever closer to than Clapper, and for years they'd gone on an annual fishing trip in June at a lodge Ross had north of Montreal. He became so emotional when Clapper's decision to retire was announced at the team's annual break-up dinner, that he was unable to deliver the short remarks he'd prepared.

Ross's first choice to replace Clapper as coach was Joe Primeau, but the former Maple Leafs star who was coaching at St. Michael's College found that the pressures of his off-ice business were too great for him to leave Toronto for an extended period. (Primeau would become coach of the Maple Leafs in 1950–51.) Instead, Ross turned to old-time Ottawa Senators star George Boucher to lead the Bruins in 1949–50. Boucher had been coaching senior amateur hockey in Ottawa for three seasons, but hadn't coached in the NHL since 1934–35. He didn't work out in Boston — although he was angry when the Bruins didn't give him another chance after his one-year deal expired. Things had been so bad at one point that Weston Adams asked Ross if he'd take over behind the bench, but Ross said "It would probably kill me at my age." Milt Schmidt was convinced to act as an advisor to Boucher, whom the Bruins didn't fire because, "we had a contract to honor."

The chance to hire a new coach, and to groom his successor as general manger, presented itself when Lynn Patrick resigned as coach of the Rangers on May 5, 1950. Lynn had just led New York to the Stanley Cup Final and a game seven double-overtime loss against Detroit, but announced he wanted to raise his family in his hometown of Victoria, British Columbia. He would also coach the minor league Cougars, which he co-owned with this father, Lester Patrick. But two months later, Ross called him in Victoria. "[He] was very persuasive," Lynn would recall for Eric Whitehead, "and he made me a great offer — twelve thousand dollars, which was big money then — and I accepted right there on the phone." When he arrived in Boston and was introduced to the media on August 1, 1950, Ross laid out his vision for the future.

"Lynn is not just filling in," declared Ross. "He is here permanently. He will coach the next two years and also will absorb the general manager's duties. He'll take over that post from me and Milt Schmidt [who was still very much active and about to embark on his Hart Trophy-winning season] will become coach if he shows he has the ability."

"The matter of Uncle Frank never came up between us," Lynn said later, but Ross had chosen a difficult time to groom a successor. For the first time since the earliest days of the franchise, the Bruins were struggling for survival.

*  *  *

Art Ross and Weston Adams had fought together against the NHL's decision to expand the season from 60 games to 70 for the 1949–50 season. "We have all kinds of school hockey and basketball and baseball all over our papers," said Adams at an NHL governors meeting on March 11, 1949, explaining why the Bruins could not stand any more games. "We have more competition in Boston than any other city in the league." The New York Rangers were also against the move, but Conn Smythe was strongly in support.

The NHL did expand the season, and the 70-game schedule drawn up for the Bruins in 1949–50 was terrible. Boston fans didn't traditionally turn their attention to hockey until after American Thanksgiving, yet the Bruins were given many of their home games early in the season. They also played too many home games on weeknights. Smythe's Leafs, on the other hand, got 23 of their 35 home games on Saturdays, Toronto's best night of the week.

Weston Adams also blamed television for cutting into the Bruins gate: not just televised sports, but the added competition from this new form of entertainment available in homes for free. Whatever the reasons, the Bruins had the lowest gate receipts in the NHL in 1949–50. Though they returned to the playoffs under Lynn Patrick in 1950–51, the team's record was only marginally better and Boston drew the lowest attendance in the league. Crowds declined by 20 percent and the Bruins lost $80,000.

The NHL was splitting, both in terms of on-ice success and box-office earnings, into the haves (Toronto, Montreal, and Detroit — whose winning ways made them immune to the problems facing the other American teams) and the have-nots (Boston, Chicago, and New York). Further complicating matters in Boston and Chicago was that the owners of the other four teams owned their own arenas, while the Bruins and Black Hawks paid rent.

Similar to the ownership in New York and Chicago, Boston was also neglecting its farm system — which only exacerbated the NHL's lopsidedness. Then, in the fall of 1951, Adams refused to finance the Bruins' training camp. The relationship between Ross and Adams had been strained, at best, as the team's fortunes declined, and this pushed it to the breaking point.

As early as 1941, it had been speculated that the Boston Garden-Arena Corporation (which operated both the Boston Garden and the Boston Arena) would buy the Bruins. Charles Adams had hoped to sell the team to the Boston Garden group in 1936, and they'd offered him $250,000, but the taxes on the transaction would have eaten up too much of the sale price. In 1941, Art Ross was willing to sell his shares (then estimated at 30 percent of the team), but the Garden wasn't looking for a minority interest. Ten years later, Ross began calling for a sale to the Garden group during the 1951 playoffs. Now, the Garden stepped up with a loan to cover the Bruins' training expenses in Hershey, which soon led to a deal for the Corporation to purchase a majority interest in the team.

The deal to buy 60 percent of the Bruins was announced on October 11, 1951. Reports in the next day's newspapers vary somewhat in different sources, with the *Boston Globe* reporting the price as $179,520 and Toronto's *Globe and Mail* as $187,680. The Boston paper said each Bruins shareholder would have the chance to sell 60 percent of his stock, although Adams and team treasurer Ralph Burkard guaranteed to make up the amount if others chose not to sell. (The *Boston Globe* claimed Adams owned 58 percent of the team, with Burkard holding 9 percent, while the Toronto paper claimed Adams held 51 percent.) Adams resigned immediately as club president, and Walter Brown of the Garden was named in his place. Adams still had something of a stake in the team however, as he owned 22 percent of the Boston Garden-Arena Corporation's stock.

It's not clear whether Art Ross sold any of his stock in 1951, but by September of 1952, he and Brown came to an agreement to buy him out. Meantime, "I'm most pleased in the change which has been made," Ross said when the sale was announced. "I'm sure under Walter Brown's rule the Bruins will regain their prestige." The bad feelings between Ross and his former boss were clear at the end of the press conference, when Ross posed for pictures with Brown but refused to do so with Adams. Later, when Adams posed for pictures with Brown in his private office, he was asked a question about the players and responded sharply, "That's the hockey department — next door."

The Bruins showed improvement on the ice under their new ownership through the end of the 1950s, reaching the Stanley Cup Final in 1953, 1956, and 1957, and drawing larger crowds and better gate receipts. However, the team would struggle for much of the 1960s. Not until the arrival of Bobby Orr in 1966–67, and the expansion of the NHL from 6 to 12 teams the following season, did the team that Art Ross built truly regain its prestige.

At the time of the sale in 1951, Walter Brown revealed that Art Ross was working under a five-year contract running until May 1, 1953. Brown said that Ross would stay on as vice president and general manager until then. His deal paid him $23,000 per year.

Detroit was the NHL's best team in 1952–53, and though the defending Stanley Cup champions were not quite as strong as they'd been the previous two seasons, the Red Wings romped to their fifth straight first-place finish with a record of 36–16–18. The Red Wings were 15 points ahead of the second-place Canadiens and 21 ahead of the Bruins, who posted a losing record of 28–29–13 but still finished in third place with 69 points. Boston met Detroit to open the playoffs, and despite having lost 10 of 14 games to them during the regular season and dropping the series opener 7–0, the Bruins beat the Red Wings in six games. It was thought that a Stanley Cup victory would be the perfect parting gift for Ross, who was expected to retire when his contract was up, but Montreal beat Boston in five games, wrapping up the series with a 1–0 victory on an overtime goal from Elmer Lach.

Walter Brown was pleased with the season. "I'm tickled with the fine job that Lynn Patrick has done coaching. Lynn and these boys have done a world of good for hockey in Boston." Patrick would remain as coach, and Milt Schmidt was confirmed to return for what turned out to be his final full season as a player in 1953–54. Woody Dumart also returned. As for the general manager, "I certainly want Ross with the Bruins," Brown said. "But essentially it is his decision."

It's only speculation made more than 60 years later, but unhappy circumstances may have made Ross's decision for him.

Muriel Ross had fallen ill on November 1, 1952, while visiting family in Montreal. She remained there all winter, but did not recover. She was finally flown back to Boston in a private plane in mid April, and in early May, she entered the hospital.

"Mrs. Ross was quite different from her husband," wrote Victor Jones in the *Boston Globe*. "Where he tends to be dour and introspective, she was habitually gay and outgoing. Though she seldom missed a Bruins game, very few fans knew she was in the Garden. Art sat on the bench, masterminding, or in more recent years, restlessly prowled the Garden, looking at the game from different points of view. Mrs. Ross was there, unseen, with friends and neighbors." She had long gotten over her anger at fans "who feel they could manage the team much better than her husband and who spend most of the game pointing this out at the top of their lungs," and as the years went by, "there never was a time when Ross came back to Boston from a bitter defeat on the road — and to him all defeats are bitter — without Mrs. Ross being at the station to meet him."

Muriel Ross died on May 10, 1953. She was 67 years old. She hadn't been there to cushion the blows for her husband during the 1952–53 season. Knowing that she never would be again, Ross may have decided to bury himself in his work one last time rather than live alone in an empty house. Two days before Muriel died, he signed a one-year contract to return as general manager. On July 2, 1953, he was re-elected to his position of vice president.

\* \* \*

Art Ross believed the 1952–53 Bruins had been their best team in five years, and that the 1953–54 version would be even better. He'd acquired veteran Cal Gardiner to bolster the roster and agreed with Lynn Patrick that Doug Mohns was ready for the NHL after leading the Barrie Flyers to the Memorial Cup. Late in the 1953–54 season, Ross acquired Gus Bodnar, who helped the Bruins finish 32–28–10 for their first winning record since 1948–49. Still, Boston's 74 points were only good enough for fourth place. In the playoffs, the second-place Canadiens swept the Bruins in their opening-round series.

On April 1, 1954, two nights after the team was eliminated, the Bruins held their annual break-up dinner. It was there that Art Ross's retirement was announced. He agreed to stay on as an advisor for six more months, but his active role in running the team was over after 30 years. Walter Brown praised Ross as, "the greatest fellow I have met in hockey," adding that Ross had retired at his own request. "Nobody wanted it to be this way," said Brown, "least of all myself. He has been one of the city's greatest professional sports operators."

Ross confirmed it was his decision, and that he'd already overstayed the time frame he'd laid out in 1950. "I'm standing by a promise I made to Lynn and Milt," he told the players, writers, and others in attendance at the dinner. "And in the 30 years since C.F. [Adams] came to Montreal to ask me to help him form this team, I have never broken a promise to a player or anyone else."

"I'm delighted to get the opportunity," Lynn Patrick admitted, "but I'm sorry Mr. Ross is retiring." Years later, he'd say, "Art Ross was the greatest boss I ever had. I loved the guy and I think the feeling was mutual."

Milt Schmidt felt the same. "The 18 years I have been with you have been wonderful ones for me," he said. "When I came to play here, I was practically a child." Dit Clapper spoke similarly. "There's only one way to say it. Art was a father to me. Everyone knows that he will be a great loss to hockey. It's a tough thing for the game to see him stepping down."

There was no word from Eddie Shore, and though the two never seemed to patch up their relationship, whenever Ross discussed the greatest players he ever saw, Shore was always the first defenceman mentioned. "I only knew one who I thought could compare to him," Ross told Fred Cusick in 1960, "and that was Hod Stuart." Of course, given all the comparisons between Stuart and Ross during his playing days, this could have been Ross's modest way of saying that Shore reminded him of himself!

Two other stars who'd left the Bruins on bad terms did send their praises. "The retirement of Ross means hockey is losing one of its great men," read a telegram from Cooney Weiland. "He has done a lot for the game; helped make it what it is in Canada as well as this country. One of the real pioneers. He'll be missed."

Bill Cowley also sent his thoughts about the man he'd quarreled with so openly at the same dinner seven years before. "He is unquestionably the greatest man in hockey. We had a misunderstanding, but after I got out into the business world myself, I realized that he was 100 percent right, and I was all wrong.

"If Art Ross were still connected with the Bruins when my son came of age to play professional hockey, I wouldn't want him to play for anybody except Mr. Ross."

# EPILOGUE

As a much younger man, nearing the end of his playing days, it was said that he never came out second best in a fight. Now that he was almost 70 years old and nearing the end of his management career, that was no longer true. No one who'd done anything for as long as he had could ever expect to win every battle, but it would have been nice to win the last one.

Art Ross, at his final NHL board meeting on September 15, 1954, moved to institute a simple revenue-sharing plan as there had been in his early years in Boston. Bruins ownership suggested that 10 percent of the net box office receipts, after deduction of the league's 5 percent share, be turned over to the visiting team. After a brief discussion, no one would even second the motion and so Ross withdrew it. There would be no revenue sharing in the NHL until the end of the lockout in 1994–95.

Two weeks later, on September 30, 1954, Ross formally announced his retirement. Over the next few years, he continued to make regular visits to the Bruins office. "I don't butt in, but the boys [Lynn Patrick and Milt Schmidt] like to talk things over with me."

"Milt and I look forward to having Mr. Ross in the office," Lynn confirmed. "After all, his advice is invaluable. If he doesn't show up for a while, I keep after him on the phone. I welcome the help he gives us."

Sadly, Ross could no longer attend games. His eyesight had been failing him since at least 1947, and the glare from the ice now induced intolerable headaches. "I listen some to the radio and follow things ... in the papers," he explained to Tom Fitzgerald of the *Boston Globe* late in 1956. His failing vision also meant he could no longer play gin rummy, an old favourite from his days of train travel. His eyes got too tired when the cards were played fast. Now, when he felt like playing cards, he went to the Charles River Country Club, where there was always a bridge game going. "When my eyes get tired," he told the *Globe*'s Arthur Siegel in 1960, I start telling a story or I start an argument and that slows everything until I'm rested."

He didn't mention it for public consumption, but something else he did in retirement was dote on his grandchildren. To them, Art Ross wasn't the hockey legend who built the Bruins. He was simply Gramp; "an endearing, kind, low key, and generous family fixture," says Art Ross III. "His place at the head of the table had nothing to do with pucks, nets, and pulling the goalie."

"I never remember him uttering a word about hockey at the table for family gatherings," says granddaughter Victoria Ross. Gramp gave her and her younger sister Valerie a new pair of figure skates every year at Christmas, but the only advice about skating he ever gave them was to make sure the laces were done up tight.

Both Art and Victoria have fond memories of their grandfather carving the roast at Sunday dinners, and the turkey at Christmas and Thanksgiving. "With surgical precision," Art recalls, adding that even with his diminished eyesight, Gramp still had the hand-eye co-ordination of a great athlete.

Youngest sister Valerie remembers that when her grandfather came to visit, "He always came to the front door wearing a sports jacket. He was warm and kind and would always — at least it seemed like it was always — bring a large jar of coins for my sister and me. We'd get so excited! We'd dump the jar of coins on the living room rug and separate all the pennies, nickels, dimes, and quarters, and then divide them up between us."

The one sad aspect of this happy domestic scene was that Art Jr. and wife Bunnie divorced in 1959. There was such a stigma at the time that no one in the family was actually told about it for several years. Bunnie would later say that the war had changed Art Jr. Over the years, Victoria came to realize, from the work she did with veterans suffering from post-traumatic stress, that her father had all the symptoms. "Yet back then," she says, "we knew virtually nothing about such problems and our family had little understanding of them."

The relationship between Art Ross and his eldest son deteriorated. They never repaired the rift. Ross had never seen his own father again after the breakup of his parents' marriage and he was probably unable to even comprehend the emotions this new divorce brought back to him. Ross made no provisions for his son in his will, but continued to look after Bunnie and the children. Years later, Art Jr. remarried and had another daughter, MacKenzie.

\* \* \*

Art Ross's health took a turn for the worse around 1962, and he moved into a nursing home. Son John (who was married, but had no children) became his primary caregiver until the end came on August 5, 1964. Funeral services were held in Boston and then in Montreal, where his remains were placed alongside those of his late wife Muriel at the Mount Royal Cemetery. A who's who of hockey turned out to mourn him, and generous eulogies appeared in many newspapers. Perhaps the most touching tribute was a simple telegram that arrived at Walter Brown's office on the evening that Ross passed away:

SORRY TO HEAR THE OLD BRUIN WARRIOR HAS GONE ALONG. GIVE MY DEEPEST SYMPATHY TO HIS FAMILY. REGARDS. CONN SMYTHE

# ACKNOWLEDGEMENTS

I decided I wanted to write a biography about Art Ross at the end of the summer in 2005. I can no longer remember if there was one thing in particular that made up my mind. I do remember thinking that if he had done all the things he did in baseball instead of hockey, there would already be several books about him.

The first person I contacted was Canadian sportswriting legend Milt Dunnell, who was just a few months shy of 100 years old at the time. Milt had written about Art Ross back in the 1940s and 1950s, but it turned out that he'd never really known him. Still, he sent me an envelope with clippings from his collection, and that's what got me started.

Next, I paid a visit to the Resource Centre at the Hockey Hall of Fame in Toronto and made photocopies of more clippings. Phil Pritchard and Craig Campbell (and, more recently Katherine Pearce) have always been very accommodating, and when I asked Phil if he had contact information for any members of Art Ross's family, he had an email address for Victoria Ross, one of Art's granddaughters. Victoria and I corresponded by email a few times in September of 2005, and then spoke on the phone on my birthday, October 20. Five days later, I received an email from

Victoria's brother, Art Ross III, who had already done extensive genealogical research on his grandfather. Well over 2,000 emails later, plus a few visits with Art and his wife Kathy, I have a new father figure in my life, and you hold this book in your hands.

I could never have written this book without Art's encouragement and support. It was a lot of work, but a lot of fun too, trying to uncover family mysteries, in which we were aided greatly by a distant Ross cousin, Serge Harvey, whom Art met online through their shared genealogical interest. Everyone should have a Serge Harvey in their life, helping them climb the branches of their own family tree! Serge also connected Art and me with another Ross cousin, Helen Webster, who has access to a treasure trove of old family letters from when Art Ross was a boy. Another relative through Ross's mother's family, Patrice MacLeod, helped me make sense of this very large family when I was just getting started. Near the end of the journey, Victoria and Valerie Ross both sent me reminiscences of their grandfather. (Valerie also earns special honours for saving my wife and me from the worst hotel room it was ever our misfortune to almost stay in!)

While this is, first and foremost, a book about a hockey legend, it was amazing where some of the research led. Anyone looking for information on someone who worked for the Hudson's Bay Company is in luck because the Archives of Manitoba houses incredibly detailed records. Leah Sander, who now works for Library and Archives Canada, was able to provide all sorts of fascinating information on the lives of Thomas Barnston Ross, Peter McKenzie, and other members of their families. Even more surprising to me, the Bank of Montreal has an archivist, and records that include the former Merchants Bank of Canada from well before it was absorbed by BMO in 1922. Yolaine Toussaint was able to provide an employment record for Art Ross from 1903 to 1906.

Richard Johnson from the Sports Museum in Boston showed great enthusiasm for this project. He also suggested contacting Harry Sinden and Bob Cleary. Neither had actually known Art Ross, but both provided some wonderful second-hand stories. Milt Schmidt — who did know Ross for years — was a delight to speak with and very gracious even though he has shared his stories many times before. Boston Bruins director of Public Relations and Information Heidi Holland was very helpful and introduced me to Bruins Alumni Coordinator Karen Wonoski. Through Karen, I was able to speak with former Bruins Johnny Peirson and Paul Ronty, who had both played while Art Ross was general manager of the team. Bill Cleary connected me with another former Bruin, Ed Sandford, who had some wonderful stories to tell.

Thank you also to Ian Ott, a PR co-ordinator with the Buffalo Sabres, and to Washington Capitals Senior Director of Communications Sergey Kocharov, for putting me in touch with Craig and Dick Patrick. And, of course, thank you to the two Mr. Patricks for sharing a few family stories. It was certainly a thrill when my phone rang one day and it was Scotty Bowman, calling in reply to an email request, and sharing an Art Ross story he'd heard from Lynn Patrick (Craig's father) when they worked together in St. Louis in 1967–68.

Thank you also to Stewart Richardson, co-author *of Dit: Dit Clapper and the Rise of the Boston Bruins*, to James Andrew Ross (no relation to Art), Roger Godin, Paul Kitchen, and my colleagues at the Society for International Hockey Research, as well as to Dan Diamond, Ralph Dinger, Paul Bontje, and James Duplacey.

When I occasionally approached publishing people about this book over the years, I generally heard a lot of variations on "hockey people don't care about history and history people don't like hockey." But when I mentioned it to Michael Melgaard of Dundurn Press in January of 2014, he couldn't wait to hear more! Thank you, Michael, for encouraging me to write as much as I wanted … and then deftly editing it all down to size.

Last — but most important of all — thank you to my family, especially my wife Barbara.

# APPENDIX: CAREER STATISTICS

## PLAYER STATS

| Year | Team | League | Season | | | | | Playoffs | | | | |
|------|------|--------|--------|---|---|-----|-----|----------|---|---|-----|-----|
| | | | GP | G | A | Pts | PIM | GP | G | A | Pts | PIM |
| 1900-01 | Westmount AAA | CAHL Int | Statistics not available | | | | | | | | | |
| 1901-02 | Westmount AAA | CAHL Int | 4 | 2 | 0 | 2 | 0 | | | | | |
| 1902-03 | Westmount AAA | CAHL Int | 5 | 4 | 0 | 4 | 0 | | | | | |
| 1904-05 | Merchants Bank | Independent | Statistics not available | | | | | | | | | |
| | Westmount AAA | CAHL | 8 | 10 | 0 | 10 | .... | | | | | |
| 1905-06 | Brandon Hockey Club | MHL | 8 | 5 | 1 | 6 | 32 | | | | | |
| | Brandon Hockey Club | Exhibition | 1 | 2 | 0 | 2 | .... | | | | | |
| | Merchants Bank | M Bankers | Statistics not available | | | | | | | | | |
| 1906-07 | Brandon Hockey Club | MHL | 9 | 5 | 0 | 5 | 21 | 2 | 1 | 0 | 1 | 3 |
| | Brandon Hockey Club | Exhibition | 2 | .... | .... | .... | .... | | | | | |
| | Kenora Thistles | Stanley Cup | | | | | | 2 | 0 | 0 | 0 | 10 |
| 1907-08 | Montreal Wanderers | ECAHA | 10 | 8 | 2 | 10 | 27 | | | | | |
| | Pembroke Lumber Kings | OVHL | 1 | 5 | 0 | 5 | .... | | | | | |
| | Montreal Wanderers | Stanley Cup | | | | | | 5 | 3 | 0 | 3 | 23 |
| | Montreal Wanderers | Exhibition | 3 | 2 | .... | 2 | .... | | | | | |
| 1908-09 | Montreal Wanderers | Stanley Cup | | | | | | 2 | 0 | 0 | 0 | 13 |
| | Montreal Wanderers | ECHA | 9 | 2 | 2 | 4 | 30 | | | | | |
| | Montreal Wanderers | Exhibition | 4 | 2 | 0 | 2 | 3 | | | | | |
| | Cobalt Silver Kings | TPHL | | | | | | 2 | 1 | 0 | 1 | 0 |

| 1909-10 | All-Montreal | CHA | 4 | 4 | 3 | 7 | 3 | | | | | |
|---|---|---|---|---|---|---|---|---|---|---|---|---|
| | Haileybury Comets | NHA | 12 | 6 | 0 | 6 | 25 | | | | | |
| 1910-11 | Montreal Wanderers | NHA | 11 | 4 | 2 | 6 | 31 | | | | | |
| 1911-12 | Montreal Wanderers | NHA | 19 | 15 | 5 | 21 | 60 | | | | | |
| | NHA All-Stars | Exhib | 3 | 4 | 0 | 4 | 0 | | | | | |
| 1912-13 | Montreal Wanderers | NHA | 18 | 11 | 2 | 13 | 58 | | | | | |
| | NHA All-Stars | Exhib | 5 | 0 | 0 | 0 | 18 | | | | | |
| 1913-14 | Montreal Wanderers | NHA | 18 | 4 | 5 | 9 | 74 | | | | | |
| 1914-15 | Ottawa Senators | NHA | 16 | 3 | 1 | 4 | 55 | 2 | 1 | 0 | 1 | 25 |
| | Ottawa Senators | Stanley Cup | | | | | | 3 | 0 | 0 | 0 | .... |
| 1915-16 | Ottawa Senators | NHA | 21 | 8 | 8 | 16 | 69 | | | | | |
| 1916-17 | Montreal Wanderers | NHA | 16 | 6 | 3 | 9 | 66 | | | | | |
| 1917-18 | Montreal Wanderers | NHL | 3 | 1 | 0 | 1 | 12 | | | | | |

## COACHING STATS

| Year | Team | League | Season | | | | Playoffs | | | |
|---|---|---|---|---|---|---|---|---|---|---|
| | | | Ga | W | L | T | Ga | W | L | T |
| 1913-14 | Montreal Wanderers | NHA | 5 | 3 | 2 | 0 | | | | |
| 1917-18 | Montreal Wanderers | NHL | 6* | 1 | 4 | 0 | | | | |
| 1922-23 | Hamilton Tigers | NHL | 24 | 6 | 18 | 0 | | | | |
| 1924-25 | Boston Bruins | NHL | 30 | 6 | 24 | 0 | | | | |
| 1925-26 | Boston Bruins | NHL | 36 | 17 | 15 | 4 | | | | |
| 1926-27 | Boston Bruins | NHL | 44 | 21 | 20 | 3 | 8 | 2 | 2 | 4 |
| 1927-28 | Boston Bruins | NHL | 44 | 20 | 13 | 11 | 2 | 0 | 1 | 1 |
| 1928-29 | Boston Bruins | NHL | 44 | 26 | 13 | 5 | 5 | 5 | 0 | 0 |
| 1929-30 | Boston Bruins | NHL | 44 | 38 | 5 | 1 | 6 | 3 | 3 | 0 |
| 1930-31 | Boston Bruins | NHL | 44 | 28 | 10 | 6 | 5 | 2 | 3 | 0 |
| 1931-32 | Boston Bruins | NHL | 48 | 15 | 21 | 12 | | | | |
| 1932-33 | Boston Bruins | NHL | 48 | 25 | 15 | 8 | 5 | 2 | 3 | 0 |
| 1933-34 | Boston Bruins | NHL | 48 | 18 | 25 | 5 | | | | |
| 1936-37 | Boston Bruins | NHL | 48 | 23 | 18 | 7 | 3 | 1 | 2 | 0 |
| 1937-38 | Boston Bruins | NHL | 48 | 30 | 11 | 7 | 3 | 0 | 3 | 0 |
| 1938-39 | Boston Bruins | NHL | 48 | 36 | 10 | 2 | 12 | 8 | 4 | 0 |
| 1941-42 | Boston Bruins | NHL | 48 | 25 | 17 | 6 | 5 | 2 | 3 | 0 |
| 1942-43 | Boston Bruins | NHL | 50 | 24 | 17 | 9 | 9 | 4 | 5 | 0 |
| 1943-44 | Boston Bruins | NHL | 50 | 19 | 26 | 5 | | | | |
| 1944-45 | Boston Bruins | NHL | 50 | 16 | 30 | 4 | 7 | 3 | 4 | 0 |
| | **NHL Totals** | | 772 | 387 | 290 | 95 | 70 | 32 | 33 | 5 |

\* Wanderers only played four games, but lost two more by default after withdrawing from NHL

# A NOTE ON THE SOURCES

The vast majority of information used in writing this book was obtained from old newspapers searched via the Internet. Many sources are noted directly in the text, and often when they are not, it's because the same information can be found in many different newspapers.

Among the newspapers that proved most valuable are the following (listed alphabetically): *Brandon Daily Sun, Boston Globe, Globe and Mail* and the *Globe* (Toronto), *Kenora Miner and News, Lethbridge Herald, Lewiston Journal, Manitoba Free Press* (Winnipeg), *Montreal Gazette, Montreal Daily Mail, Ottawa Citizen, Ottawa Journal, Pittsburgh Press, Toronto Star, Toronto World, Vancouver Sun, Vancouver World, Westmount News, Winnipeg Free Press, Winnipeg Telegram, Winnipeg Tribune.*

Certain articles were so useful, I feel I must list them individually:

- An eight-part series written by Frank Patrick for the *Boston Sunday Globe* between January 27 and March 17, 1935;
- a seven-page autobiography by Lester Patrick for sportswriter Andy Lytle circa 1947, generously shared by Jason Beck of the British Columbia Sports Hall of Fame;

- Sprague Cleghorn with Frederick Edwards, "It's a Tough Game," *Maclean's Magazine* (four-part series beginning December 1, 1934);
- Arthur Siegel, "A Visit with Art Ross," (undated article, likely from a Boston Bruins program, found in the Hockey Hall of Fame's Art Ross folder). The article originally appeared as "Art Ross Sees Local Boys Making the Bruins," *Daily Boston Globe*, March 13, 1960, A7;
- Arthur Siegel "Built Game, Title Team in Boston Ross Dies … Hockey Genius," *Boston Globe*, August 6, 1964, 1;
- John Gillooly, "The Man Who Made Hockey — Part 1— Life of Art Ross," *Boston Sunday Advertiser*, December 4, 1949; and
- *Playing the Field* by Dink Carroll, "A Story About Art Ross," *Montreal Gazette*, September 13, 1951, 16.
- Arthur S. Ross, Jr. and Bob Considine, "God Said Bail Out," *Cosmopolitan* Magazine, February, 1945.

Quotations by, and information about, Art Ross and Walter Smaill in Cobalt come mainly from "Great Hockey Plays and Players No. 2 — Art Ross," *Montreal Standard*, January 3, 1914, found in the Art Ross folder at Hockey Hall of Fame; "Real Puck War Staged In Canadian Silver Camps Was Toughest Game Art Ross, Now With Bruins, Ever Played In," *Lewiston Daily Sun*, December 24, 1924, 9; John Gillooly, "The Man Who Made Hockey — Part 2 — Life of Art Ross," *Boston Daily Record*, December 5, 1949, 68; Speaking on Sports by Milt Dunnell, "Bet At Rate of $2,000 Per Minute," *The Toronto Daily Star*, February 11, 1950, 12; "Bruising contest recalled by old-time hockey star," *The Leader-Post* (Regina), February 5, 1963, 18; and from other sources noted in the text.

Stories about Ross's defensive scoring system are from Gordon Walker, "Ross Invents Point Plan As Defensive Rewards," *Toronto Star*, January 11, 1947; Bobby Hewitson, "Give Defensive Player Credit That Is Due Him, *The Evening Telegram* (Toronto), January 11, 1947; Leo MacDonell, "Art Ross Proposes New Hockey Plan Bruin Boss Would Reward Defensive Play," *Detroit Times*, January 13, 1947; and The Passing Sport Show by Baz O'Meara, *Montreal Daily Star*, February 14, 1947. All are from the Art Ross file at the Hockey Hall of Fame.

Art Ross III and his uncle, John Ross (who died in 2002), made a series of audio recording circa 2000 that are both valuable and entertaining. Most quotes attributed to John Ross in this book come from these recordings. Art Ross III also provided an audio recording of the WEEI interview between Art Ross and Fred Cusick. The exact date has not been preserved but it is from 1960, during the playoffs after the 1959–60 NHL regular season.

James Andrew Ross generously provided a copy of his 2008 Ph.D. thesis from London's University of Western Ontario *Hockey Capital: Commerce Culture, and the National Hockey League, 1917–1967*. This provided me with much information on Thomas Duggan, the birth of the Bruins, and the team's economic troubles in the early 1950s. Andrew also provided bits and pieces of other research, including Charles Adams' quote about Ross being "lukewarm" on Boston (found in a Lionel Hitchman scrapbook at Library and Archives Canada) and Michael Rodden's quote about Eddie Shore wanting to sign with the St. Patricks (found in the Michael Rodden fonds at Queen's University Archives).

All references to Montreal street addresses come from Lovell's Montreal city directories. Henderson's street directories of Brandon, Manitoba, 1906 and 1907, were also valuable.

# SELECTED BIBLIOGRAPHY

Bowlsby, Craig H. *Empire of Ice: The Rise and Fall of the Pacific Coast Hockey Association, 1911–1926*. Vancouver: Knights of Winter Publishing, 2012.

Coleman, Charles L. *The Trail of the Stanley Cup, Vol. 1*. National Hockey League, 1966.

_____. *The Trail of the Stanley Cup, Vol. 2*. National Hockey League, 1969.

_____. *The Trail of the Stanley Cup, Vol. 3*. National Hockey League, 1976.

Cosentino, Frank. *The Renfrew Millionaires: The Valley Boys of Winter 1910*. Burnstown: General Store Publishing House, 1990.

Diamond, Dan et al., eds. *Total Hockey: The Official Encyclopedia of the National Hockey League*. New York: Total Sports, 1998.

Fischler, Stan. *The Burly Bruins: Hockey's Tempestuous Team*. Englewood Cliffs: Prentice-Hall, Inc., 1971.

Fischler, Stan and Shirley. *Heroes & History: Voices from the NHL's Past!* Whitby: McGraw-Hill Ryerson, 1994.

Frayne, Trent. *The Mad Men of Hockey*. New York: Dodd Mead, 1974.

Hardy, Stephen. "Long Before Orr." In *The Rock the Curse and the Hub: a Random History of Boston Sports.* Cambridge, MA and London: Harvard University Press, 2005.

Harper, Stephen J. *A Great Game: The Forgotten Leafs and the Rise of Professional Hockey.* Toronto: Simon & Schuster Canada, 2013.

Hiam, C. Michael. *Eddie Shore and That Old Time Hockey.* Toronto: McClelland & Stewart, 2010.

Holzman, Morey, and Joseph Nieforth. *Deceptions and Doublecross: How the NHL Conquered Hockey.* Toronto: Dundurn Press, 2002.

Howey, Florence R. *Pioneering on the C.P.R.* Ottawa: Mutual Press Limited, 1938.

Jenish, D'Arcy. *The Montreal Canadiens: 100 Years of Glory.* Toronto: Doubleday Canada, 2008.

_____. *The NHL: A Centennial History.* Toronto: Doubleday Canada, 2013.

Keene, Kerry. *Tales from the Boston Bruins Locker Room: A Collection of the Greatest Bruins Stories Ever Told.* New York: Skyhorse Publishng, Inc., 2011.

Kitchen, Paul. *Win, Tie or Wrangle: The Inside Story of the Old Ottawa Senators 1883–1935.* Manotick, ON: Penumbra Press, 2008.

McFarlane, Brian. *The Bruins: Brian McFarlane's Original Six.* Toronto: Stoddart Publishing Co. Ltd., 1999.

McParland, Kelly. *The Lives of Conn Smythe: From the Battlefield to Maple Leaf Gardens: A Hockey Icon's Story.* Toronto: FENN/McClelland & Stewart, 2011.

O'Hara, Aidan. *Common Ice: The Culture of Ice Hockey in Greater Boston, 1920–1933.* (Unpublished: Courtesy of Hockey Hall of Fame.)

Richardson, Stewart and Richard Leblanc. *Dit: Dit Clapper and the Rise of the Boston Bruins.* PACTS Management Inc., 2012.

Roche, Wilfrid Victor (Bill) ed. *The Hockey Book.* Toronto: McClelland & Stewart, Ltd., 1953.

Ross, Art III. *Looking Back … Two Centuries of Ross Heritage in North America.* Sale Creek, TN: Self-Published, 2008.

Smythe, Conn and Scott Young. *Conn Smythe: If You Can't Beat 'Em in the Alley.* Toronto: McClelland & Stewart, 1981.

Vantour, Kevin. *The Bruins Book.* Toronto: ECW Press, 1997.

Wesley, Sam, with David Wesley. "Art Ross's Team." In *Hamilton's Hockey Tigers.* Toronto: James Lorimer & Company, 2005.

Whitehead, Eric. *Cyclone Taylor: A Hockey Legend.* Toronto: Doubleday Canada Limited, 1977.

_____. *The Patricks: Hockey's Royal Family.* Toronto: Doubleday Canada Limited, 1980.

Wong, John Chi-Kit. *Lords of the Rink: The Emergence Of The National Hockey League 1875–1936.* Toronto, Buffalo London: University of Toronto Press, 2005.

Young, Scott and Astrid Young. *O'Brien: From Water Boy to One Million a Year.* Toronto: Ryerson Press, 1967.

# INDEX

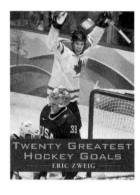

**Twenty Greatest Hockey Goals**
Eric Zweig

Every hockey fan remembers certain goals scored that stand out from all others. But if one had to name just 20 as the greatest ever accomplished, what would they be?

There's Paul Henderson's third game-winning goal in 1972, the one that clinched the Summit Series for Canada against the Soviet Union. Also Mike Eruzione's upset "Miracle on Ice" winner for the United States against the Soviets at Lake Placid in 1980. And don't forget the famous Stanley Cup winners by the Toronto Maple Leafs' Bill Barilko in 1951 and the Boston Bruins' Bobby Orr in 1970.

From the goal by the Montreal Victorias against the Winnipeg Victorias in the 1896 Stanley Cup rematch that truly made hockey's most famous hardware a national event, to Wayne Gretzky's 77th goal in 1982 that beat Phil Esposito's single-season record for goals, to Sidney Crosby's "golden goal" in the 2010 Vancouver Winter Olympics, Zweig serves up a slice of exceptional hockey moments that's sure to provoke heated discussion.

**Hope and Heartbreak in Toronto**
Life as a Maple Leafs Fan
Peter Robinson

For many, being a Toronto Maple Leafs fan has become a curse from cradle to grave.

False hope, hollow promises, and a mind-numbing lack of success — these words describe the Toronto Maple Leafs and the hockey club's inexplicable mediocrity over much of the past decade.

Author Peter Robinson has attended some 100 games over the past six seasons and has little to show for it except an unquenched thirst that keeps him coming back. Why does a team that hasn't won a Stanley Cup since 1967, long before many of its followers were even born, have such a hold on its fans? Robinson tries to answer that question and more while detailing what it's like to love one of the most unlovable teams in all of professional sports.

Being a Leafs fan requires a leap of faith every year, girding against inevitable disappointment. This book tells what that's like, how it got to be that way, and what the future holds for all who worship the Blue and White.

**Sudden Death**
The Incredible Saga of the 1986 Swift Current
Broncos
Leesa Culp

A true story of hockey heartbreak, tragedy, and triumph.

*Sudden Death* brings to life the incredible ongoing saga of the Swift Current Broncos hockey team. After a tragic game-day bus accident on December 30, 1986, left four of its star players dead, the first-year Western Hockey League team was faced with nearly insurmountable odds against not only its future success but its very survival. The heartbreaking story made headlines across North America, and the club garnered acclaim when it triumphantly rebounded and won the Canadian Hockey League's prestigious Memorial Cup in 1989.

Many of the surviving Broncos continued their successful hockey careers in the NHL, among them 2012 Hockey Hall of Famer Joe Sakic, Sheldon Kennedy, and *Sudden Death* co-author Bob Wilkie. Years later the Broncos' tragedy-to-triumph tale was overshadowed when the team's former coach, Graham James, was convicted of sexual assault against Sheldon Kennedy, Theoren Fleury, and Todd Holt, all of whom played for him.